Robert Buist

Buist's Almanac and Garden Manual for the Year 1888

Designed to furnish concise hints to cottagers, farmers and planters, on the cultivation of vegetables, with other useful information on gardening

Robert Buist

Buist's Almanac and Garden Manual for the Year 1888
Designed to furnish concise hints to cottagers, farmers and planters, on the cultivation of vegetables, with other useful information on gardening

ISBN/EAN: 9783337377359

Printed in Europe, USA, Canada, Australia, Japan

Cover: Foto ©Lupo / pixelio.de

More available books at **www.hansebooks.com**

1828
ESTABLISHED 60 YEARS
1888

ALMANAC

FOR THE YEAR
1888

AND GARDEN MANUAL

DESIGNED TO FURNISH

Concise Hints to Cottagers, Farmers and Planters,

ON THE

CULTIVATION OF VEGETABLES,

WITH OTHER USEFUL INFORMATION ON GARDENING,

BY

ROBERT BUIST, Jr.

GROWER OF BUIST'S CELEBRATED GARDEN SEEDS.

THE ONLY BRAND OF SEEDS IN THIS COUNTRY WHICH ARE GROWN EXCLUSIVELY FROM SELECTED SEED STOCKS.

———◆———

SEED WAREHOUSE:
Nos. 922 and 924 Market Street,
Adjoining the new Post-Office,
PHILADELPHIA.

BUIST'S GARDEN MANUAL
FOR
❋ 1888 ❋
WE WISH YOU A HAPPY NEW YEAR.

PHILADELPHIA has long been famous for her many manufacturing and commercial industries, and the products are found in almost all the various markets of the world. One of these industries, and by no means the least in importance, is the growing and shipping of garden seeds. It is a well-known fact that Philadelphia seeds bear a greater reputation for purity and reliability than those from any other section of the country. The largest market for seeds is found in the Southern States and foreign tropical countries. One-half the seeds used in these sections are supplied from this city, where two of the largest and oldest seed firms are located.

Our establishment was founded in 1828 by the father of the present proprietor, and has been in successful operation for sixty years, passing through the various commercial panics and stagnations of trade, without making a retrograde step; from the most humble beginning to the most extensive now in the trade. Our motto has been "Onward!" always growing the best and most improved seeds regardless of cost, feeling assured that seeds of value will always find a market. The result is that Buist's seeds are sold and sought after in every section of the country, and annual shipments are made to the leading merchants and gardeners of Europe, East and West Indies, South America, Australia, China, Japan and the extreme southern portions of Africa.

The great secret of our success and the popularity of our seeds is their reliability, which is attributed to the care exercised in growing them exclusively from selected seed stocks—that is, to select each year the most perfect specimens from the crop while growing and the seed product to be sown for the following year's crop. This causes a continued improvement in their quality and keeps Buist's Garden Seeds up to the highest standard of excellence.

For a successful garden, good soil, good seed and good culture are three important requirements, without which success will not crown your efforts. If you are not already a purchaser of Buist's seeds, do not fail to sow them this season, as they are acknowledged to be not only the most reliable, but *are* the best known.

I am, yours truly,

Robert Buist

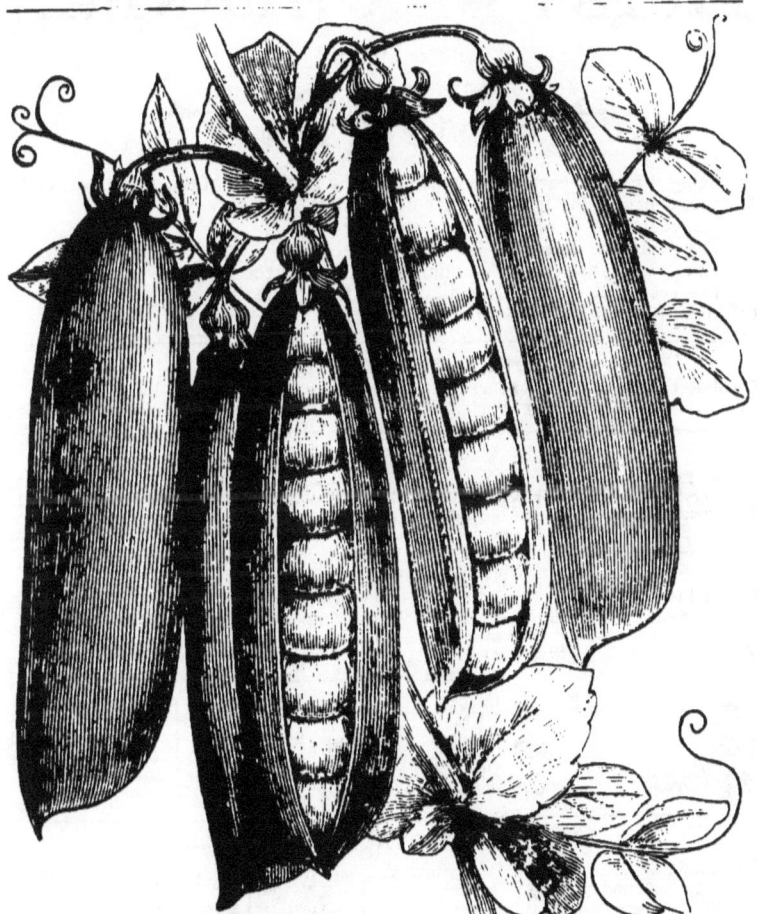

Copyrighted, 1887.

Buist's Early Morning-Star Pea.
THE EARLIEST PEA IN THE WORLD. THE LARGEST-PODDED EXTRA EARLY KNOWN.

We introduced this extraordinary variety of EXTRA EARLY PEA the past year, two thousand bushels of which were sold and sent to almost every section of the United States, and especially to the districts devoted to market-gardening. There has been but one verdict, and that is, "It proved the Earliest and Best ever Grown."

It was raised from a three years' selection from the earliest podded stock of our famous PREMIER EXTRA EARLY, which is so celebrated with market-gardeners, which has given it an established habit for extreme earliness, dwarf but robust growth, great increase in the size of its pods, and unusual hardiness. It is not only the earliest variety known, but the most productive and the largest podded. One of its greatest features is to withstand great changes and severity of weather, which of late years have proved so damaging to the early crop of Peas, especially in the South. It is the most profitable variety for the market-gardener because the earliest and most productive.

They are sold only in our Sealed Packages, as follows: Papers, 10 cts.; ½ Pint, 15 cts.; Pint, 25 cts.; Quart, 40 cts.; 4 Quarts, $1.25. Leaded Sealed Sacks, etc.; ¼ Bushel, $2.00; ½ Bushel, $3.50; Bushel, $6.50.

BUIST'S CALENDAR
—FOR—
1888.

Being the latter part of the 112th and the beginning of the 113th year of the Independence of the United States of America. Also,
The year 7396-97 of the Byzantine Era;
The year 5648-49 of the Jewish Era;
The year 2641 since the foundation of Rome, according to Varro;
The year 1306 of the Mohammedan Era, or the Era of the Hegira, which begins on the 7th day of September, 1888.

CHRONOLOGICAL CYCLES.

Dominical Letters........ A G | Golden Number............... 8 | Roman Indiction.......... 1
Epact............................17 | Solar Cycle.......................21 | Julian Period............ ...6601

THE SEASONS.   Washington Time.

Vernal Equinox (Spring begins).. March   19, 11 h. P.M.
Summer Solstice (Summer begins).. June   20, 7 h. P.M.
Autumnal Equinox (Autumn begins)...................................... Sept.   22, 10 h. A.M.
Winter Solstice (Winter begins)... Dec.   21, 4 h. A.M.

ASTRONOMICAL SIGNS.

☉ The Sun.   ♂ Mars.   ☌ Conjunction.   ☽ First Quarter.
⊕ The Earth.   ♃ Jupiter.   ☍ Opposition.   ○ Full Moon.
☿ Mercury.   ♄ Saturn.   ☊ Ascending Node.   ☾ Last Quarter.
♀ Venus.   ♅ Herschel.   ☋ Descending Node.   ● New Moon.

Aries, or Ram.   Cancer, or Crab.   Libra, or Balance.   Capricornus, or Goat.
Taurus, or Bull.   Leo, or Lion.   Scorpio, or Scorpion.   Aquarius, or Waterman.
Gemini, or Twins.   Virgo, or Virgin.   Sagittarius, or Bowman.   Pisces, or Fishes.

FIXED AND MOVABLE FESTIVALS.

Epiphany................Jan. 6 | Palm Sunday..........Mar. 25 | Whit Sunday..........May 20
Septuagesima Sunday " 29 | Good Friday............ " 30 | Trinity Sunday....... " 27
Quinquagesima— | Easter Sunday ....April 1 | Corpus Christi........ " 31
  Shrove Sunday.....Feb. 12 | Low Sunday............ " 8 | St. John Bapt.........June 24
Ash Wednesday...... " 15 | Rogation Sunday......May 6 | Michaelmas ....Sept. 29
1st Sunday in Lent..... " 19 | Ascension Day— | 1st Sunday in Advent Dec 2
St. Patrick.............Mar. 17 | Holy Thursday........May 10 | Christmas............... " 25

ECLIPSES FOR THE YEAR 1888.

In the year 1888 there will be five eclipses, three of the Sun and two of the Moon.
  I. A Total Eclipse of the Moon, January 28. Visible more or less to the world generally, except to the Pacific Ocean.
  II. A Partial Eclipse of the Sun, February 11. Invisible to the United States. Visible to the Antarctic Ocean and Southern Patagonia.
  III. A Partial Eclipse of the Sun, July 9. Invisible to the United States. Visible to the Southern Indian Ocean.
  IV. A Total Eclipse of the Moon, July 22-23. Visible to the larger part of the world, except Eastern Europe and Asia.
  V. A Partial Eclipse of the Sun, August 7. Invisible to the United States. Visible to the Arctic Ocean and adjacent regions, including Norway and Sweden.

Buist's Seeds are Grown by Buist.

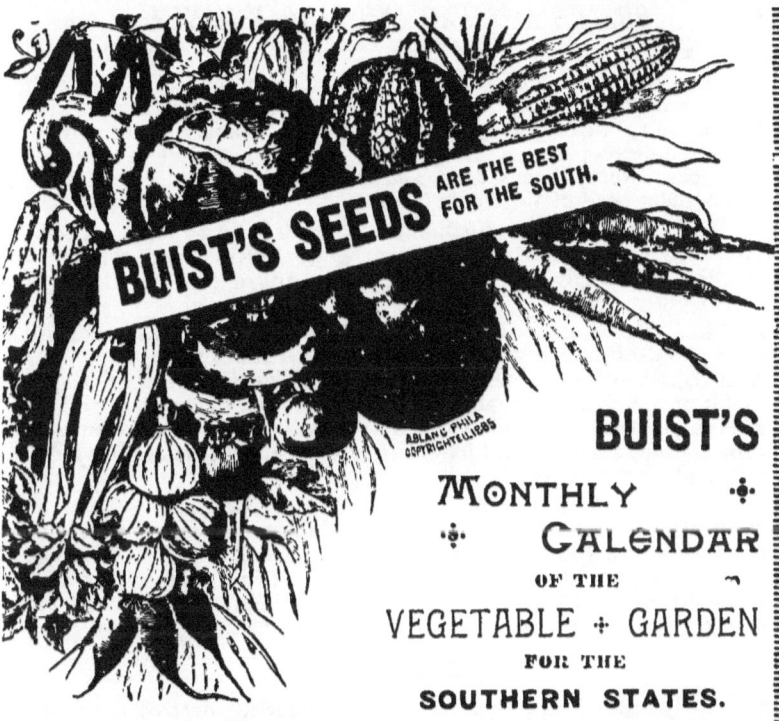

BUIST'S
MONTHLY ✢
✢ CALENDAR
OF THE
VEGETABLE ✢ GARDEN
FOR THE
SOUTHERN STATES.

VEGETABLE GARDENING for the South in monthly operations cannot be accurately given, as the active months in this department are January, February, March, April, October, November, and December. We therefore merely throw out hints of cropping and about the period they should be attended to in latitudes south of Charleston. The adaptation to time in the various States can be readily adopted by common observation of season and climate.

There are several points, however, that must be held strictly in view to insure success.

1st. PLANT RELIABLE SEEDS from a RELIABLE HOUSE. AVOID COMMISSIONED SEEDS, as they are like the QUACK MEDICINES OF THE COUNTRY, producing a great show on paper, but accomplishing nothing but poor results and disappointment to those who sow them. If you have not been successful in obtaining Reliable Seeds, then try BUIST'S. They have a world-wide reputation, and especially so in the Southern States; the cultivation and improvement of varieties adapted to that section of the country are made a specialty by devoting a portion of their extensive farms exclusively to the growth of such varieties. Personal attention is given to the purity of every crop grown, and they guarantee their Seeds in a favorable season to prove entirely satisfactory. If you desire that your gardening operations should prove both a success and a pleasure, then ALWAYS PLANT BUIST'S SEEDS. If your merchant does not keep them, order direct from our house.

THEY HAVE BEEN AWARDED GRAND PRIZES FOR THEIR GREAT PURITY, AND FINE QUALITY IN ALMOST EVERY SEED MARKET OF THE WORLD.

BUIST'S ALMANAC AND GARDEN MANUAL.

2d. Select for your garden a location where the soil is both rich and of a mellow nature, not likely to become surface-baked and capable of being worked very early in spring. Manure it thoroughly with well-decomposed stable manure, plow and subsoil it, or spade it at least twenty inches deep, and lay it out similar to illustration given under head of Vegetable Garden.

3d. A thorough eradication of all weeds must be made; a complete hoeing and clearing up every two weeks will insure this; stirring the soil deeply and frequently will guard against the damages of drought.

4th. Never, under any circumstance, allow a weed to seed upon your premises; every year you will then have fewer to destroy. Our habit is, when we see one growing either in the field or way-side, to pull it up. Remember that a single plant of Dock will produce enough seed to plant an acre, a Carrot will surprise you with its industry in propagating, a Thistle will lodge its seed in every part of your farm, and finally overrun it.

5th. PRACTICE INDUSTRY. An indolent gardener can never be successful; he is continually putting off for to-morrow what should be done to-day; if you have one of this stamp, change him, as there can be no profit in anything he produces. Failure in a crop with him is generally attributed to the season; he is not impressed with the old adage, that "TIME AND TIDE" wait for no man.

JANUARY.

Early frosts in the Southern States frequently destroy early gardens; but this is no reason why you should not try and have one, for if your early plantings are destroyed, you will then have ample time to re-seed; remember, an early garden of one acre, if not damaged by frost, will produce more than a two-acre garden planted late; therefore, January should be a very active month in Texas, Louisiana, Mississippi, Georgia, Alabama and Florida, and the following seeds should be planted. If your Hot-Bed has not been already prepared, attend to it at once for the sowing of Early Tomatoes, Peppers, Egg-Plant, and other early seeds. (Read remarks about its preparation.)

Beets. As soon as the season will permit, sow the seed in drills, about twenty inches apart, very thinly and evenly, about half an inch deep. Before covering up the seed, sprinkle a few seeds of Long Scarlet Radish in the drills; they will come up at once, and show where the rows are. The soil can be hoed, and the Radishes will be used within four weeks; the Beets when thinned out should stand six inches apart. Select Buist's Extra Early, Early Egyptian, Buist's Othello, and Early Blood Turnip. During moist weather the young plants of Beet can be as successfully transplanted as the Cabbage.

Carrots. Sow similar to Beets. Select Early Horn and Half-long Scarlet Danver's; distinguish the rows by a few seeds of Turnip Radish; the Radish crop will be off before the Carrots are advanced for thinning out.

Cabbage Seed. If you overlooked sowing last month, attend to it at once. Buist's Large York, Jersey Wakefield, Winnigstadt, and Buist's Improved Flat Dutch and Drumhead will give you a succession of heads during April and May. Recollect that Buist's improved varieties of Cabbage have no superior in this country; they have been awarded 22 first premiums in a single season, and are very popular throughout the entire country, and especially so in the South, where so much difficulty is experienced in heading Cabbage. Always sow them, and you will never fail in growing fine heads. But please observe that the two latter varieties are only sold in our original sealed packages. See Page 3.

Cauliflower and Brocoli planted in the AUTUMN will commence heading, and should the weather be cold, give them a slight protection of straw or other covering. Select Erfurt, Snowball and Half Early Paris Cauliflower, and Walcheren Brocoli, for such plantings; also sow Cauliflower in frames, to be transplanted next March.

Peas are a very important crop in every garden and must not be overlooked; to keep up a regular succession of crops make sowings every two weeks throughout the season, and put in plenty of them, as they are a general favorite; there is a great difference in the quality of this vegetable, and it would be folly to grow inferior varieties when you can obtain those of superior quality at the same price. I will here remark, and beg that it shall be observed, that where the ground is dry there should be water run in the drills before the peas are sown.

Form the drills two feet apart and three inches deep, dropping the peas to stand about half an inch apart. Cover up, and the moisture will at once vegetate the seeds. As soon as up, hoe well, and keep clear of weeds; when they are about one foot high give them stakes or put in rods six feet apart and run strong twine of any cheap kind along them.

Most cultivators permit their peas to become too far advanced before using them; the proper time to have them in all their perfection is when the pods have swelled and the peas formed. When more fully advanced they always lose their delicacy of flavor. The French always use them at this stage of ripening, and for this reason the American tourist is always impressed with the delicious flavor of French Peas, they also thoroughly understand the great importance of proper seasoning, which is very much neglected both in England and America. We recommend the following varieties as the most desirable to plant:

PLANT BUIST'S PREMIER EXTRA EARLY AND BUIST'S MORNING STAR. The latter variety is sold only in our Sealed Packages, Pints, Quarts, Pecks, Half-Bushels and Bushels. These two varieties are the earliest known, producing large crops of sweet and luscious Peas. The latter variety is our New Extra Early, and offered this season for the first time, it will be found a very great acquisition, it is a bonanza for the Market Gardener. Do not overlook planting it.

Premium Little Gem. This variety is, indeed a gem of the first water, is as dwarf as the Tom Thumb, and twice as productive.

CARTER'S STRATEGEM, PRIDE OF THE MARKET AND TELEPHONE are the cream of varieties for a general crop, the latter produces pods as large as that of the Lima Bean.

Champion of England. A very luscious pea, a general favorite and should be grown by all. Sow in rows three feet apart, but, not unless the soil is warm; cold, moist weather destroys the germ.

1st Month. JANUARY, 1888.

MOON'S PHASES.

MIDDLE STATES.				SOUTHERN STATES.			
	D.	H.	M.		D.	H.	M.
Last Quarter	6	6	46 M.	Last Quarter			
New Moon	13	3	42 M.	New Moon			
First Quarter	20	11	53 A.	First Quarter			
Full Moon	28	6	23 A.	Full Moon			

D. of M.	D. of W.	Lat. of Middle States.				Constellations.	Equation of Time.	Lat. of Southern Sta.			
		The Sun		The Moon				The Sun		The Moon	
		Ris.	Sets.	R & S.	Souths			Ris.	Sets.	R & S.	S
		h. m.	h. m.	h. m.	h. m.			h. m.	h. m.	h. m.	h
1	S	7 25	4 43	7 18	1 45	♑	10 S.	7 3	5 5	7 36	
2	M	7 25	4 44	8 24	2 39	♑	24	4 7	3 5	6	8 38
3	Tu	7 25	4 45	9 32	3 31	♒	7	5 7	3 5	6	9 43
4	W	7 25	4 46	10 41	4 23	♒	21	5 7	3 5	7	10 46
5	Th	5 7 25	4 47	11 50	5 13	♓	5	6 7	3 5	8	11 51
6	Fr	6 7 25	4 48	morn	6 4	♓	19	6 7	4 5	9	morn
7	Sa	7 7 25	4 49	0 59	6 55	♈	4	6 7	4 5	10	0 55
8	S	8 7 25	4 50	2 9	7 48	♈	18	7 7	4 5	10	2 1
9	M	9 7 24	4 51	3 19	8 42	♉	2	7 7	4 5	11	3 7
10	Tu	10 7 24	4 52	4 28	9 38	♉	16	8 7	4 5	12	4 12
11	W	11 7 24	4 53	5 34	10 36	♊	0	8 7	4 5	13	5 16 1
12	Th	12 7 24	4 54	6 34	11 33	♊	14	9 7	3 5	14	6 15 1
13	Fr	13 7 23	4 55	sets	Ev. 30	♊	28	9 7	3 5	15	sets
14	Sa	14 7 23	4 56	6 30	1 23	♋	11	9 7	3 5	16	6 47
15	S	15 7 23	4 57	7 32	2 14	♋	24	10 7	3 5	16	7 46
16	M	16 7 22	4 58	8 33	3 2	♌	7	10 7	3 5	17	8 44
17	Tu	17 7 22	4 59	9 33	3 47	♌	19	10 7	3 5	18	9 40
18	W	18 7 21	5	1 10 32	4 30	♍	1	11 7	2 5	19	10 35
19	Th	19 7 21	5	2 11 29	5 12	♍	13	11 7	2 5	20	11 28
20	Fr	20 7 20	5	3 morn	5 54	♎	25	11 7	2 5	21	morn
21	Sa	21 7 20	5	4 0 26	6 36	♎	7	12 7	1 5	22	0 21
22	S	22 7 19	5	5 1 23	7 20	♏	19	12 7	1 5	23	1 14
23	M	23 7 18	5	6 2 21	8 6	♏	1	12 7	1 5	24	2 8
24	Tu	24 7 17	5	8 3 19	8 54	♐	13	12 7	0 5	25	3 3
25	W	25 7 17	5	9 4 17	9 46	♐	26	13 7	0 5	26	3 59
26	Th	26 7 16	5	10 5 13	10 39	♑	9	13 6	59 5	27	4 54 1
27	Fr	27 7 15	5	11 6 7	11 34	♑	22	13 6	59 5	28	5 48 1
28	Sa	28 7 14	5	12 rises	morn	♒	5	13 6	58 5	29	rises
29	S	29 7 14	5	14 6 11	0 29	♒	19	13 6	58 5	30	6 27
30	M	30 7 13	5	15 7 20	1 24	♓	3	14 6	57 5	31	7 31
31	Tu	31 7 12	5	16 8 30	2 17	♓	17	14 6	56 5	32	8 37

JEWISH CALENDAR.—5648. January 14, Sh

NOTABLE MONTHLY EVENTS.

4, 1492, West Indies discovered. — 14, 1797, Battle of Rivoli. Franklin born.—19, 1736, James Watt born.—22, 1788, Lord Byron bo Pacific lost.—30, 1649, Charles I. beheaded.

CONJECTURES OF THE WEATHER

1-5, clear and cold; 6-10, milder; 11-16, cloudy and snow; 17-2 cloudy; 27-29, snow; 30-31, milder.

Copyrighted August 1, 1881.

BUIST'S CABBAGE AWARDED THE

Marrowfat. This class of Pea is no favorite of ours, but in the Southern States it is popular with all. Select the Dwarf White, which produces longer pods and is more productive, than the tall growing variety. Sow in drills four feet apart; between each drill sow a row of broad-leaved Spinach, which will be off before the Peas shade the ground.

Lettuce. Transplant plants from Fall-sown seed, and sow the following varieties. These to head will require very rich ground; sow in very shallow drills twelve inches apart; the seed requires very little covering of soil; when up, thin out to six inches apart; select Buist's Prize Head, Boston Market, Dutch Butter, Large Passion, Hubbard Market and the Improved Royal Cabbage.

Sow **Buist's Garnishing Parsley, Collard, Spinach, Spring and Red-Top Turnips.** MUSTARD, CRESS, LEEK, PARSNIP, ONION-SETS, SHALLOTS, and GARLIC may still be planted; earth up CELERY, and ENDIVE should be tied up for blanching as required. Plant CUCUMBERS in hot-beds for forcing. Select the large ENGLISH varieties or BUIST'S LONG GREEN.

In planting ONION-SETS, always select the Philadelphia-grown, as they produce much finer Onions than those raised from Western-grown; besides, they are not so liable to shoot to seed.

DRESS your ASPARAGUS-BED with manure and salt, and spade it in carefully. All Fall-sown crops should now be well cultivated.

Onion. Sow in very rich ground in shallow drills six inches apart, cover lightly, rake the ground evenly, tramp it all over with the feet, and rake gently again; when up, keep down the weeds; they will make button-bulbs, that can be kept in a cool, dry room till next October, when they can be planted out, and grow to good bulbs for kitchen use. The Improved Bermuda, if sown very early on rich soil, will produce very large bulbs the same season.

Potatoes. There is not yet an early potato superior to the Vermont Early Rose for earliness, productiveness, and quality; it has also a strong healthy foliage; plant in rows two and a half feet apart, and eighteen inches in the row; rich ground well cultivated will give a good return; where only a few are grown, plant in hills two feet apart each way. I have seen fine large potatoes grown from sets the size of marbles. THE EXTRA EARLY VERMONT and EARLY OHIO are also very desirable early varieties, but for a later crop in the South, plant the PEERLESS. Should the potato-bugs make their appearance later in the season, dust the foliage with a mixture of one-fourth paris green to three-fourths plaster, or a preparation called slug shot, these are really the only applications that will settle them.

FEBRUARY.

This is strictly the gardening month for all the Gulf States; every garden amateur must be up and doing; if a frost should cut off any crop, do not despair, sow it again; if any seed has failed, sow again. If the sowing of any variety recommended to be attended to in January has been overlooked, attend to it at once: delay is always a loss in gardening operations.

Hot-beds will now require daily attention; give air by slightly raising the sash from the back during fine weather, always closing them before evening, and never permitting the young plants to be-

2d Month FEBRUARY, 1888. 29 Days.

MOON'S PHASES.

MIDDLE STATES.	D.	H.	M.	SOUTHERN STATES.	D.	H.	M.
Last Quarter	4	2	30 A.	Last Quarter	4	2	6 A.
New Moon..........................	11	6	56 A.	New Moon..........................	11	6	32 A.
First Quarter......................	19	9	3 A.	First Quarter......................	19	8	39 A.
Full Moon	27	7	1 M.	Full Moon	27	6	37 M.

D. of W.	D. of M.	Lat. of Middle States. The Sun Ris. h. m.		The Sun Sets. h. m.		The Moon R & S. h. m.		The Moon Souths h. m.		Constel-	lations.	Equation of Time.	Lat. of Southern States. The Sun Ris. h. m.		The Sun Sets. h. m.		The Moon R & S. h. m.		The Moon Souths h. m.		Aspects of Planets and Remarkable Days for both Latitudes.
W	1	7	11	5	17	9	40	3	9	♎	2	S.	6	56	5	33	9	43	3	9	☌♅☾.
Th	2	7	10	5	18	10	50	4	1	♎	16	14	6	55	5	34	10	48	4	1	*Purification.*
Fr	3	7	9	5	20	11	59	4	52	♏	0	14	6	54	5	34	11	52	4	52	Ve. r. 4.30 M.
Sa	4	7	8	5	21	morn		5	44	♏	15	14	6	54	5	35	morn		5	44	☾ ***4th.***
S	5	7	7	5	22	1	8	6	38	♏	29	14	6	53	5	36	0	57	6	38	☌♃☾.
M	6	7	6	5	23	2	17	7	32	♐	13	14	6	52	5	37	2	2	7	32	♆ stationary.
Tu	7	7	5	5	25	3	24	8	28	♐	26	14	6	51	5	38	3	6	8	28	Mars r. 10.52 A.
W	8	7	4	5	26	4	24	9	24	♑	10	14	6	50	5	39	4	5	9	24	☌♀☾. ◡
Th	9	7	2	5	27	5	19	10	20	♑	23	14	6	50	5	40	5	0	10	20	Aldeb. so. 7.11 A.
Fr	10	7	1	5	28	6	9	11	13	♒	6	14	6	49	5	41	5	51	11	13	Cap. s. 7.46 A
Sa	11	7	0	5	29	sets		Ev.	5	♒	19	14	6	48	5	42	sets		Ev.	5	● ***11th.***
S	12	6	59	5	31	6	20	0	53	♓	2	14	6	47	5	43	6	32	0	53	☌☿☾.
M	13	6	58	5	32	7	20	1	40	♓	15	14	6	46	5	44	7	28	1	40	Jupiter r. 1.32 M.
Tu	14	6	56	5	33	8	19	2	24	♓	27	14	6	45	5	44	8	23	2	24	*St. Valentine.*
W	15	6	55	5	34	9	17	3	6	♈	9	14	6	44	5	45	9	17	3	6	*Ash Wednesday*
Th	16	6	53	5	36	10	14	3	48	♈	21	14	6	43	5	46	10	10	3	48	☿ in perihelion.
Fr	17	6	53	5	37	11	11	4	30	♉	3	14	6	42	5	47	11	4	4	30	☾ in apogee.
Sa	18	6	51	5	38	morn		5	14	♉	15	14	6	41	5	48	11	58	5	14	Saturn s. 5.18 M.
S	19	6	50	5	39	0	8	5	58	♉	27	14	6	40	5	49	morn		5	58	☾ ***19th.*** [A.
M	20	6	48	5	40	1	6	6	45	♊	9	14	6	39	5	50	0	53	6	45	Can. s. 8.20
Tu	21	6	47	5	42	2	4	7	34	♊	21	14	6	38	5	50	1	47	7	34	Uran. r. 9.12 A.
W	22	6	45	5	43	3	0	8	25	♋	4	14	6	37	5	51	2	42	8	25	Sirius so. 8.31 A.
Th	23	6	44	5	44	3	54	9	19	♋	17	14	6	36	5	52	3	35	9	19	☿ stationary. ◠
Fr	24	6	43	5	45	4	45	10	14	♌	0	13	6	35	5	53	4	27	10	14	*St. Matthias.*
Sa	25	6	41	5	46	5	33	11	9	♌	14	13	6	34	5	54	5	16	11	9	☾ in ☊. [N.
S	26	6	40	5	48	6	15	morn		♌	28	13	6	32	5	55	6	1	morn		☿ gr. hel. lat.
M	27	6	38	5	49	rises		0	4	♍	12	13	6	31	5	55	rises		0	4	○ ***27th.***
Tu	28	6	37	5	50	7	23	0	58	♍	27	13	6	30	5	56	7	27	0	58	♀ in ☋.
W	29	6	35	5	51	8	36	1	52	♎	11	13	6	29	5	57	8	35	1	52	☌♅☾: ☾ in per.

JEWISH CALENDAR.—5648. February 13, Adar.

NOTABLE MONTHLY EVENTS.

1, 1789, Washington President.—7, 1812, Charles Dickens born.—8, 1586, Mary Stuart beheaded.—9, 1886, General Hancock died.—13, 1779, Captain Cook killed.—21, 1813, Ogdensburg taken.—28, 1776, Battle of Long Island.

CONJECTURES OF THE WEATHER.

1-6, very cold; 7-10, milder; 11-15, light snow; 17-22, clear and colder; 23-26, cloudy · 27-29, warmer, with heavy fall of snow.

Copyrighted August 1, 1881.

Buist's Seeds are the Most Reliable.

come chilled. Should the weather become cold, cover the sash at night with mats, in order to retain the heat. If the plants stand too thickly in the rows, thin them out in order to form stronger plants, or which is far better, transplant them into another prepared frame.

Plant Snap Beans. The Early Mohawk is the best for the first crop; it is more hardy than the others, and about a week earlier. If the weather is favorable however, run the risk and plant the Shippers' Favorite, which is the best of all the green podded varieties producing very long pods which when young are entirely stringless. Plant in rows twenty inches apart, drop the seed about an inch apart, and cover three inches deep; when up keep clean, and earth up a few inches of the stem. SECOND SOWING, say in two weeks, may be the Valentine, or, what is still better than them all, Buist's Selected Golden Wax, which is stringless and luscious, producing a waxy-colored pod, which, when properly prepared for the table, is as rich as marrow itself; to have fresh and tender Snapshorts there should be a few sown every two weeks throughout the season. We recommend planting Buist's Selected Wax Beans, because they are strictly pure and very early, being fit for table use in six weeks from planting. One-half of the Wax Beans sold throughout the country are all mixed up with green podded varieties, which are both tough and stringy, occasioned by growing them too close to other varieties, and selling the product for seed.

Plant another succession of PEAS, as advised last month. Sow CABBAGE and COLLARDS for a succession, to head later than last month's sowings; sow also FLAT DUTCH TURNIPS, BEETS, SQUASH, MELONS, SPINACH, LETTUCE, CRESS, RADISH, CARROT, CUCUMBER, PARSNIP, and if the weather is mild, make a planting of ADAMS'S EXTRA EARLY, and EXTRA EARLY DWARF SUGAR CORN. CUCUMBERS, SQUASH, and MELONS should always be protected early in the season by a covering of boxes at night, to prevent injury from cold.

Egg-Plant. If you have overlooked sowing, sow at once on a rich bed, covered with sash; it will be the end of March before they are fit to plant out; they require richer ground than any other vegetable, and must have a free supply of water in dry weather; another sowing should be made in March. Don't sow the common Egg Plant of the trade called by various names, such as New York Purple, &c., nearly all of which is the seed of the common mixed Egg-Plant grown in the South by inexperienced persons and are frequently of almost every shape and color, but purchase Buist's Improved Large Purple. We have never seen its equal for size, color or purity.

Celery. Sow thinly in rich soil, raked fine and tramp the ground evenly and rake again, as advised for onion seed; it delights in moist ground, and must have it, or a constant supply of water in some way. When the plants are six inches high, select damp weather, and plant them in rows two and a half feet apart and six inches from plant to plant; the drill for planting them should be a few inches under the level; mulch them with short manure, and water every two or three days. Select Buist's Mammoth White Solid and Golden Dwarf.

Transplant CABBAGE, LETTUCE, CAULIFLOWER; and ASPARAGUS ROOTS can also be planted for the formation of new beds.

Salsify, or Vegetable Oyster. Sow thinly in drills two inches deep, and twenty inches from row to row; when two inches

3d Month. **MARCH, 1888.** 31 Days.

MOON'S PHASES.

MIDDLE STATES.	D.	H.	M.		SOUTHERN STATES.	D.	H.	M.	
Last Quarter	4	10	30	A.	Last Quarter	4	10	6	A.
New Moon	12	11	25	M.	New Moon	12	11	1	M.
First Quarter	20	3	47	A.	First Quarter	20	3	23	A.
Full Moon	27	5	11	A.	Full Moon	27	4	47	A.

D. of W.	D. of M.	Lat. of Middle States. The Sun Ris. h. m.	The Sun Sets. h. m.	The Moon R. & S. h. m.	The Moon Souths h. m.	Constel-	lations.	Equation of Time.	Lat. of Southern States. The Sun Ris. h. m.	The Sun Sets. h. m.	The Moon R. & S. h. m.	The Moon Souths. h. m.	Aspects of Planets and Remarkable Days for both Latitudes.
Th	1	6 34	5 52	9 48	2 45	♍	26	S.	6 28	5 58	9 43	2 45	*St. David.*
Fr	2	6 32	5 53	11 0	3 39	♎	11	12	6 27	5 59	10 51	3 39	Venus r. 4.52 M.
Sa	3	6 31	5 54	morn	4 33	♎	25	12	6 25	5 59	11 57	4 33	☌ ☿ ☉ inferior.
S	4	6 29	5 55	0 10	5 28	♏	9	12	6 24	6 0	morn	5 28	☾ *4th.* [A.
M	5	6 28	5 56	1 18	6 24	♏	23	11	6 23	6 1	1 0	6 24	Capel. s. 6.12
Tu	6	6 26	5 57	2 20	7 20	♐	7	11	6 22	6 2	2 1	7 20	Rigel so. 6.9 A. ☋
W	7	6 24	5 59	3 16	8 15	♐	20	11	6 20	6 2	2 57	8 15	Mars r. 9.14 A.
Th	8	6 23	6 0	4 6	9 8	♑	3	11	6 19	6 3	3 47	9 8	Canop. s. 7.13 A.
Fr	9	6 21	6 1	4 49	10 0	♑	16	10	6 18	6 4	4 33	10 0	☌ ♀ ☾ : ☾ in ☋.
Sa	10	6 19	6 2	5 27	10 48	♑	29	10	6 16	6 5	5 15	10 48	☌ ☿ ☾.
S	11	6 18	6 3	6 1	11 35	♒	11	10	6 15	6 5	5 52	11 35	● Sir. s. 7.20 A.
M	12	6 16	6 4	sets	Ev. 19	♒	23	10	6 14	6 6	sets	Ev. 19	*12th.*
Tu	13	6 15	6 5	7 7	1 2	♓	5	9	6 13	6 7	7 9	1 2	Castor s. 7.59 A.
W	14	6 13	6 6	8 6	1 44	♓	17	9	6 11	6 8	8 4	1 44	Proc. so. 8.1 A.
Th	15	6 11	6 7	9 3	2 27	♓	29	9	6 10	6 8	8 57	2 27	Pollux so. 8.2 A.
Fr	16	6 10	6 8	9 59	3 9	♈	11	9	6 9	6 9	9 50	3 9	☿ stat. : ☾ in ap.
Sa	17	6 8	6 9	10 57	3 53	♈	23	8	6 7	6 10	10 44	3 53	*St. Patrick.*
S	18	6 6	6 11	11 54	4 38	♉	5	8	6 6	6 11	11 38	4 38	Saturn s. 3.19 M.
M	19	6 5	6 12	morn	5 26	♉	17	8	6 5	6 11	morn	5 26	☽ *Spring beg.*
Tu	20	6 3	6 13	0 49	6 15	♉	29	7	6 4	6 12	0 31	6 15	*20th.*
W	21	6 1	6 14	1 43	7 6	♊	12	7	6 2	6 13	1 24	7 6	☿ in ☋ : ♃ stat. ☊
Th	22	6 0	6 15	2 34	7 59	♊	25	7	6 1	6 13	2 15	7 59	☌ ♄ ☾.
Fr	23	5 58	6 16	3 23	8 53	♋	8	6	6 0	6 14	3 5	8 53	☾ in ☋.
Sa	24	5 56	6 17	4 6	9 48	♋	21	6	5 58	6 15	3 52	9 48	Uranus r. 7.1 A.
S	25	5 55	6 18	4 46	10 42	♌	5	6	5 57	6 15	4 35	10 42	*Annunciation.*
M	26	5 53	6 19	5 23	11 36	♌	20	6	5 56	6 16	5 17	11 36	○ Spica s. 1.3
Tu	27	5 51	6 20	rises	morn	♍	5	5	5 54	6 17	rises	morn	*27th.* [M.
W	28	5 50	6 21	7 27	0 30	♍	20	5	5 53	6 18	7 24	0 30	☌ ♂ ☾ : ☾ in per.
Th	29	5 48	6 22	8 41	1 25	♎	5	5	5 52	6 18	8 33	1 25	Nept. s. 10.2 A.
Fr	30	5 46	6 23	9 55	2 21	♎	20	4	5 50	6 19	9 42	2 21	*Good Friday.*
Sa	31	5 45	6 24	11 7	3 18	♏	5	4	5 49	6 20	10 50	3 18	☌ ♃ ☾ : ☿ in aph.

JEWISH CALENDAR.—5648. March 13, Nissan.

NOTABLE MONTHLY EVENTS.

5, 1770, Boston Massacre.—7, 1844, Florida becomes a State.—14, 1767, Andrew Jackson born.—15, 1820, Maine admitted a State.—23, 1808, Madrid taken.—26, 1649, John Winthrop died.—29, 1807, Planet Vesta discovered.

CONJECTURES OF THE WEATHER.

1-4, clear and cold; 5-10, milder; 11-12, hail or snow; 13-19, cold; 20-23, cloudy and snow; 25-28, clear and cold, 29-31, cloudy.

Copyrighted August 1, 1881.

BELLE AND BEAUTY ARE THE BEST TOMATOES.

high, thin out to four inches apart; the more cultivation, the finer the roots, which go deep and resist the heat and drought, sow the Mammoth.

Stock-Beets, such as MANGEL WURZEL and WHITE SUGAR, should now be sown; for shallow soil select Buist's Golden Globe; and for deep soil, Buist's Mammoth Long Red Mangel. The cultivation of stock-roots is greatly on the increase in this country, being found by the agriculturist an invaluable crop for cattle food during the winter.

Plant EARLY ROSE, EXTRA EARLY VERMONT and PEERLESS Potatoes. In Louisiana and other extreme Southern States, this is the month to plant for a general crop. Start your SWEET POTATOES in beds for sprouting.

MARCH.

This month is the basis of our crops for the production of what we will call *vegetable fruits*. In all warm, light soils, such productions succeed admirably, and there is no country where the melon, in all its varieties, is grown in such beauty and perfection as in the Southern States.

Beans. *The Lima and the Sewee*, especially the former is the cream of all the shelled-bean family; they require good soil, and planted in hills; if the ground is still cold, defer planting until later, as they are liable to rot.

First put in strong poles four feet each way, place a handful of rich compost at its base, and with the hoe or plow draw or furrow some soil over it; plant five good sound beans, eye downwards, around the pole, and cover with an inch of earth. When they have grown about a foot, tie the vines to the poles, and they will then provide for themselves, and produce beautiful crops from June till November; another planting can be made in May.

German Wax Pole, Dwarf Black Wax and Golden Wax Beans, plant by all means; they are luscious varieties, but are used as a snap, and not as a shelled-bean like the Lima. Their pods are of a beautiful golden color and entirely stringless.

Beets. Make another sowing of either Buist's Extra Early Turnip, Early Blood Turnip, Egyptian or Othello.

Corn. Plant, for first, a little of Adams; next, Early Sugar, Mammoth Sugar, followed by *Stowell's Evergreen Corn*. A planting of either of the two latter should be made every two or three weeks till August or September, thereby securing one of the finest table vegetables for six months of the year.

Cucumber. Sow in hills the *Perfection White Spine and Long Green*. If you wish only one sort, select the former, and make a small planting every month till August.

Cress and Mustard. A small sowing for Salad along with curled Lettuce. Select the Mammoth Curled Mustard—it is the best.

Nasturtium, where desired for pickles, should be sown; they fruit best when tied to trellises or poles.

Okra, or Gombo. Sow in rows three feet apart, and thin out to four inches apart in the row. Buist's Dwarf is the prominent and best variety.

4th Month. **APRIL, 1888.** 30 Days.

MOON'S PHASES.

MIDDLE STATES.	D.	H.	M.		SOUTHERN STATES.	D.	H.	M.	
Last Quarter	3	7	45	M.	Last Quarter	3	7	21	M.
New Moon	11	4	12	M.	New Moon	11	3	48	M.
First Quarter	19	6	56	M.	First Quarter	19	6	32	M.
Full Moon	26	1	26	M.	Full Moon	26	1	2	M

D. of W.	D of M.	Lat. of Middle States. The Sun Ris. h. m.		The Sun Sets. h. m.		The Moon R & S. h. m.		The Moon Souths h. m.		Constellations	Equation of Time.	Lat. of Southern States. The Sun Ris. h. m.		The Sun Sets. h. m.		The Moon R & S. h. m.		The Moon Souths h. m.		Aspects of Planets and Remarkable Days for both Latitudes.
S	1	5	43	6	25	morn		4	16	20	S.	5	48	6	20	11	55	4	16	Regul. s. 9.19 A.
M	2	5	41	6	26	0	13	5	14	4	3	5	46	6	21	morn		5	14	♀ in aph.
Tu	3	5	40	6	27	1	13	6	11	17	3	5	45	6	22	0	53	6	11	*3d.*
W	4	5	38	6	28	2	5	7	5	0	3	5	44	6	22	1	46	7	5	☍ ♅ ☉.
Th	5	5	36	6	29	2	50	7	57	13	3	5	42	6	23	2	33	7	57	☾ in ☋. [A.
Fr	6	5	35	6	30	3	29	8	47	26	2	5	41	6	24	3	15	8	47	Deneb. so. 10.40
Sa	7	5	33	6	31	4	3	9	33	8	2	5	40	6	25	3	53	9	33	Spica so. 0.16 M.
S	8	5	32	6	32	4	34	10	18	20	2	5	39	6	25	4	28	10	18	☌ ☿ ☾: ☌ ♀ ☾.
M	9	5	30	6	33	5	2	11	0	2	1	5	37	6	26	4	59	11	c	Mars r. 6.28 A.
Tu	10	5	28	6	34	5	30	11	42	14	1	5	36	6	27	5	31	11	42	☍ ♂ ☉.
W	11	5	27	6	36	sets		Ev.	24	2(	1	5	35	6	27	sets		Ev.	24	*11th.*
Th	12	5	25	6	37	7	53	1	7	8	1	5	34	6	28	7	44	1	7	☾ in apogee.
Fr	13	5	24	6	38	8	50	1	50	20	0	5	32	6	29	8	38	1	5c	☌ ☿ ♀.
Sa	14	5	22	6	39	9	47	2	35	2	0	5	31	6	29	9	32	2	35	☌ ♆ ☾.
S	15	5	21	6	40	10	44	3	21	14	fast	5	30	6	30	10	26	3	21	Jupiter r. 9.30 A.
M	16	5	19	6	41	11	38	4	10	2(		5	29	6	31	11	19	4	10	Alphac. s. 1.51 M.
Tu	17	5	18	6	42	morn		4	59	8	1	5	28	6	32	morn		4	59	Ant. s. 2 39 M.
W	18	5	16	6	43	0	29	5	51	20	1	5	26	6	32	0	9	5	51	☌ ♄ ☾.
Th	19	5	15	6	44	1	17	6	43	3	1	5	25	6	33	0	59	6	43	*19th.*
Fr	20	5	13	6	45	2	2	7	35	1(	1	5	24	6	34	1	45	7	35	Saturn s. 1.11 M.
Sa	21	5	12	6	46	2	42	8	27	c	1	5	23	6	35	2	28	8	27	☿ gr. hel. lat. S.
S	22	5	10	6	47	3	19	9	20	14	2	5	22	6	35	3	10	9	20	Uranus s. 4.38 M
M	23	5	9	6	48	3	54	10	14	28	2	5	21	6	36	3	49	10	14	*St. George.*
Tu	24	5	8	6	49	4	28	11	8	13	2	5	20	6	36	4	28	11	8	☌ ♂ ☾.
W	25	5	6	6	50	5	2	morn		28	2	5	19	6	37	5	7	morn		*St. Mark.*
Th	26	5	5	6	51	rises		0	4	14	2	5	18	6	38	rises		0	4	*26th.*
Fr	27	5	3	6	52	8	44	1	1	29	3	5	17	6	39	8	29	1	1	☌ ♃ ☾.
Sa	28	5	2	6	53	9	57	2	1	14	3	5	16	6	40	9	38	2	1	Vega so. 4.6 M.
S	29	5	1	6	54	11	2	3	1	29	3	5	15	6	41	10	42	3	1	Nept. s. 8.4 A.
M	30	4	59	6	55	morn		4	0	13	3	5	14	6	41	11	40	4	0	Deneb. s. 9.6 A.

JEWISH CALENDAR.—5648. April 12, Iyar.

NOTABLE MONTHLY EVENTS.

6, 1831, Revolution in Brazil.—9, 1886, St. Louis Railroad Riots.—13, 1791, James Buchanan born.—15, 1564, Shakespeare born.—17, 1655, Massacre of Waldenses.—24, 1814, Washington burned.—28, 1758, James Monroe born.—30, 1725, Battle of Fontenoy.

CONJECTURES OF THE WEATHER.

1-3, clear and cool; 4-7, cloudy; 8-12, snow or rain; 13-17, clear and pleasant; 18-22, warmer; 23-27, showers; 28-30, pleasant.

Copyrighted August 1, 1881.

BUIST'S ARE THE PRIZE MEDAL SEEDS.

Pumpkins of every desired variety should be planted in hills like Corn. The many new and wonderful sorts, with the most extravagant descriptions, are all excelled by the old *Cashaw*.

Radish. Sow White Summer and Buist's Yellow Summer, as the red varieties would now become spongy. They will come off in six weeks; thin this crop, when up, to an inch apart. Radishes should, however, always be sown between other crops, as they soon come off the ground.

Squash. There are several kinds in use, all of which have their peculiar qualities. *Bush Squash* does not run, comes soon to maturity, and to have a succession must be frequently sown. *Summer Crook Neck* or *Yellow* continues to run and grow, producing throughout the season. The *London Marrow* White Squash has also the quality of growing and producing for months.

Tomatoes. Independent of sowing in hot-beds for a later crop, sow in a warm bed or corner of the garden, covered at night or from cold winds until the season is favorable; as soon as they are four inches high, plant out into hills three feet apart, and two plants to a hill; as they grow, tie them to stakes, and as soon as three feet high, pinch off the points of the vines, which will cause them to mature their fruit earlier. Do not overlook planting the BELLE and BEAUTY, they are the finest varieties ever introduced, being early, solid, beautiful and perfect. Other desirable varieties are ACME, LIVINGSTON'S FAVORITE, and TROPHY.

Herbs. Now is the time for sowing a full assortment of these. If the weather is favorable, and the soil warm, all early hot-bed plants, such as Tomatoes, Egg Plant, and Peppers, can be transplanted to the open ground, and also transplant Cabbage and Lettuce from your winter-beds, if not already done.

Continue planting PEAS, BUIST'S MORNING STAR and PREMIER EXTRA EARLY, ADVANCER, CHAMPION, ALPHA, and PREMIUM GEM, and a further supply of BUIST'S DWARF GOLDEN WAX and VALENTINE BEANS. Sow DUTCH BUTTER, ROYAL CABBAGE and SALAMANDER LETTUCE, as they withstand the heat, and are not so liable to shoot to seed as the early varieties; sow also SPINACH, CARROT, MELON, ONION, and LEEK, and, in fact, any other vegetables that you require, as the season is sufficiently advanced for any variety to do well. Give all the growing crops your attention. Just remember that good cultivation is almost as powerful a stimulant to the growth of plants as manure. Look out for weeds; they are enemies in your camp, and will rob your ground of a good portion of the nourishment that is intended for your crops.

APRIL.

The vegetable garden is now in its exuberance of growth; cultivate well, and look out for weeds. Thin out all young crops, to prevent crowding. Water when dry; CAULIFLOWER requires copious watering at the roots when forming heads. Celery-seed beds and plants are also in need of water; if, however, labor and care are deficient, those vegetables will not make a return for planting; as soil can never be too rich for them. Where BEETS are too thick, they can be transplanted; cut off the large thick leaves, lift carefully, and dibble them into rows, or amongst other crops that are too thin; do this in moist weather.

5th Month. **MAY, 1888.** 31 Days.

MOON'S PHASES.

MIDDLE STATES.	D.	H.	M.	SOUTHERN STATES.	D.	H.	M.
Last Quarter	2	6	51 A.	Last Quarter	2	6	27 A.
New Moon	10	8	27 A.	New Moon	10	8	3 A.
First Quarter	18	6	9 A.	First Quarter	18	5	45 A.
Full Moon	25	8	44 M.	Full Moon	25	8	20 M.

D. of W.	D. of M.	Lat. of Middle States. The Sun Ris. h. m.	The Sun Sets. h. m.	The Moon R & S. h. m.	The Moon Souths h. m.	Constellations.		Equation of Time.	Lat. of Southern States. The Sun Ris. h. m.	The Sun Sets. h. m.	The Moon R & S. h. m.	The Moon Souths h. m.	Aspects of Planets and Remarkable Days for both Latitudes.
Tu	1	4 58	6 56	0 0	4 58	♐	26	F.	5 13	6 42	morn	4 58	☾ *St. Phil. St.*
W	2	4 57	6 57	0 50	5 53	♑	9	3	5 12	6 42	0 32	5 53	*2d* [*James.*
Th	3	4 56	6 58	1 31	6 44	♑	22	3	5 11	6 43	1 17	6 44	Venus r. 4.26 M.
Fr	4	4 54	6 59	2 7	7 32	♒	5	3	5 10	6 44	1 56	7 32	Spica so. 10.26 A.
Sa	5	4 53	7 0	2 38	8 17	♒	17	4	5 9	6 45	2 30	8 17	☌♅♂.
S	6	4 52	7 2	3 7	9 0	♒	29	4	5 8	6 45	3 3	9 0	Arct. so. 11.9 A.
M	7	4 51	7 3	3 35	9 42	♓	11	4	5 7	6 46	3 34	9 42	Mars s. 3.37 M.
Tu	8	4 50	7 4	4 2	10 24	♓	23	4	5 6	6 47	4 5	10 24	☌♀☾.
W	9	4 49	7 5	4 29	11 6	♈	5	4	5 5	6 47	4 36	11 6	● ☿ in ☊.
Th	10	4 47	7 6	4 55	11 48	♈	17	4	5 4	6 48	5 7	11 48	*10th.*
Fr	11	4 46	7 7	sets	Ev. 33	♈	29	4	5 4	6 49	sets	Ev. 33	☌♆☾.
Sa	12	4 45	7 8	8 39	1 19	♉	11	4	5 3	6 50	8 21	1 19	Alph. so. 0.8 M.
S	13	4 44	7 9	9 34	2 7	♉	23	4	5 2	6 50	9 15	2 7	Jupiter r. 7.27 A.
M	14	4 43	7 9	10 26	2 56	♊	5	4	5 1	6 51	10 6	2 56	☿ in perihel. ⌓
Tu	15	4 42	7 10	11 15	3 47	♊	17	4	5 1	6 52	10 56	3 47	☌♆☿.
W	16	4 42	7 11	morn	4 38	♋	0	4	5 0	6 53	11 42	4 38	☌♄☾ : ☾ in ☊.
Th	17	4 41	7 12	0 0	5 29	♋	12	4	4 59	6 53	morn	5 29	☽ Ant. so. 0.41
Fr	18	4 40	7 13	0 40	6 20	♋	25	4	4 59	6 54	0 26	6 20	*18th.* [M.
Sa	19	4 39	7 14	1 17	7 11	♌	9	4	4 58	6 55	1 7	7 11	☌♆☉.
S	20	4 38	7 15	1 51	8 2	♌	23	4	4 58	6 55	1 45	8 2	☌♃β' scorpii.
M	21	4 37	7 16	2 24	8 53	♍	7	4	4 57	6 56	2 22	8 53	☌♂☾ : ☌♅☾.
Tu	22	4 36	7 17	2 58	9 47	♍	22	4	4 56	6 57	3 1	9 47	☍♃☉ : ♂ stat
W	23	4 36	7 18	3 32	10 43	♎	7	3	4 56	6 57	3 39	10 43	Vega so. 2.28 M.
Th	24	4 35	7 18	4 10	11 41	♎	22	3	4 55	6 58	4 22	11 41	○ ☌♃☾.
Fr	25	4 34	7 19	rises	morn	♏	7	3	4 55	6 59	rises	morn	*25th.*
Sa	26	4 34	7 20	8 43	0 41	♏	22	3	4 55	6 59	8 24	0 41	Uran. s. 2.21 M.
S	27	4 33	7 21	9 47	1 43	♐	7	3	4 54	7 0	9 27	1 43	Alt. so. 3.24 M. ◡
M	28	4 33	7 22	10 41	2 43	♐	21	3	4 54	7 1	10 22	2 43	Arct. so. 9.42 A.
Tu	29	4 32	7 23	11 28	3 41	♑	5	3	4 54	7 1	11 11	3 41	Nept. r. 4.33 M.
W	30	4 32	7 23	morn	4 36	♑	18	3	4 53	7 2	11 53	4 36	☾ in ☋.
Th	31	4 31	7 24	0 7	5 27	♒	1	2	4 53	7 2	morn	5 27	*Corpus Christi.*

JEWISH CALENDAR.—5648. May 11, Sivan.

NOTABLE MONTHLY EVENTS.

4, 1886, Anarchist Riot in Chicago.—8, 1846, Battle of Palo Alto.—12, 1607, Jamestown settled.—18, 1846, Matamoras taken.—19, 1536, Anna Boleyn beheaded.—26, 1564, John Calvin died.—29, 1871, Paris burned.—30, 1853, Dr. Kane sails.

CONJECTURES OF THE WEATHER.

1-4, warm; 5-7, cloudy and sultry; 8-11, showers; 12-17, clear and pleasant· 18-23, warmer; 24-27, cloudy; 28-31, heavy fog and rain.

Copyrighted August 1, 1881.

FOR PROFIT, SOW BUIST'S SEEDS.

Do not overlook planting a few BEANS, PEAS, CORN, CUCUMBER, LETTUCE, LEEK, MELON, SUMMER RADISH, and in fact, all varieties named for last month's sowing can be still sown, which will afford an ample succession of crops.

If Melons or any crops have not come up well, stir the ground and replant at once; whenever you have had your supply of seeds, make a note of failures, and acquaint the parties with it; such action will benefit yourself and others. See to tying up ENDIVE for blanching before use; at this season it will blanch in eight or ten days.

About the last of the month sow a supply of Buist's Improved Flat Dutch, Buist's Drumhead, and Drumhead Savoy Cabbage, for June Planting, to head in Fall; these varieties will always produce fine heads in the South. At this season of the year the small cabbage-fly is very destructive to the young plants, and frequently destroys them as fast as they make their appearance above ground; always keep them well dusted with plaster, or apply strong tobacco-water until they are sufficiently large to withstand such attacks.

Spring-Sown Cabbage is now ready for transplanting; the soil for their culture must be rich to insure fine heads. Sow Celery for main crop, hill up Potatoes and keep them well cultivated. Train the Lima Bean vines to poles, and stake all Peas planted last month. Do not neglect your Asparagus-bed; keep it well cultivated and loosened with a hoe until the shoots commence appearing.

MAY.

We now fully repeat the observations of last month; the warm season is approaching, when many of the crops cease growing. Fresh and young crops from the second or third sowing will continue to grow whenever moisture is supplied. Irrigation and good cultivation is the whole secret in successful culture in dry, warm climates. Sweet Potato sprouts, for a late crop, should be planted; these tubers, prepared in every variety of cooking, are a grateful dish on our table three times a day.

Plant Snap-short and Pole Beans for a succession; sow late Cabbage for Winter-heading; also Cauliflower and Brocoli; sow Salamander Lettuce—it is the only variety that will now stand the heat without shooting to seed. Sow Buist's Yellow Summer and White Summer Radish. Melons, Cucumbers and Squashes may still be planted for a succession. Look out for weeds, as they will now rapidly overgrow your crops.

CORN, for late roasting-ears, should be planted in the early part, and also the last of this month. The old-fashioned New England Sugar, Mammoth Sugar and Stowel's Evergreen are the best.

YOUR TOMATO SEEDS have produced the finest fruit I ever saw. One of my customers assured me that he had grown some of your Belle the past season that weighed 1¼ pounds.
August 11, 1887. WILLIAM ANDERSON, of Florida.

It affords me pleasure to say that Buist's seeds produced by far the best vegetables of any seeds I have ever sown.
August 19, 1887. J. E. SPRINGER, of Texas.

I have used Buist's seeds for fifteen years; they always give perfect satisfaction.
March 8, 1887. G. L. McCREARY, of Alabama.

Your seeds are the best that I have ever sown.
February 25, 1887. PRINCE HUNTER, of Louisiana.

6th Month. JUNE, 1888. 30 Days.

MOON'S PHASES.

MIDDLE STATES.	D.	H.	M.	SOUTHERN STATES.	D.	H.	M.
Last Quarter	1	7	57 M.	Last Quarter	1	7	33 M
New Moon	9	11	38 M.	New Moon	9	11	14 M.
First Quarter	17	1	54 M.	First Quarter	17	1	30 M.
Full Moon	23	4	11 A.	Full Moon	23	3	47 A.
Last Quarter	30	10	56 A.	Last Quarter	30	10	32 A.

D. of W.	D. of M.	Lat. of Middle States. The Sun Ris. h. m.	The Sun Sets. h. m.	The Moon R & S. h. m.	The Moon Souths h. m.	Constel-	lations.	Equation of Time.	Lat. of Southern States. The Sun Ris. h. m.	The Sun Sets. h m.	The Moon R & S. h m.	The Moon Souths h m.	Aspects of Planets and Remarkable Days for both Latitudes.
Fr	1	4 31	7 25	0 40	6 14	♓	14	F.	4 53	7 3	0 31	6 14	☾ 1st. ☌♆♀.
Sa	2	4 30	7 26	1 10	6 58	♓	26	2	4 52	7 3	1 5	6 58	Ve.r.4.19M.
S	3	4 30	7 26	1 38	7 41	♈	8	2	4 52	7 4	1 37	7 41	Spica so. 8.28 A
M	4	4 29	7 27	2 5	8 23	♈	20	2	4 52	7 4	2 8	8 23	Arctur.so.9.15A.
Tu	5	4 29	7 28	2 31	9 4	♉	2	2	4 52	7 5	2 37	9 4	♂ in ☋.
W	6	4 29	7 28	2 58	9 47	♉	14	1	4 52	7 5	3 8	9 47	☌♅♂: ☾ in apo.
Th	7	4 29	7 29	3 28	10 30	♉	26	1	4 51	7 6	3 42	10 30	☌♆☾.
Fr	8	4 28	7 29	4 1	11 16	♊	8	1	4 51	7 6	4 18	11 16	● ☌♀☾.
Sa	9	4 28	7 30	sets	Ev. 3	♊	20	1	4 51	7 7	sets	Ev. 3	9th.
S	10	4 28	7 30	8 23	0 53	♋	2	1	4 51	7 7	8 3	0 53	Alph.so.10.10 A.
M	11	4 28	7 31	9 13	1 44	♋	14	0	4 51	7 8	8 53	1 44	*St. Barnabas.* ☊
Tu	12	4 28	7 31	10 0	2 35	♋	27	0	4 51	7 8	9 42	2 35	☿gr.el.E.24° 24′
W	13	4 28	7 32	10 43	3 26	♌	9	0	4 51	7 8	10 27	3 26	Ant. so. 10.51 A.
Th	14	4 28	7 32	11 20	4 17	♌	22	sl.	4 51	7 9	11 8	4 17	Jupiter s. 3 23M.
Fr	15	4 28	7 33	11 54	5 7	♍	5	0	4 51	7 9	11 46	5 7	☽ Vega s. 0.57
Sa	16	4 28	7 33	morn	5 56	♍	19	1	4 51	7 10	morn	5 56	17th. [M.
S	17	4 28	7 33	0 27	6 46	♎	3	1	4 51	7 10	0 23	6 46	☿ in ☋: ☌♂☾.
M	18	4 28	7 34	0 59	7 37	♎	17	1	4 51	7 10	0 59	7 37	☌♅☾.
Tu	19	4 28	7 34	1 31	8 30	♏	1	1	4 52	7 11	1 36	8 30	♅ stat.: ♀ in ☊.
W	20	4 28	7 34	2 5	9 25	♏	16	1	4 52	7 11	2 15	9 25	*Summer begins.*
Th	21	4 29	7 34	2 43	10 23	♐	1	2	4 52	7 11	2 58	10 23	☌♃☾: ☾ in per.
Fr	22	4 29	7 35	3 27	11 23	♐	16	2	4 52	7 11	3 46	11 23	○ Uran.s.0.34
Sa	23	4 29	7 35	rises	morn	♑	1	2	4 53	7 11	rises	morn	23d. [M.
S	24	4 29	7 35	8 27	0 24	♑	15	2	4 53	7 11	8 7	0 24	*St John, Bapt.* ☋
M	25	4 30	7 35	9 19	1 25	♑	29	2	4 53	7 11	9 0	1 25	☿ stationary.
Tu	26	4 30	7 35	10 3	2 22	♒	13	3	4 53	7 12	9 48	2 22	☾ in ☋.
W	27	4 31	7 35	10 41	3 16	♒	26	3	4 54	7 12	10 30	3 16	☿ in aphelion.
Th	28	4 31	7 35	11 13	4 6	♓	9	3	4 54	7 12	11 6	4 6	Nept. r. 2.39 M.
Fr	29	4 31	7 35	11 41	4 53	♓	22	3	4 54	7 12	11 38	4 53	☾ *St. Peter. St.*
Sa	30	4 32	7 35	morn	5 37	♈	5	3	4 55	7 12	morn	5 37	30th. [*Paul*

JEWISH CALENDAR.—5648. June 10, Tammuz.

NOTABLE MONTHLY EVENTS.

2, 1814, Treaty of Paris.—4, 1871, Telegraph to China.—9, 1800, Battle of Montebello.—14, 1800, Battle of Marengo.—18, 1880, Gen. Sutter died.—26, 1813, Battle of Lundy's Lane.—28, 1880, Seewanhaka burned.—30, 1530, Montezuma died.

CONJECTURES OF THE WEATHER.

1–4, pleasant; 5–7, cloudy; 8–12, rain; 13–17, clear and warm; 18–20, cloudy and sultry; 21–22, thunderstorms; 23–27, pleasant; 28–30, warm.

Copyrighted August 1, 1881.

BUIST'S SEEDS SPROUT QUICKLY.

JUNE.

The gardener of the South and the garden amateur have much to reflect upon in this glorious month of bearable sunshine. Renew all crops as advised; plant Snap-short Beans; look over Melons, Cucumbers, and Squashes; destroy bugs and every other enemy; weeds abhor with the vengeance of destruction. Stir up the soil to keep in moisture, and allow the air and dew to penetrate; all will assist to keep the growing life in crops. Transplant Cauliflower, Brocoli, Buist's Drumhead and Flat Dutch Cabbage, which must be liberally supplied with water; perseverance will always insure success in your gardening operations.

Buist's Perfection Early White Spine Cucumber

—IS THE—

BEST TABLE AND THE MOST PROFITABLE SHIPPING VARIETY.

This Stock is put up and sold only in our Sealed Papers and Cartoons. We send out no Seed of this variety in bulk.

The first and most important feature in growing cucumbers for market is to obtain the choicest seed stock for planting. Most of the crops grown are very much mixed, and of inferior quality. Buist's Perfection is regarded by growers as the finest and purest stock known. It is not only the very earliest, but it produces cucumbers of the finest form and most salable size for shipping purposes. It was introduced by us three years since, and is already being grown by the most extensive cucumber cultivators in this country. Our crop the past season, grown especially for seed, was over 150 acres.

| Price per oz., - 20 cents. | Price per lb., - - $1.50 |
| " " ¼ lb., - 40 " | " " 10 lbs., - $12.50 |

6th Month.	JULY, 1888.	31 Days.

MOON'S PHASES.

MIDDLE STATES.	D.	H.	M.	SOUTHERN STATES.	D.	H.	M.
New Moon	9	1	20 M.	New Moon	9	0	56 M.
First Quarter	16	7	17 M.	First Quarter	16	6	53 M.
Full Moon	23	0	49 M.	Full Moon	23	0	25 M.
Last Quarter	30	3	33 A.	Last Quarter	30	3	9 A.

D. of W.	D. of M.	Lat. of Middle States. The Sun Ris. h. m.	The Sun Sets. h. m.	The Moon R. & S. h. m.	The Moon Souths h. m.	Constel-	lations.	Equation of Time.	Lat. of Southern States. The Sun Ris. h. m.	The Sun Sets. h. m.	The Moon R. & S. h. m.	The Moon Souths h. m.	Aspects of Planets and Remarkable Days for both Latitudes.
S	1	4 32	7 35	0 8	6 20	♓	17	S.	4 55	7 12	0 8	6 20	Alph. so, 8.48 A.
M	2	4 33	7 34	0 35	7 2	♓	29	4	4 56	7 12	0 39	7 2	Venus r. 4.48 M.
Tu	3	4 33	7 34	1 2	7 44	♈	11	4	4 56	7 12	1 10	7 44	☉ apog.: ☾ in ap.
W	4	4 34	7 34	1 30	8 27	♈	22	4	4 57	7 11	1 42	8 27	□ ♅ ☉.
Th	5	4 35	7 34	2 0	9 12	♉	4	4	4 57	7 11	2 17	9 12	☌ ♆ ☾.
Fr	6	4 35	7 33	2 36	9 58	♉	16	5	4 58	7 11	2 55	9 58	Ant. so. 9.21 A
Sa	7	4 36	7 33	3 17	10 47	♉	29	5	4 58	7 11	3 38	10 47	Mars s. 11.54 A.
S	8	4 37	7 33	4 1	11 38	♊	11	5	4 58	7 11	4 23	11 38	☌ ☿ ☉ inf. ☊
M	9	4 38	7 32	sets	Ev. 30	♊	23	5	4 59	7 10	sets	Ev. 30	9th. ☾ in ☊.
Tu	10	4 38	7 32	8 42	1 22	♋	6	5	4 59	7 10	8 25	1 22	☌ ♄ ☾.
W	11	4 39	7 32	9 21	2 14	♋	19	5	5 0	7 10	9 7	2 14	☌ ♀ ☉ superior.
Th	12	4 39	7 31	9 56	3 5	♌	2	5	5 1	7 9	9 47	3 5	Vega so. 11.7 A.
Fr	13	4 40	7 31	10 29	3 54	♌	16	6	5 1	7 9	10 24	3 54	Jupit. s. 1.22 M.
Sa	14	4 41	7 30	11 1	4 44	♍	0	6	5 2	7 9	11 0	4 44	☌ ♅ ☾.
S	15	4 41	7 30	11 34	5 33	♍	14	6	5 2	7 8	11 37	5 33	☌ ♂ ☾.
M	16	4 42	7 29	morn	6 24	♍	28	6	5 3	7 8	morn	6 24	*16th.*
Tu	17	4 43	7 28	0 7	7 16	♎	12	6	5 4	7 8	0 15	7 16	☌ ♃ ☾.
W	18	4 44	7 28	0 42	8 11	♎	26	6	5 4	7 7	0 55	8 11	☿ gr. hel. lat. S.
Th	19	4 45	7 27	1 22	9 9	♏	11	6	5 5	7 7	1 39	9 9	☿ stat.: ☾ in per.
Fr	20	4 45	7 26	2 7	10 8	♏	25	6	5 6	7 6	2 28	10 8	Fom. s. 2.57 M.
Sa	21	4 46	7 25	3 0	11 8	♐	10	6	5 6	7 6	3 22	11 8	Sat. s. 7.34 A. ☋
S	22	4 47	7 25	3 58	morn	♐	24	6	5 7	7 5	4 20	morn	□ ♂ ☉.
M	23	4 48	7 24	rises	0 7	♑	8	6	5 8	7 4	rises	0 7	*23d.*
Tu	24	4 49	7 23	8 35	1 3	♑	21	6	5 8	7 4	8 22	1 3	Mark. so. 2.49 M.
W	25	4 50	7 22	9 10	1 55	♒	4	6	5 9	7 3	9 1	1 55	*St. James.*
Th	26	4 51	7 21	9 41	2 44	♒	17	6	5 10	7 2	9 36	2 44	Uran. s. 10.17 A.
Fr	27	4 52	7 20	10 9	3 30	♓	0	6	5 10	7 2	10 8	3 30	☌ ♄ ♀.
Sa	28	4 53	7 19	10 36	4 14	♓	13	6	5 11	7 1	10 39	4 14	Ant. so. 7.54 A.
S	29	4 54	7 18	11 3	4 57	♓	25	6	5 11	7 0	11 10	4 57	
M	30	4 55	7 17	11 31	5 39	♈	7	6	5 12	7 0	11 42	5 39	*30th.*
Tu	31	4 56	7 16	morn	6 22	♈	19	6	5 13	6 59	morn	6 22	☾ in apogee.

JEWISH CALENDAR.—5648. July 9, Ab.

NOTABLE MONTHLY EVENTS.

1, 1781, Battle of Porto Novo.—5, 1811, Independence of Venezuela.—13, 1815, Napoleon surrendered.—14, 1789, Bastile captured.—24, 1862, Martin Van Buren died.—28, 1833, Wilberforce died.—30, 1718, William Penn died.

CONJECTURES OF THE WEATHER.

1-6, very warm; 7-10, cloudy and rain; 11-15, clear and warm; 16-20, hot and sultry; 21-25, showers; 26-31, clear and pleasant.

Copyrighted August 1, 1881.

BUIST'S MORNING STAR, EARLIEST and BEST PEA.

BUIST'S ALMANAC AND GARDEN MANUAL.   21

JULY.

If there is any month in the twelve where there may be some cessation of labor by the gardener of the South, it is July—ground is dry, atmosphere hot. Seeds may be sown, but they do not vegetate; weeds, however, grow, and they must be kept under. Snap Beans will grow, and plant them for succession; water Celery or mulch it; towards the end of the month, if moist, sow Ruta Baga Turnip; select Buist's Improved Yellow, which is by far the finest variety; plant Cucumber seed for pickles; transplant Drumhead and Flat Dutch Cabbage under showers; prepare ground for crops in the ensuing month; sow Squash, Spinach, and also a supply of Turnips and Sugar Corn.

The Turnip-fly is a very destructive insect on the Ruta Baga and Turnip crop, frequently eating off the young plants just as fast as they make their appearance above ground. Examine closely and if they are discovered, dust them with plaster. Frequent failures are often experienced in securing a good stand of plants; do not become disheartened, but re-seed at once.

Turnip Seed is always a very uncertain article to purchase, as the great object with some growers the past few years appears to be to raise it cheaply, regardless of quality. To guard against any such disappointment, PURCHASE and SOW BUIST'S GROWTH; all the leading merchants throughout the Southern States generally keep this brand, but in purchasing, observe that the packages are distinctly marked GROWN BY BUIST. The great popularity of our seed has caused some northern dealers who are not growers, (but who are compelled to purchase all the seed they sell,) to imitate our style of putting up in order to sell their inferior stocks of the common Imported or inferior American seed.

OPINION OF OUR CUSTOMERS
ABOUT THE QUALITY OF
Buist's Garden Seeds.

No seed came nearer to perfection than those I bought of you last season.
April 29, 1887.   W. W. SMITH, of North Carolina.

I consider Buist's garden seeds the best of all, especially your Improved Flat Dutch Cabbage and Belle Tomato. They cannot be recommended too highly, as they are unequalled by any for quality.
March 11, 1887.   W. L. SAXON, of Georgia.

I have used your garden seeds for many years, and prefer them to any others.
February 7, 1887.   W. M. JACKSON, of Alabama.

Your seeds are fine.
February 28, 1887.   FRANK CLAYTON, of Florida.

I have been using your garden seeds for many years, and never had them fail.
February 14, 1887.   W. J. AUSTIN, of Louisiana.

I have planted Buist's garden seeds for over ten years, and will use no others when I can get them.
August 1, 1887.   B. H. TAYLOR, of South Carolina.

I have had splendid results from all of your seeds, and can recommend them heartily.
May 4, 1887.   J. H. LYNCH, of Indian Territory.

Have used Buist's garden seeds exclusively in my garden this year with great satisfaction. Your Extra Early Peas are the best I ever grew.
May 28, 1887.   MRS. H. BRISCO, of Virginia.

Have tested your seeds, and have never grown better.
June 1, 1887.   A. F. THERIOT, of Texas.

8th Month. **AUGUST, 1888.** 31 Days.

MOON'S PHASES.

MIDDLE STATES.	D.	H	M.	SOUTHERN STATES.	D.	H.	M.
New Moon	7	1	25 A.	New Moon	7	1	1 A.
First Quarter	14	11	48 M.	First Quarter	14	11	24 M.
Full Moon	21	11	24 M.	Full Moon	21	11	0 M.
Last Quarter	29	9	22 M.	Last Quarter	29	8	58 M.

D. of W.	D. of M.	Lat. of Middle States. The Sun Ris. h. m.	The Sun Sets. h. m.	The Moon R & S. h. m.	The Moon Souths h. m.	Constellations.		Equation of Time.	Lat. of Southern States. The Sun Ris. h. m.	The Sun Sets. h. m.	The Moon R & S. h. m.	The Moon Souths h. m.	Aspects of Planets and Remarkable Days for both Latitudes.
W	1	4 57	7 15	0 1	7 6	♉	1	S.	5 14	6 58	0 16	7 6	☌♆☾: ☌♄☉.
Th	2	4 58	7 14	0 34	7 52	♉	13	6	5 14	6 57	0 52	7 52	Venus s. 7.18 A.
Fr	3	4 58	7 13	1 11	8 40	♉	25	6	5 15	6 56	1 32	8 40	Vega so. 9.41 A.
Sa	4	4 59	7 12	1 55	9 30	♊	7	6	5 16	6 55	2 17	9 30	Alt. so. 10 49A. ⌓
S	5	5 0	7 10	2 44	10 21	♊	19	6	5 16	6 55	3 6	10 21	☌☿☾: ☿ in ☊.
M	6	5 1	7 9	3 40	11 14	♋	2	6	5 17	6 54	4 1	11 14	● ☌♄☾.
Tu	7	5 2	7 8	sets	Ev. 7	♋	15	5	5 18	6 53	sets	Ev. 7	*7th.* ☌♀☾.
W	8	5 3	7 7	7 53	0 59	♋	29	5	5 18	6 52	7 42	0 59	Mars s. 10.34 A.
Th	9	5 4	7 5	8 29	1 50	♌	12	5	5 19	6 51	8 23	1 50	Fomal. s. 1.39 M.
Fr	10	5 5	7 4	9 3	2 41	♌	26	5	5 20	6 50	9 1	2 41	☿ in perihelion.
Sa	11	5 6	7 3	9 35	3 31	♍	10	5	5 21	6 49	9 38	3 31	☌♅☾.
S	12	5 7	7 1	10 7	4 21	♍	25	5	5 21	6 48	10 14	4 21	Jupit. s. 11.21 A.
M	13	5 8	7 0	10 41	5 13	♎	9	5	5 22	6 47	10 53	5 13	☽ ☌♂☾.
Tu	14	5 9	6 59	11 19	6 6	♎	23	4	5 23	6 46	11 36	6 6	*14th.*
W	15	5 10	6 58	morn	7 0	♏	7	4	5 23	6 45	morn	7 0	♀ gr. hel. lat. N.
Th	16	5 11	6 56	0 2	7 59	♏	21	4	5 24	6 43	0 22	7 59	Mark. s. 1.19 M.
Fr	17	5 12	6 54	0 52	8 58	♐	5	4	5 25	6 42	1 13	8 58	Alge. s. 2.23 M. ⌣
Sa	18	5 13	6 53	1 48	9 56	♐	19	3	5 25	6 41	2 10	9 56	Saturn r. 4.22 M.
S	19	5 14	6 52	2 49	10 52	♑	3	3	5 26	6 40	3 10	10 52	☾ in ☋.
M	20	5 15	6 50	3 53	11 45	♑	16	3	5 26	6 39	4 12	11 45	○ □♃☉.
Tu	21	5 16	6 49	rises	morn	♒	0	3	5 27	6 38	rises	morn	*21st.*
W	22	5 17	6 47	7 40	0 35	♒	13	3	5 28	6 37	7 33	0 35	Pol. so. 3.13 M.
Th	23	5 18	6 46	8 9	1 22	♒	26	2	5 29	6 35	8 6	1 22	☌☿☉ superior.
Fr	24	5 19	6 44	8 37	2 7	♓	8	2	5 29	6 34	8 38	2 7	*St. Bartholom.*
Sa	25	5 20	6 43	9 4	2 51	♓	21	2	5 30	6 33	9 9	2 51	Uran. s. 8.23 A.
S	26	5 21	6 41	9 31	3 34	♈	3	1	5 31	9 32	9 40	3 34	Acher. so. 3.13 M.
M	27	5 22	6 40	10 0	4 16	♈	15	1	5 31	6 31	10 13	4 16	Vega so. 8.6 A.
Tu	28	5 23	6 38	10 32	5 0	♈	27	1	5 32	6 29	10 48	5 0	☾ ☌♆☾.
W	29	5 24	6 37	11 7	5 45	♉	8	1	5 33	6 28	11 27	5 45	*29th.*
Th	30	5 25	6 35	11 48	6 31	♉	20	0	5 33	6 27	morn	6 31	Nept. r. 10.32 A.
Fr	31	5 26	6 33	morn	7 20	♊	2	0	5 34	6 26	0 9	7 20	Fomal. s. 0.12 M.

JEWISH CALENDAR.—5648. August 8, Elul.

NOTABLE MONTHLY EVENTS.

2, 1563, Plague in London.—4, 1886, Samuel J. Tilden died.—8, 1815, Napoleon banished.—11, 1831, Barbadoes devastated.—12, 1676, King Philip shot.—16, 1857, Capture of Delhi.—27, 1776, Battle of Long Island.—31, 1886, Earthquake at Charleston.

CONJECTURES OF THE WEATHER.

1–4, very warm; 5–10, cloudy and rain; 11–13, clear and warm; 14–17, hot and sultry, 18–20, threatening; 21–25, rain; 26–31, clear and pleasant.

Copyrighted August 1, 1881.

Buist's Perfection Cucumber, Best Market Variety.

BUIST'S ALMANAC AND GARDEN MANUAL. 23

AUGUST.

Whatever was omitted last month execute at once, and push on with the following, now in season; if no rain, water freely. This is the great month for sowing Turnip and Ruta Baga seeds, and too much attention cannot be bestowed upon the importance of this crop. It is invaluable, supplying nutritious food for both man and beast, during the Fall and Winter months, with little or no care, after once preparing the ground and sowing the seed. But an important feature is to secure pure seed, as the market has been flooded the past two or three years with a very inferior quality of Turnip seed, produced without the expensive process of transplanting and selecting the roots. Seed grown in this manner produces knotty and degenerated bulbs, having a disagreeable, strong flavor. To guard against any such disappointment, purchase your seed from Buist, who is the largest and most successful Turnip-seed grower in this country (who grows every grain of seed from transplanted and selected roots on his farms near Philadelphia). and you will grow roots of unsurpassed quality. If the weather is pleasant and soil in good order, the following varieties may now be planted; but if hot and dry, defer them until next month. Beets, Improved Long Blood and Blood Turnip for Winter; sow Brocoli and Cauliflower in rich ground, transplant them in September in very rich soil to head in December. Snap Beans; Early Horn and Half Long Carrot; Radish of all sorts; Buist's Morning Star and Premier Extra Early Peas; plant Onion-sets; plant Early Rose potatoes for Winter use; the crop matured in May will do to plant now; transplant late Cabbage and late Celery; Onions that matured in June can now be planted to use in Winter; sow Endive to blanch in November; Butter Lettuce sown now will head in November; sow Savoy Cabbage for Winter heading; this variety is as delicate as Brocoli.

Buist's Cabbage Seed
IS MORE POPULAR THAN EVER IN THE SOUTH.

5 Millions of Packets, 25,000 lbs. of seed in bulk Sold the past year
—OF—
BUIST'S IMPROVED FLAT DUTCH.
BUIST'S IMPROVED DRUMHEAD.
WHY IS IT?
Simply because they have proved to be the only brand of Seed that will invariably produce large solid heads in that section of our Country. (See Page 3.)

BUIST'S CABBAGE BEATS THEM ALL, BOTH NORTH AND SOUTH.

I never had success with cabbage until I planted Buist's Improved Seed. The heads were quite a show; they sold for thirty cents each. Your seeds are fine.
March 28, 1887.   W. B. STRING, of Alabama.

Out of ten varieties of cabbage I grew last year, yours was the best, and took the premium at our fair.
February 22, 1887.   G. JEHU, of Minnesota.

9th Month. SEPTEMBER, 1888. 30 Days.

MOON'S PHASES.

MIDDLE STATES.

	D.	H.	M.	
New Moon	6	0	0	M.
First Quarter	12	5	4	A.
Full Moon	20	0	28	M.
Last Quarter	28	3	34	M.

SOUTHERN STATES.

	D.	H.	M.	
New Moon	5	11	36	A.
First Quarter	12	4	40	A.
Full Moon	20	0	4	M.
Last Quarter	28	3	10	M.

D. of W.	D. of M.	Lat. of Middle States. The Sun Ris. h. m.	The Sun Sets. h. m.	The Moon R. & S. h. m.	The Moon Souths h. m.	Constel-	lations.	Equation of Time.	Lat. of Southern States. The Sun Ris. h. m.	The Sun Sets. h. m.	The Moon R. & S. h. m.	The Moon Souths h. m.	Aspects of Planets and Remarkable Days for both Latitudes.
Sa	1	5 27	6 32	0 34	8 11	♏	15	F.	5 35	6 24	0 56	8 11	Venus s. 7.4 A ⌓
S	2	5 28	6 30	1 27	9 3	♏	27	1	5 35	6 23	1 49	9 3	☾ in ☊.
M	3	5 29	6 28	2 26	9 55	♐	10	1	5 36	6 22	2 47	9 55	☌♄☾.
Tu	4	5 30	6 27	3 30	10 48	♐	24	1	5 36	6 20	3 47	10 48	● ♆ stat.
W	5	5 31	6 25	4 36	11 40	♑	8	2	5 37	6 19	4 50	11 40	*5th.*
Th	6	5 32	6 24	sets	Ev.32	♑	22	2	5 38	6 18	sets	Ev.32	☌☿☾: ☌♀☾.
Fr	7	5 33	6 22	7 36	1 24	♒	6	2	5 38	6 16	7 36	1 24	☌♅☾.
Sa	8	5 34	6 20	8 9	2 16	♒	20	3	5 39	6 15	8 14	2 16	Mars s. 9.33 A.
S	9	5 35	6 18	8 43	3 8	♓	5	3	5 39	6 14	8 53	3 8	☾ in perigee
M	10	5 36	6 17	9 20	4 2	♓	20	3	5 40	6 12	9 35	4 2	☌♂☾. ☌♃☾.
Tu	11	5 37	6 15	10 1	4 58	♈	4	4	5 41	6 11	10 20	4 58	☽ ☌♂♃.
W	12	5 38	6 14	10 49	5 55	♈	18	4	5 42	6 10	11 10	5 55	*12th.*
Th	13	5 39	6 12	11 43	6 52	♉	2	4	5 42	6 8	morn	6 52	☿ in ☋.
Fr	14	5 40	6 10	morn	7 50	♉	16	5	5 43	6 7	0 5	7 50	Altair s. 8.8 A ◡
Sa	15	5 41	6 9	0 41	8 45	♉	29	5	5 44	6 6	1 3	8 45	☾ in ☋.
S	16	5 42	6 7	1 42	9 38	♊	13	5	5 44	6 4	2 2	9 38	Saturn r. 2.45 M.
M	17	5 43	6 5	2 47	10 29	♊	26	6	5 45	6 3	3 4	10 29	Fomal. s. 11.1 A.
Tu	18	5 44	6 4	3 52	11 16	♋	9	6	5 46	6 2	4 5	11 16	☌☿♀.
W	19	5 45	6 2	4 56	morn	♋	21	7	5 46	6 0	5 4	morn	○ ☌☉☿.
Th	20	5 46	6 0	rises	0 2	♌	4	7	5 47	5 59	rises	0 2	*20th.*
Fr	21	5 47	5 59	7 5	0 46	♌	17	7	5 48	5 58	7 8	0 46	*St. Matthew.*
Sa	22	5 48	5 57	7 32	1 28	♌	29	8	5 48	5 56	7 39	1 28	*Autumn begins.*
S	23	5 49	5 55	8 0	2 11	♍	11	8	5 49	5 55	8 11	2 11	☿ in aphelion.
M	24	5 50	5 54	8 29	2 55	♍	23	8	5 49	5 54	8 45	2 55	☌♆☾.
Tu	25	5 51	5 52	9 3	3 39	♎	5	9	5 50	5 52	9 22	3 39	☾ in apogee.
W	26	5 52	5 50	9 42	4 25	♎	16	9	5 51	5 51	10 2	4 25	Uranus s. 6.23 A.
Th	27	5 53	5 48	10 25	5 12	♎	28	9	5 51	5 50	10 47	5 12	☾ Pol s.o.52 M.
Fr	28	5 54	5 47	11 14	6 1	♏	10	10	5 52	5 48	11 36	6 1	*28th.*
Sa	29	5 55	5 45	morn	6 52	♏	23	10	5 53	5 47	morn	6 52	*Michaelmas.*
S	30	5 56	5 43	0 9	7 43	♐	5	10	5 54	5 46	0 30	7 43	☌♄☾.

JEWISH CALENDAR.—5649. September 6, Tishri (5649th year).

NOTABLE MONTHLY EVENTS.

5, 1854, Cholera in London.—8, 1855, Capture of Sebastopol.—13, 1759, Quebec taken.—15, 1847, Scott takes Mexico.—16, 1812, Moscow burned.—18, 1872 Charles XV. died.—26, 1777, Philadelphia taken.—27, 1854, Steamer Arctic lost.

CONJECTURES OF THE WEATHER.

1–5, warm; 6–10, fog and rain; 11–13, clear and cool; 14–17, warmer; 18–21, cloudy and rain; 22–25, clear and pleasant; 26–30, cool.

Copyrighted August 1, 1881.

BUIST'S SEEDS ARE THE GARDENERS' CHOICE.

SEPTEMBER.

Activity must prevail in the garden this month; it is really the beginning of the vegetable year in the "Sunny South." Remember, good, clean, deep, rich ground, and Buist's seeds, are the gardener's foundation.

Transplant Cabbage and Cauliflower; plant Onions, Shallots, and Garlic. Shallot is a kind of Onion used for seasoning delicate cookery; plant them in drills four inches apart, and twenty inches from row to row; cover two inches deep.

Cultivate thoroughly all growing crops; Peas planted last month will require sticking, and potatoes hilling up; sow Leek and Endive, and transplant Lettuce; sow Parsley for Spring use; sow CARROTS and BUIST'S MORNING STAR and PREMIER EXTRA EARLY PEAS for using in December: all varieties of RADISH are now in season, make several sowings of them; and enrich the ground to a great degree for frequent sowings of SPINACH and CORN SALAD; early in the month make the last planting of SNAP-SHORT BEANS.

Be sure that the Early Celery is well supplied with soapsuds every wash-day, or any other rich water; stir up the soil freely before watering, and also a few days after it, and begin to earth it up next month. If your sowing of Turnips of last month failed, or has been overlooked, it is still time; sow Buist's Late Flat Dutch Drumhead and Drumhead Savoy Cabbage about the last of this month, and plenty of Georgia Collards; transplant as usual, which will continue growing all Winter, and head in early Spring; the leaves of Collards can be stripped off and used throughout the growing season.

BUIST'S SEEDS IN PAPERS

Are for sale by the leading Country Merchants. But look out for the cheap Auction Seeds, put up in imitation of our brand. See that every paper has the name of Buist on it.

Every paper of seeds from our house is now put up in an illustrated package, and, that every one may readily distinguish them at sight, from all other brands, please observe the following points:

1st. Every paper bears our trade-mark as represented on third page of cover, with illustration of the vegetable thereon, and distinctly printed, GROWN AND WARRANTED BY ROBERT BUIST, JR. Those put up in any other style, and represented as Buist's, are either a spurious imitation or old stock.

2d. The entire face of the bag and illustration is always printed in one solid color.

3d. The small or half-size papers are all printed in plain black.

4th. The large or whole papers are all printed in bright colors, as red, blue, green or purple, but no whole papers in black.

By observing the above you will prevent the worthless commission and spurious seeds, with which the country is flooded, from falling into your hands and causing disappointment in the product of your garden.

IF YOUR MERCHANT DOES NOT KEEP THEM, ORDER DIRECT FROM US. IF YOU DESIRE PAPERS, WE MAIL TWENTY-FIVE SMALL SIZE OR FIFTEEN LARGE SIZE FOR ONE DOLLAR. FOR PRICES OF SEEDS BY THE OUNCE, POUND, QUART OR BUSHEL, SEE LAST PAGES.

10th Month. OCTOBER, 1888. 31 Days.

MOON'S PHASES.

MIDDLE STATES.	D.	H.	M.	SOUTHERN STATES.	D.	H.	M.
New Moon	5	9	38 M.	New Moon	5	9	14 M.
First Quarter	12	0	33 M.	First Quarter	12	0	9 M.
Full Moon	19	4	13 A.	Full Moon	19	3	49 A.
Last Quarter	27	9	0 A.	Last Quarter	27	8	36 A.

D. of W.	D. of M.	Lat. of Middle States. The Sun Ris. h. m.	The Sun Sets. h. m.	The Moon R & S. h. m.	The Moon Souths h. m.	Constellations.	Equation of Time.	Lat. of Southern States. The Sun Ris. h. m.	The Sun Sets. h. m.	The Moon R & S. h. m.	The Moon Souths h. m.	Aspects of Planets and Remarkable Days for both Latitudes.
M	1	5 57	5 42	1 10	8 35	18	F.	5 54	5 44	1 29	8 35	Altair so. 7.1 A.
Tu	2	5 58	5 40	2 15	9 27	2	11	5 55	5 43	2 31	9 27	Venus s. 6.41 A.
W	3	5 59	5 38	3 23	10 19	16	11	5 56	5 42	3 35	10 19	Fomal. so. 9.59 A.
Th	4	6 0	5 37	4 34	11 11	0	12	5 56	5 40	4 40	11 11	Mark. s. 0.2
Fr	5	6 1	5 35	sets	Ev. 3	15	12	5 57	5 39	sets	Ev. 3	*5th.* [A.
Sa	6	6 2	5 33	6 40	0 57	0	12	5 58	5 38	6 48	0 57	☌♀☾ : ☌☿☾.
S	7	6 3	5 32	7 16	1 52	15	12	5 58	5 36	7 29	1 52	☾ in perigee.
M	8	6 4	5 30	7 57	2 49	29	13	5 59	5 35	8 14	2 49	☌♃☾.
Tu	9	6 5	5 29	8 44	3 48	14	13	6 0	5 34	9 4	3 48	☌☿♀ : ☌♂☾.
W	10	6 6	5 27	9 36	4 47	29	13	6 1	5 33	9 58	4 47	☌♁☉.
Th	11	6 7	5 26	10 34	5 45	13	13	6 1	5 32	10 56	5 45	Mars s. 8.50
Fr	12	6 8	5 24	11 36	6 42	26	14	6 2	5 30	11 57	6 42	*12th.* [A.
Sa	13	6 9	5 22	morn	7 35	10	14	6 3	5 29	morn	7 35	☿ gr. hel. lat. S.
S	14	6 10	5 21	0 39	8 26	23	14	6 4	5 28	0 57	8 26	Jupiter s. 7.43 A.
M	15	6 11	5 19	1 42	9 14	6	14	6 4	5 27	1 57	9 14	Polar. so. 11.37 A.
Tu	16	6 13	5 18	2 45	9 59	18	15	6 5	5 26	2 56	9 59	Acher. s. 11 49 A.
W	17	6 14	5 16	3 47	10 43	1	15	6 6	5 24	3 53	10 43	Algol so. 1.16 M.
Th	18	6 15	5 15	4 48	11 25	13	15	6 7	5 23	4 50	11 25	*St. Luke,*
Fr	19	6 16	5 13	5 47	morn	25	15	6 7	5 22	5 45	morn	*19th.* [*Ev.*
Sa	20	6 17	5 12	rises	0 8	7	15	6 8	5 21	rises	0 8	☿ stationary.
S	21	6 18	5 11	6 29	0 51	19	15	6 9	5 20	6 44	0 51	☌♆☾.
M	22	6 19	5 9	7 3	1 35	1	16	6 10	5 19	7 21	1 35	☾ in apogee.
Tu	23	6 20	5 8	7 40	2 20	13	16	6 10	5 18	8 0	2 20	Aldeb. so. 2.21 M.
W	24	6 21	5 6	8 20	3 7	25	16	6 11	5 17	8 42	3 7	Uran. r. 5.14 M.
Th	25	6 23	5 5	9 6	3 55	7	16	6 12	5 16	9 29	3 55	Cap. s. 2.52. M.
Fr	26	6 24	5 4	9 58	4 44	19	16	6 13	5 15	10 20	4 44	☾ in ☊.
Sa	27	6 25	5 2	10 55	5 34	1	16	6 14	5 14	11 15	5 34	*27th.*
S	28	6 26	5 1	11 56	6 25	13	16	6 15	5 13	morn	6 25	*St. Sim. St. Jude.*
M	29	6 27	5 0	morn	7 15	26	16	6 15	5 12	0 13	7 15	Nept. r. 6.33 A.
Tu	30	6 28	4 59	1 1	8 6	10	16	6 16	5 11	1 15	8 6	Canop. s. 3.45 M.
W	31	6 30	4 57	2 9	8 56	24	16	6 17	5 10	2 18	8 56	☌☿☉ inferior.

JEWISH CALENDAR.—5649. October 6, 'Heshvan.

NOTABLE MONTHLY EVENTS.

1, 1807, Fulton's First Steamboat Trip.—2, 1780, Major Andre hung.—9, 1871, Fire in Chicago.—11, 1799, General Pulaski died.—17, 1777, Burgoyne surrendered.—19, 1812, Moscow evacuated.—23, 1641, Irish Rebellion.

CONJECTURES OF THE WEATHER.

1-4, cloudy and rain; 5-10, clear and cool; 11-12, warmer; 13-17, cloudy · 18-22, rain; 23-26, clear and pleasant; 27-31, cool.

Copyrighted August 1, 1881.

THIS IS THE 60th YEAR FOR BUIST'S SEED'S.

OCTOBER.

See that all crops are clean and in good growing order. What ever was omitted last month do not overlook. Take opportunity of the weather to transplant Cabbage, Lettuce, and Savoy Cabbage; earth up Celery; first stir up the earth with plow and hoe, throwing it close to the plants; then keep the leaves close with one hand, and with a trowel or short hoe draw the earth up as far as the heartleaves; every two or three weeks repeat the operation while the plants continue growing. Sow another supply of Lettuce and Radish; plant Buist's Premier Extra Early and Black-Eyed Marrowfat Peas. About the end of this month, or next, make new beds of Strawberries—deep, rich ground is their delight. Make another sowing of Turnips. Water the Cauliflower plants; keep a basin of earth around them, and fill it frequently with water.

If the Endive has grown to be eight to ten inches in the leaves, draw them neatly together, and tie them closely with any material, such as bark, a few threads of soft twine, or matting; in two weeks the heart will be blanched white, and fit for table Salad, it is hard and unfit for use, unless tied up to blanch tender. Thin out late Carrots and Beets. Turnips should be well hoed or harrowed; thin them out to three or six inches apart; sow a few more seed for a late, or rather Spring crop. Spinach can still be sown. Plant Onion-sets for Winter and Spring use.

OPINION OF OUR CUSTOMERS

—ABOUT THE QUALITY OF—

BUIST'S GARDEN SEEDS.

FROM LOUISIANA.

I enclose you a photograph of a specimen of a cabbage which was grown from your Improved Seed the past season by James Cure of Jefferson Parish, in this State, which weighed thirty pounds. The seed was sown August 4, and headed in January. He made a very fine and profitable crop. The following gardeners in the same parish had equal success with your seed: Mr. John Betz, A. Barhorow, James Spanord, Frank Larreshell, Peter Betz, Valentine Betz, and J. Fortie. The latter party said he never saw cabbage produce such fine large heads in the parish before. Your Premier Extra Early Peas also gave great satisfaction. Mr. Cure and Mr. Fortie said they were the earliest and most productive they ever grew.
July 11, 1887. R. T. KAMPEN, of Louisiana.

FROM VIRGINIA.

A mammoth cabbage was exhibited yesterday at the store of Faulkner & Craighill, weighing eighteen pounds. It was raised by a colored man (Ruffin Mason), near the fair-grounds, from Buist's Improved Flat Dutch, and was fertilized with the famous fertilizer of Wright & Craighill.
Copied from LYNCHBURG PAPER, July 8, 1887.

FROM TENNESSEE.

The cabbage seed I ordered from you last season gave great satisfaction. I raised the finest crop I ever saw.
May 5, 1887. S. W. MARTIN.

FROM ALABAMA.

I have been planting Buist's garden seeds for the past ten years side by side with other leading brands, and have never yet found their equal; they are undoubtedly the best for the Southern States. Your Improved Cabbage is as sure to head as it is to grow.
February 8, 1887. J. W. CHAPPELL.

11th Month. NOVEMBER, 1888. 30 Days.

MOON'S PHASES.

MIDDLE STATES.	D.	H.	M.	SOUTHERN STATES.	D.	H.	M.
New Moon	3	7	6 A.	New Moon	3	6	42 A.
First Quarter	10	11	20 M.	First Quarter	10	10	56 M.
Full Moon	18	10	20 M.	Full Moon	18	9	56 M.
Last Quarter	26	0	24 A.	Last Quarter	26	0	0 A.

D. of W.	D. of M.	Lat. of Middle States. The Sun Ris. h. m.	The Sun Sets. h. m.	The Moon R & S. h. m.	The Moon Souths h. m.	Constellations.		Equation of Time.	Lat. of Southern States. The Sun Ris. h. m.	The Sun Sets. h. m.	The Moon R & S. h. m.	The Moon Souths h. m.	Aspects of Planets and Remarkable Days for both Latitudes.
Th	1	6 31	4 50	3 20	9 45	♎	8	F.	6 18	5 9	3 24	9 45	*All Saints' Day*
Fr	2	6 32	4 55	4 32	10 38	♎	23	16	6 19	5 8	4 31	10 38	☿ in ☊.
Sa	3	6 33	4 54	5 46	11 33	♏	8	16	6 20	5 7	5 40	11 33	***3d.*** ☌☿☾.
S	4	6 34	4 53	sets	Ev. 30	♏	23	16	6 21	5 6	sets	Ev. 30	☾ in perigee.
M	5	6 36	4 52	6 33	1 30	♐	8	16	6 22	5 6	6 53	1 30	☌♃☾: ☌♀☾.
T	6	6 37	4 50	7 24	2 32	♐	23	16	6 23	5 5	7 46	2 32	☿ in perihelion.
W	7	6 38	4 49	8 22	3 33	♑	8	16	6 24	5 4	8 45	3 33	☌♂☾.
Th	8	6 39	4 48	9 25	4 32	♑	22	16	6 24	5 3	9 47	4 32	☿ stationary.
Fr	9	6 41	4 47	10 30	5 29	♒	6	16	6 25	5 2	10 50	5 29	☾ in ☋.
Sa	10	6 42	4 46	11 35	6 21	♒	19	16	6 26	5 2	11 52	6 21	***10th.***
S	11	6 43	4 45	morn	7 10	♓	2	16	6 27	5 1	morn	7 10	□♄☉.
M	12	6 44	4 44	0 40	7 56	♓	15	16	6 28	5 0	0 52	7 56	Mars s. 8.30 A.
Tu	13	6 45	4 44	1 42	8 40	♓	28	15	6 29	5 0	1 49	8 40	♀ in aphelion.
W	14	6 46	4 43	2 42	9 23	♈	10	15	6 30	4 59	2 45	9 23	Algen. so. 8.29 A.
Th	15	6 47	4 42	3 41	10 5	♈	22	15	6 31	4 59	3 40	10 5	Jupiter s. 6.1 A.
Fr	16	6 49	4 41	4 39	10 47	♉	4	15	6 32	4 58	4 34	10 47	☿ gr. hel. lat. N.
Sa	17	6 50	4 40	5 37	11 30	♉	16	15	6 33	4 58	5 28	11 30	☿ gr. el. W. 19° 34'
S	18	6 51	4 40	rises	morn	♉	28	15	6 34	4 57	rises	morn	***18th.***
M	19	6 52	4 39	5 38	0 15	♊	10	14	6 34	4 57	5 58	0 15	Pol. s. 9.20 A.
Tu	20	6 54	4 38	6 18	1 2	♊	22	14	6 35	4 56	6 40	1 2	Saturn r. 10.48 A.
W	21	6 55	4 38	7 2	1 49	♋	4	14	6 36	4 56	7 25	1 49	Acher. so. 9.27 A.
Th	22	6 56	4 37	7 51	2 38	♋	16	14	6 37	4 56	8 14	2 38	☍♆☉.
Fr	23	6 57	4 37	8 46	3 28	♋	28	13	6 38	4 56	9 7	3 28	☾ in ☊.
Sa	24	6 58	4 36	9 44	4 18	♌	10	13	6 39	4 55	10 3	4 18	☌♄☾. [M.
S	25	6 59	4 36	10 46	5 7	♌	22	13	6 40	4 55	11 2	5 7	Uran. r. 3.17
M	26	7 0	4 36	11 51	5 56	♍	5	12	6 41	4 55	morn	5 56	***26th.***
Tu	27	7 1	4 35	morn	6 44	♍	18	12	6 42	4 54	0 3	6 44	Aldeb. s. 11 59 A.
W	28	7 2	4 35	0 58	7 33	♎	2	12	6 42	4 54	1 5	7 33	Nept. s. 6.15 M.
Th	29	7 3	4 34	2 7	8 23	♎	16	11	6 43	4 54	2 9	8 23	☌♂☾.
Fr	30	7 4	4 34	3 19	9 15	♏	1	11	6 44	4 54	3 16	9 15	*St. Andrew.*

JEWISH CALENDAR.—5649. November 5, Kislev.

NOTABLE MONTHLY EVENTS.

2, 1873, Vienna Exhibition closed.—3, 1870, Napoleon III. surrenders.—7, 1811, Battle of Tippecanoe.—15, 1777, Fort Mifflin taken.—23, 1792, France a Republic.—27, 1825, Stereotyping invented.—28, 1859, Washington Irving died.

CONJECTURES OF THE WEATHER.

1-3, light frost; 4-7, cloudy and rain; 8-13, clear and cold; 14-18, cloudy; 19-22, rain or snow; 23-26, clear and warmer; 27-31, cloudy and rain.

Copyrighted August 1, 1881.

MARKET GARDENERS PRAISE BUIST'S SEEDS.

NOVEMBER.

A judicious system of preserving the crops of the season should share a liberal portion of our ideas in economy and security, at the least possible cost.

Early in the month sow Parsnips for early Summer use, earth up Celery, tie up Endive as it is required for the table. If a new planting of Asparagus is required, it may be done now or next month. Cover the old bed with a few inches of manure, to lay till January, and then fork it in with the top-soil. To have this vegetable crisp and large, use stimulants freely.

Plant Buist's Morning Star, Premier Extra Early, Tom Thumb, and Little Gem Peas, and stake up others if required.

These are all dwarf varieties, and are well adapted for sowing at this season of the year in the South—if they withstand the Winter they will be ready for the table in early Spring. From their dwarf habit they can very readily be protected during severe weather, although they will make very little progress in growing while it is cold, yet they will become thoroughly established before spring, and crop abundantly.

Transplant Cabbage, if not already done, for Spring heading; sow Lettuce on sheltered borders, and a few sowings of Radish will also prove successful.

To make cheap-covered beds for Lettuce, Radish, or any other tender Winter vegetable, raise the ground one foot high in front, eighteen inches at the back, of any convenient length. Take four pieces of board, three inches wide, nail them together to make a frame six feet long and three feet wide; tack tightly over it muslin to fit, give it a coat of oil, and when dry, it will suit the purposes of glazed sash for cold weather, to be placed over the bed you have made to keep out all frost or cold winds, but of course in mild weather these muslin frames are taken off; these beds must be watered in dry weather. Transplant Rhubarb in rich ground, and early in Spring mulch the ground to retain moisture and to prevent injury from dry weather. Sow Onion seed to transplant in February to form bulbs; you will thereby have good roots the first season. Onion-sets can still be planted.

In Louisiana, Texas, Southern Mississippi, and Florida, almost every variety of seed can now be planted, such as BEET, CABBAGE, LETTUCE, CARROT, PARSNIP, SALSIFY, SPINACH, ENDIVE, RADISH, MUSTARD, PEAS, etc.; it is also a very favorable month for the sowing of BUIST'S FLAT DUTCH and DRUMHEAD CABBAGE, which will form large and beautiful heads in Spring. Manure for the hot-bed should now be looked after in these States, for the starting of early vegetable plants. Read remarks about its preparation under the head of Hot-Beds.

The Gardener's Price List will be found on the last pages of this Almanac. If your Merchant keeps our Seeds he will supply you at the prices quoted, and give you the following discounts on Garden Seeds in bulk:

On Orders of $5.00 and over 10 Per Cent. Discount.
                  10.00   "   12½   "   "
                  25.00   "   15   "   "
                  50.00   "   20   "   "

12th Month. DECEMBER, 1888. 31 Days.

MOON'S PHASES.

MIDDLE STATES.	D.	H.	M.		SOUTHERN STATES.	D.	H.	M.	
New Moon	3	5	9	M.	New Moon	3	4	45	M.
First Quarter	10	1	50	M.	First Quarter	10	1	26	M.
Full Moon	18	5	45	M.	Full Moon	18	5	21	M.
Last Quarter	26	1	4	M.	Last Quarter	26	0	40	M.

D. of W.	D. of M.	Lat. of Middle States. The Sun Ris. h. m.	The Sun Sets. h. m.	The Moon R & S. h. m.	The Moon Souths h. m.	Constellations.		Equation of Time.	Lat. of Southern States. The Sun Ris. h. m.	The Sun Sets. h. m.	The Moon R & S. h. m.	The Moon Souths h. m.	Aspects of Planets and Remarkable Days for both Latitudes.
Sa	1	7 5	4 34	4 34	10 12	♎	16	F.	6 45	4 54	4 25	10 12	☌☿☾.
S	2	7 6	4 33	5 50	11 11	♏	1	10	6 46	4 54	5 36	11 11	☌♃☾.
M	3	7 7	4 33	sets	Ev. 12	♏	16	10	6 46	4 54	sets	Ev. 12	3d.
Tu	4	7 8	4 33	6 3	1 15	♐	2	9	6 47	4 54	6 26	1 15	Venus s. 7.24 A.
W	5	7 9	4 33	7 6	2 18	♐	17	9	6 48	4 54	7 29	2 18	☌♀☾. ◡
Th	6	7 10	4 33	8 14	3 19	♑	1	8	6 49	4 54	8 35	3 19	*St. Nicholas.*
Fr	7	7 11	4 33	9 22	4 15	♑	15	8	6 50	4 54	9 40	4 15	Algen. so. 6.59 A.
Sa	8	7 12	4 33	10 28	5 7	♑	29	8	6 51	4 54	10 42	5 7	☌♃☉
S	9	7 13	4 33	11 32	5 55	♒	12	7	6 51	4 54	11 41	5 55	Mars s. 8.24
M	10	7 14	4 33	morn	6 40	♒	24	7	6 52	4 54	morn	6 40	10th. [A.
Tu	11	7 15	4 33	0 34	7 24	♓	7	6	6 53	4 55	0 38	7 24	Pol. so. 7.53 A.
W	12	7 15	4 33	1 33	8 6	♓	19	6	6 54	4 55	1 34	8 6	Acher. so. 8.5 A
Th	13	7 16	4 33	2 32	8 48	♈	1	5	6 54	4 55	2 28	8 48	Algol so. 9.28 A
Fr	14	7 17	4 34	3 30	9 31	♈	13	5	6 55	4 55	3 22	9 31	Jupiter r. 6.38 M.
Sa	15	7 18	4 34	4 28	10 15	♈	25	4	6 55	4 56	4 17	10 15	☌♆☾.
S	16	7 18	4 34	5 26	11 0	♉	7	4	6 56	4 56	5 11	11 0	☌☿♃: ☾ in apo.
M	17	7 19	4 35	6 23	11 48	♉	19	3	6 57	4 57	6 5	11 48	Ald. s. 10.41
Tu	18	7 20	4 35	rises	morn	♊	1	3	6 57	4 57	rises	morn	18th. [A.
W	19	7 20	4 35	5 46	0 37	♊	13	2	6 58	4 58	6 9	0 37	Cap. s. 11.12 A. ⌓
Th	20	7 21	4 36	6 40	1 27	♊	25	2	6 58	4 58	7 2	1 27	☿ in aph. ☾ in ☊
Fr	21	7 21	4 36	7 38	2 15	♋	7	1	6 59	4 58	7 58	2 15	*Winter beg. St.*
Sa	22	7 21	4 37	8 40	3 6	♋	19	1	6 59	4 59	8 57	3 6	☌♄☾. [*Thomas*
S	23	7 22	4 38	9 43	3 55	♌	2	slow	7 0	5 0	9 56	3 55	Uran. r. 1.31 M.
M	24	7 22	4 38	10 48	4 43	♌	15		7 0	5 0	10 56	4 43	Rigel so. 10.53 A.
Tu	25	7 23	4 39	11 53	5 30	♌	28	1	7 1	5 1	11 56	5 30	*Christmas.*
W	26	7 23	4 39	morn	6 18	♍	12	1	7 1	5 1	morn	6 18	26th.
Th	27	7 23	4 40	1 0	7 7	♍	26	2	7 1	5 2	0 59	7 7	*St. John, Ev.*
Fr	28	7 24	4 41	2 11	7 58	♎	10	2	7 2	5 3	2 5	7 58	*Innocents.*
Sa	29	7 24	4 42	3 24	8 53	♎	25	3	7 2	5 3	3 14	8 53	Nept. s. 4.10 M.
S	30	7 24	4 42	4 38	9 51	♏	10	3	7 2	5 4	4 23	9 51	☌♃☾.
M	31	7 24	4 43	5 51	10 52	♏	25	4	7 3	5 5	5 32	10 52	☉ perigee.

JEWISH CALENDAR.—5649. December 5, Tebeth.

NOTABLE MONTHLY EVENTS.

7, 1815, Marshal Ney shot.—11, 1816, Indiana admitted.—12, 1873, Bazaine sentenced.—14, 1799, Washington died.—19, 1813, Battle of Niagara.—23, 1858, Revolution in Hayti.—24, 1814, Treaty of Ghent.—29, 1809, Wm. E. Gladstone born.

CONJECTURES OF THE WEATHER.

1–5, clear and cold; 6–7, cloudy and snow; 8–13, warmer; 14–17, cloudy and cold; 18–22, snow; 23–26, clear and cold; 27–28, cloudy; 29–31, snow.

Copyrighted August 1, 1881.

COMMISSION SEEDS ARE GREAT TRAVELERS.

DECEMBER.

If, for the want of time, you have left anything undone, see now to have all worked up that is desired—your ground clean, and your crops ready for use or protection. Observe, through all your practice, to undertake only what you can keep thoroughly; it is a bad policy to "*let it go,*" when a small exertion will hold it.

Transplant late Cabbage, and sow Buist's Large York, Winnigstadt, and Jersey Wakefield Cabbage, to head in February and March; also sow Buist's Flat Dutch and Drumhead, which will form better heads in the South from present sowing than at any other season of the year. Sow Radish, Lettuce, and another planting of Buist's Premier Extra Early Peas. Onion-sets may still be planted, and thin out Spinach as required for use.

Plant Horse Radish; dig the ground deep and manure well; rake it off finely, and with a line mark the rows; and, with a long dibble, put a hole twelve inches deep and a foot apart in the row; put into it a piece of root, four to six inches long; they will grow in February or March; hoe and cultivate well, and you will have fair roots in one year, and very fine roots in two years; the third year the crop should be renewed.

If you desire to force early Tomatoes, start them the last of this month, and select Buist's Belle and Beauty, Acme and Paragon; the two first are the cream of the lot, especially the Belle; sow it by all means; it is the largest and finest formed variety, and decidedly the most profitable to grow for market; it is very solid, carries well, and its great beauty sells it at a greater profit.

In purchasing Buist's Improved Flat Dutch and Drumhead Cabbage, always be sure that you obtain it in our original sealed packages, as we do not send it out in any other way. The great reputation it has attained has caused some unprincipled dealers to try to sell their ordinary seed as Buist's Improved.

Now is the time to form new and good resolutions for another year's guidance; if your garden affairs have not proved satisfactory, note the difficulty, to insure better success another season, as experience is always the best teacher; we can read and listen to that of others, but are better satisfied and impressed with our own. Draw out your plans, study and reflect over them, and improve if possible; when perfected, live and work up to them, and you will be astonished to see what can be accomplished. "GOING IT BLIND" is a poor and disastrous policy in any business, and especially in gardening and planting operations.

This is also your month to make out your Spring list of seeds, required. Remember that the foundation of a good garden is first good seeds, and then good culture.

Always avoid the Commissioned Seeds, which are piled in boxes at almost every Cross Road Store in the country, as they are inferior seeds, occasioned either by age or adulteration, which can only be sold by consignments. Commission Seeds, after they are once put up in papers, are sent out year after year until sold, regardless of their age. BUIST'S GARDEN SEEDS (which are exclusively the product of our own farms), with proper culture, we guarantee will please you, and if you are not already a purchaser of them, try them the coming season; but, in purchasing, observe that the seeds you receive bear one of our trade-mark labels, given on the fourth page of cover of this Almanac with the name of Buist in bold letters on each—THOSE BEARING ANY OTHER MARKS ARE SPURIOUS.

They are, without question, the most reliable seeds of the present age, and are, undoubtedly the most popular in this country. In some sections of the South and West, where other Seeds had held undisputed sway for years, and merchants knew no others, they could only be induced to handle them by the persistent demand of their customers; numerous cases of this kind have occurred; and, when introduced, they have almost entirely superseded other brands in two seasons. The great secret of this is in their purity and fine quality; and next, a very important regulation of our house, and that is, to cut out of papers, every September, all seeds left over from the previous season. Buist's is the only house in the trade that does this—a great loss in the eyes of many—but we regard it a very profitable investment; therefore, ask your merchant if he has ordered a fresh supply of BUIST'S SEEDS; if yes, obtain them through him; if not, make out your own order from our price-list, which will be found in this Almanac, and send direct to us, with a remittance, and they will be sent to you by return of mail or express.

Early Winnigstadt Cabbage (The Prussian Prize Stock)

This stock of Winnigstadt is famous for its earliness, size of head and great uniformity in heading. We have again secured for this season the entire crop of a celebrated grower in Northern Prussia, which will be found far superior to any ever sold in this country. Price per oz., 40 cts.; per 4 oz., $1.00; per ℔., $3.00.

Your seeds advertise themselves. For the past six years people in this vicinity have been trying to grow vegetables from the boxes of commission seeds left for sale at our stores, only to find failure for the result; while my experience with Buist's seeds is success every year. Good seeds are always sure to grow and give satisfaction even on poor soil.

January 1, 1887.   H. G. FOSTER, of North Carolina.

You must never expect success in your garden if you sow commission seeds, as the most of them are weak and inferior from age. Occasionally a few new seeds are mixed in with the old ones to impart, if possible, a little vigor to the rest; this is cruelty, as age should always command greater respect.   ROBT. BUIST, JR.

Suggestions to Mail Correspondents.

When you make out your order, write it distinctly in regular columns, and not in the body of your letter. Observe that your Post-Office address, as well as your name, is distinctly written; hundreds of letters are annually received, where one or the other of these important items are omitted, and the writer, after patiently waiting for his order to arrive, frequently pens a sharp reprimand for neglect, when the fault is one of his own making; this omission has become so popular of late years, that we are obliged to have a file especially for such letters.

From our increased facilities for conducting business, no order is allowed to remain on our books, at the utmost, forty-eight hours; in order to carry out this rule during the busy months, it always occasions a great effort on our part, but it is generally accomplished, no matter to what extent the demand upon us may be; we, however, always regard it as a special favor when our customers send in their orders early.

When you remit, obtain Post-Office orders or drafts; it is really not safe to inclose bank-bills in letters, and we cannot hold ourselves responsible for such, should they be lost. Where money is sent by Express, prepay the expense of transmitting it, or it will be deducted from the remittance. When only a portion of the amount required for the order is remitted, we can only send goods to that amount; we have been compelled to adopt this rule on account of the great difficulty in collecting these small balances.

When bills are to be collected through the Express Co., the expense of making such collections are always charged on the invoice; but no perishable goods, as ONION-SETS, POTATOES, or PLANTS, will be sent in this way; remittances for such must always be made with the order; in fact, there is no necessity to have orders sent C. O. D., and be at the extra expense of return-charges, when one can so readily refer to our prices in this catalogue and ascertain the exact cost of any order.

We personally conduct our business, just as much for pleasure as for profit; our heart is in it as well as our purse, and we therefore guarantee satisfaction to all who may favor us with their orders; where errors occur we will esteem it a very great favor to be promptly advised, to enable us to make an immediate correction. Strangers who have never visited our establishment should not fail to call when in Philadelphia.

Shopping by Mail.

Seeds can be sent by mail to any part of the United States, in packages of four pounds and under, with both promptness and safety, therefore customers located in the most remote parts of this country, can just as readily obtain our seeds as those residing in our own city. **We mail papers, ounces and quarter pounds, free of postage, pounds and quarts at an additional cost of 16 cents per pound, and 30 cents per quart. Besides, we guarantee their safe delivery.** We do not permit our customers to assume any risk whatever in ordering, but place those located at the most distant parts, on the same footing with those who personally call at our store, and order their purchases sent home. The mail department of our establishment is a very extensive one, and perfect in all its details to insure the prompt and correct execution of orders.

For distant purchasers, who cannot obtain Buist's Seeds from their merchant, it will certainly pay them to mail their orders direct to us, rather than purchase such seeds as are generally left for sale at country stores, as they will almost invariably prove an unprofitable investment if perchance they grow; a paper of Cabbage for instance will frequently surprise you in producing Kale, and a paper of Turnip will often grow all tops and no root; there is no accounting for such magic turns; but more frequently the contents of the papers do not appear to have much heart to grow from the straggling sort of way they fight for their existence. Such seeds are what are known as commissioned seeds, purchased from cheap sources, regardless of quality, and left in packages until their vitality is completely exhausted. Fine vegetables can never be produced from seeds having weak germinating qualities, and very seldom from those picked up by seedsmen who are compelled to purchase their stocks, which are frequently the seeds saved from cullings after the best vegetables have been marketed.

Why Seeds Sometimes Fail to Grow.

Seeds, like people, have their peculiarities and different natures, and to know the nature of the various varieties is one of the principles of successful gardening; some sorts will withstand great moisture, while others will perish; some are liable to attacks of insects, and are completely eaten up, while others can withstand such assaults.

Lima Beans, Okra, Cucumber, Squash, Melon, Pumpkin, Corn, and Wrinkled Peas have very delicate germs, and if a succession of cold, wet weather succeed their planting, they will invariably perish in the ground; on the contrary, Peas, Radish, Lettuce, Turnip, Onion, Beet, Snap Beans, Carrot, Salsify, and Spinach will withstand quite a spell of such weather; therefore, many failures result from the inexperience of the planter in either selecting an improper time for sowing, or in covering small, delicate seeds too deep, but when failure occurs with a person who is familiar with the sowing of seeds, the reason is invariably because they are worthless from either bad harvesting or too old to grow; the latter is really the principal cause, and to guard against this, purchase your supplies from BUIST. Turnip and Cabbage Seed when grown out of doors are frequently eaten off by a small fly as rapidly as the young plants appear, and often before any leaves are expanded, and unless the planter is aware of this, he certainly must condemn the seed. When dry weather follows the sowing of Turnip and Ruta-Baga Seeds, they will not germinate freely, and those that do make their appearance are invariably eaten off; therefore harrow and re-seed before or after the first rain, and this is the only plan to adopt when a sowing fails from this cause. Ruta Baga Turnip is particularly liable to be eaten off before the plant is really visible to the eye without a close examination; and to guard against this, it is best to sow quite thickly, at the rate of two pounds to the acre, and thin out if the plants come up too close, or dust them with plaster if they are being destroyed by insects.

Many years since, we established a valuable rule by which we are always familiar with the growing qualities of every seed in our stock; a register-book is kept with every sack of seed noted down in it in alphabetical order, and when there are a number of sacks of one variety, each is designated with a number, a sample is taken from each, tested, and the strength of growing noted down in the register-book; every sack in our warehouse goes through this process twice a year, and the new crops are always tested as soon as they are received from our farms; those that prove defective are at once thrown out. By this regulation it is almost a matter of impossibility for seeds lacking vitality to be received from us. There are, unfortunately, some dealers who continue selling seeds just as long as they remain in stock, regardless of age or the disappointments that will surely follow their planting, "NEVER THINKING THAT GOOD SEEDS, UNLIKE GOOD WINE, ARE NOT IMPROVED BY BEING AGED."

MARKET GARDENING.

This is a laborious occupation, yet one that pays a very handsome percentage on the investment. Ten acres in vegetables, well cultivated and properly managed, will prove more profitable than a fifty-acre farm producing the ordinary farm crops. I have frequently observed, in my business relations with the Farmer and Market Gardener, a vast difference in the accumulation of means between them. The one will commence under very favorable prospects, on a farm leased for a series of years, will labor industriously and study economy, and rarely realize much more than a comfortable living for his family. The other, commencing under less favorable circumstances, with equal energy, does not only pay an annual rent of from thirty to sixty dollars per acre (as is the case with many of our Philadelphia Market Gardeners who occupy valuable grounds in the city), and support a large family, but in a very few years realizes sufficient to purchase the place. A few heads of Cabbage will, in frequent seasons, sell for as much as a bushel of Corn, and a bunch of early Asparagus for as much as a bushel of Wheat. Good Vegetables will always sell at a good profit, and our hungry cities can rarely be overstocked with them.

In Locating a Garden, observe that the soil is light, and situation convenient to the city; a few dollars additional rent is nothing, if the ground is suitable; and with industry and reasonable economy the cultivator will annually realize a handsome income.

A Poor Investment for the Gardener.

The Seeds Sent out to Country Stores to be Sold on Commission are almost as Valuable as Wooden Nutmegs.

The following report, which was published in the Rural New Yorker of tests made by Prof. Beal, of the Michigan Agricultural College, shows that the seeds sent out by commission seedsmen are almost as great a plague as the grasshoppers of a few years ago. He purchased the seeds of four of the leading commission seedsmen (their names, of course, we withhold, but he gives them), and planted fifty seeds from each of nine varieties, under the most favorable circumstances. By actual count, only twenty-three per cent. of the first grew; the second, thirty-seven per cent.; the third, forty-seven per cent.; and the fourth, forty-nine per cent. This tells its own tale.

The Importance of Sowing Good Seed.

Vegetables of good quality cannot be grown without first sowing reliable seeds; it is exceedingly annoying, after plowing, sowing and cultivating your garden for an entire season, to find that instead of having spent your time and money profitably, you have lost heavily in obtaining a spurious article; this is really a growing evil among Seed Dealers, who have been springing up all over the country the last few years, like so many mushrooms, without having any knowledge of their business, or brains enough to conduct it if they were acquainted with it; they do not exercise the care in selecting their stock that they should, and very frequently make errors in handing out, or putting up in orders the wrong variety. If druggists were as careless in compounding their prescriptions as many are in selling seeds, they certainly would gain great notoriety in the courts of justice. When you make your purchases, be satisfied that the parties from whom you obtain your supplies are reliable, or that such a house has a good reputation, and expect to pay a fair price for what you obtain. There are plenty of cheap seeds, as well as any other article in the market, and it would be always advisable to guard against them; a dollar saved in that line is not always a dollar earned, but very frequently you will lose twenty for every one invested.

It has been our aim, since we established our business (fifty-nine years ago), to supply the public with seeds grown from selected stocks, and which are in every instance, fresh and pure; to accomplish this, all seeds from our establishment are either grown by us or especially for us, and the crops carefully inspected, while growing, to insure

BUIST'S ALMANAC AND GARDEN MANUAL. 37

their purity. This continued care has established to BUIST'S GARDEN SEEDS the enviable reputation of the present day, and where they are sold in competition with those of other houses they invariably become the most popular; this has been demonstrated with several cities and towns that we could mention, where, a few years since, we had not a single customer, but, by hard pressure, succeeded in introducing our seeds, and now supply the entire demand of those places. Annual supplies are shipped to customers in almost all parts of the United States, Canada, East and West Indies, South America and Mexico, and there is scarcely a town or village in this country where they are not either sold or yearly planted by some of its inhabitants.

BUIST'S SEEDS IN INDIA.

FROM A LETTER RECEIVED BY THE AGRICULTURAL AND HORTICULTURAL SOCIETY OF INDIA.

I beg to report for your information that I consider the seeds supplied to your society by Robert Buist, Jr., of Philadelphia, excellent, and request you will always send me a collection. I have grown his seeds now for years in this district, and have always produced the finest vegetables; in fact, I am in a position to prove that Buist is one of the best seed-growers of the day.   W. HELYS, of India.

Our attention to the production of seeds best adapted to warm climates has met with a high appreciation in India, and our exports to that country are only second to our trade in the Southern States. Our first large shipment was made to Calcutta in 1876, embracing many thousands of dollars' worth of seeds; since then the demand has wonderfully increased—their quality was their own advertisement—and to-day we have orders from Bombay, Calcutta, Allahabad, Benares, and other cities of India from the Punjab and Assam on the north to the Isle of Ceylon on the south.

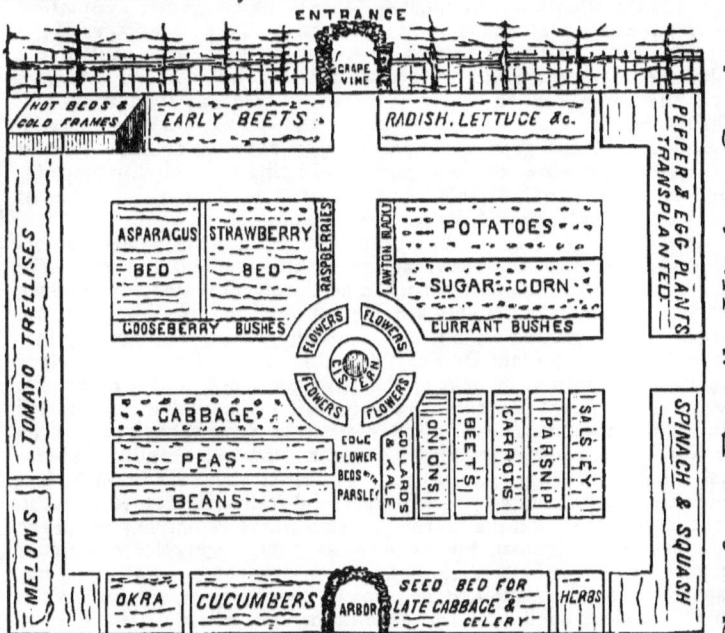

Plan for a Family Kitchen Garden.

The Kitchen Garden.

The Vegetable Garden, in our estimation, is the most important appendage to a country villa; the lawn is certainly very beautiful with its velvety carpet and graceful trees, and is without doubt the most attractive object for any rural home; but the garden, from which you draw your daily supply of vegetables, is a source of great economy, and the amount thus saved would create quite a snug fund in a single season; independent of this, is it not a great pleasure to enjoy a dish, the first of the season, of Extra Early Peas; to be able to cut a bunch of Asparagus before your neighbor, or to present a basket of Cauliflowers to a friend; and do you not also think the vegetables grown in your own garden are always more delicate in flavor than those you obtain elsewhere? Yes! that is always the general opinion, whether it is imaginary or not.

Simple as the cultivation of vegetables is considered by many, yet to cultivate them successfully requires skill acquired only by experience; book learning, as the farmer terms it, will certainly give you the general principles, but there are a great many minor features in their culture that you can only become familiar with by practice. A good garden, properly cultivated, should supply the table with a succession of crops throughout the growing season, and a stock for winter use; but many console themselves with a single crop, and purchase the balance of their vegetables in our city markets. We cannot in this condensed Guide, propose to treat fully on the subject, but will give all the information that is required for the inexperienced. The first and most important consideration in selecting a spot for the garden is the situation; the most suitable is a very gentle inclination towards the east or southeast, that it may have all the advantages of the morning sun. The next preferable exposure is south or southwest; if sheltered from the north or northwest, so much the better. Always avoid the neighborhood of large spreading trees, as their roots will exhaust the soil, and their shade injure the crops. In selecting the ground, it is of the greatest importance to have the soil of a healthy quality, being mellow, dry and capable of being worked with a spade. The best soils are of a friable and loamy texture; the worst, those of a very light sandy, or stiff clayey description.

After a proper location has been selected, the next most important consideration is to have it laid out in a convenient and attractive manner; a garden containing half an acre well cultivated will produce sufficient vegetables to supply a moderate-sized family throughout the the year. The garden should be enclosed by a board fence, against the inside of which plant DWARF PEARS, APRICOTS, PEACHES, or NECTARINES, and train as espaliers; the fruit produced in this manner is always of the finest quality. Our illustration of a kitchen garden will give an idea about what is required in order to have convenient spaces for all the important vegetables, and their location (excepting Asparagus) should be changed every year. A border about six to eight feet wide should surround the whole garden, and walks laid out from four to six feet wide. Shou'd the bottom, or subsoil, be retentive, trench the ground at least eighteen inches deep, as good vegetables can never be produced on sour or shallow soil. By trenching, I mean dig out a space two spades wide and one spade deep, placing the soil taken out to one side; then turn up the bottom soil, where it lies, at least the full depth of the spade, throw the top of the next trench on the first subsoil, and so on until the whole is finished. The general method of trenching is to turn the top side down, and the subsoil up, this is attended with evil consequences, as many years will elapse before the bad soil, which has been turned up, can be made equal to the surface soil, which has been turned under. In spading and trenching, we, of course, refer to small gardens; the more extensive ones should be plowed and subsoiled. The inclination of the soil of one foot in forty, or merely sufficient to carry off the water, is all that is required; a greater slope than this would, during our heavy rains, sweep soil, manure and seeds to the lowest ground.

Rotation of Crops.—There should always be a rotation of crops; that is, no two crops of a similar nature, such as Beets, Carrots and Parsnips, should be grown two years in succession on the same ground, it is not only very exhausting to the soil, but the crops thus grown are less productive. To facilitate this rotation, the garden should be divided into squares of nearly uniform size; say into six or eight squares, with cross-walks of from three to four feet wide. Constant stirring of the soil, destroying all weeds, and manuring freely, is one of the secrets of a gardener's success.

Manure.—Well-decomposed barnyard manure is the most reliable material for general purposes. From twenty to thirty tons is sufficient for an acre. For contingencies, or special purposes, use Peruvian Guano, at the rate of three hundred pounds to the acre, applied in moist weather; but even frequent uses of this will injure the soil. Ground raw bones (if pure) is also a valuable manure, and can be used occasionally with excellent effect; but above all, avoid superphosphate, unless you know, by actual experience of yourself or friends, that the brand you purchase is reliable, as thousands of tons are annually sold that the farmer actually receives not a particle of benefit from. A very beneficial liquid manure is made by dissolving guano at the rate of one pound to five gallons of water, to promote the growth of vegetables already started. Soapsud water in an excellent liquid manure for some garden crops, especially for Celery, which if applied every other day during its growing season, the stocks will be crisp and of a mammoth size.

HOT-BED FRAME.

In order to secure a supply of early vegetables, a hot-bed frame is indispensable. It can be constructed by any man, at a very small cost; it consists of a wooden frame, generally six feet wide, and from six to sixteen feet long, according to the supply of early vegetables required; one side to be at least six inches higher than the other; the frame to be subdivided by cross-bars, and each division covered by a glazed sash; the sides and ends should be joined by hooks and staples, to admit of its being taken apart, and stored away when not required. After completion, place it on the manure-bed, prepared in the following manner: The frame should face the south or southeast; fill in about ten inches of rich pulverized soil, and allow it to stand a few days, giving it air by slightly raising the sash, so that the fiery vapor or steam may escape. The seeds of Cabbage, Cauliflower, Egg-Plant, Peppers, Tomatoes and many other varieties may be sown, and the plants planted out as soon as the frosty weather is over.

Preparing Manure for Hot-Beds.—Fresh stable manure only, not exceeding six weeks old, is suitable for this purpose. Turn it over into a compact heap, protected from heavy rains or snow; allow it to remain so for about eight days, when it should be made up into the requisite form to suit the frame. If there is a scarcity of manure, use with it one-half fresh tanner's bark. Egg-Plant seed requires a strong heat to make it vegetate; for such the hot material will require to be two feet thick. Where the ground is quite dry, a very good method is to dig a space about eighteen inches deep, and put the manure therein; tramp it firmly and evenly; place thereon the frame and sash; put in the rich earth, and in about four days sow the seed, having previously stirred the earth freely, to destroy any seeds of weeds therein.

Cold Frame is a simple construction of boards for wintering Cabbage, Lettuce, Cauliflower, or Brocoli, for planting out early in Spring. Select a dry southern exposure; form a frame from four to six feet wide, and as long as is required. The back should be fourteen inches, and the front six inches high, with a cross-tie every six feet. Seeds of Cabbage, Lettuce, Cauliflower, and Brocoli, sown in the open border early in September, will be ready to plant into the cold frame about the end of October. The soil should be well prepared and smoothly raked before planting. Admit air freely on all pleasant days, but keep closed in severe weather.

Cold Pit.—This is a structure in very general use for growing Cauliflowers during Winter. The situation must be dry and well sheltered, having a south or southeast exposure. Dig out a space of two feet deep, and eight feet wide, if for brick and nine feet wide if for stone. Build the back wall four and a half feet high; that will be two and a half feet above ground, and three feet high in the front. If the ground is not dry, and is subject to under-water, and draining cannot be effected, do not dig so deep, and surround the walls with two feet thick of earth, which will keep the frost from penetrating them. If Cauliflower is to be planted, put into the pit three feet of leaves from the woods, tramp them firmly, over which put one foot of rich earth; after it remains for two weeks, it will be ready for the plants. Six plants for each sash of four feet will be enough. The space may be filled up with Lettuce and Radish.

Hot Pit.—Constructed in the same manner as the Cold Pit, but having the appliances of artificial warmth, either by hot manure and leaves, about half and half, firmly trampled into the bottom, two and a half to three feet thick; or one half fresh tanner's bark, half dried, mixed with hot manure, is very efficient, over which place about one foot of earth. In about two weeks the heat will have subsided sufficiently to admit of Cucumbers being planted, or any other seeds or roots requiring artificial warmth to forward their growth. These materials are readily obtained by every farmer and gardener.

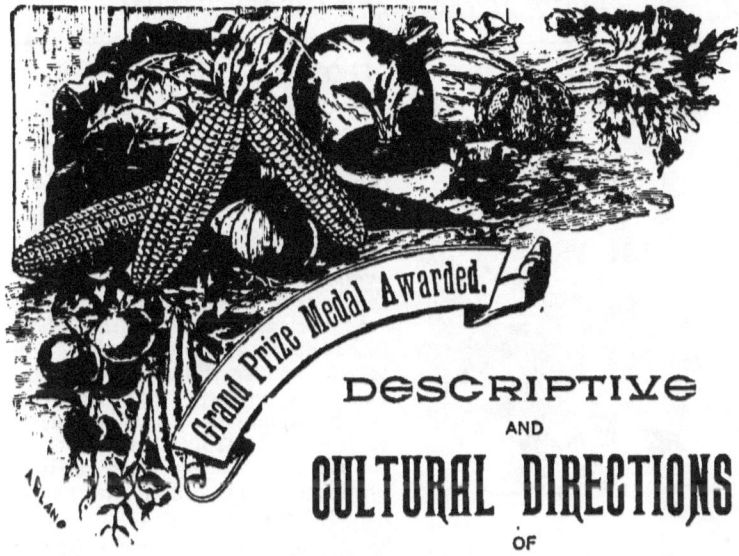

DESCRIPTIVE AND CULTURAL DIRECTIONS OF

THE STANDARD SEEDS

For Growth and Purity.

GROWN AND FOR SALE BY

ROBERT BUIST, JR.

SEED FARMS:—Rosedale, Waterford and Morrisville.

SEED WAREHOUSES:

922 and 924 Market St., ab. Ninth

(Adjoining the Post-Office),

———AND———

Storage Warehouses, Lombard Street,

PHILADELPHIA.

ARTICHOKE.

Artichaut (Fr.).   Artischoke (Ger.).   Alcachofa (Sp.).

Large Green Globe.—This is not a popular vegetable in this country, and is cultivated to a very limited extent. It is a very coarse-growing plant, occupying much space, while only a small portion is available for food, which is the receptacle of the flower. Plant the seed early in Spring, in rows three inches apart, and one foot from row to row; cover with fine earth one-quarter of an inch; when one year old, transplant them two feet apart each way, in deep, rich soil. Where the winters are severe, they must be protected with dry litter, or a bed of leaves, or by raising around them about eight inches of earth; manure and dig annually between the rows. The heads are boiled, and eaten with butter and salt; the bottom of these heads is very fleshy, and is cooked in various ways, sometimes being dried for winter use. The French are very partial to this vegetable.

Artichoke Roots—Jerusalem.—This variety is quite distinct from the above, and is only produced from the root or tuber; are planted and cultivated the same as the potato; is immensely productive and a fattening food for hogs; is also highly esteemed for pickling.

ASPARAGUS.

Asperge (Fr.).   Spargel (Ger.).   Esparraggos (Sp.).

The **Asparagus** is a favorite vegetable with all; almost every rural family have a patch or bed of it in their garden, and there is generally great competition among neighbors in cutting the first bunch of the season. There are really but two varieties, the Green Top and the Purple Top; either of these, if grown on very rich soil, will produce very large stalks, which many cultivators call the Giant, Mammoth, Colossal, &c. The seed should be soaked and sown early in Spring, two inches deep, and eighteen inches from row to row; the soil should be of a rich, sandy loam, well manured and prepared. After the plants are either one or two years old, transplant them into permanent beds, prepared in the following manner:—

The ground should be thoroughly trenched, burying in plenty of manure, as no more can be supplied after the beds are planted (except by surface dressings); the soil can scarcely be too rich, for the sweetness and tenderness of the shoots depend on the rapidity of their growth. A plot of ground twenty feet wide and fifty feet long will be large enough to supply a moderate-sized family; over it sow about one hundred pounds of salt, incorporating it with the soil to the depth of four inches. After being properly levelled, divide it off into beds four feet wide, with alleys of two feet between them. Drive in a strong stake at each corner, take up the plants carefully from the seed-rows with a spading-fork, expose them to the air as little as possible, keep them covered during the time of planting, and do not allow the roots to become dry. Stretch a line the length of the bed, nine inches from the edge, and with a spade cut a small furrow six inches deep; set a row of plants along the trench, nine inches apart, with the crown of the roots two inches below the surface; having finished a row, cover them directly, rake evenly, and proceed to open another furrow, a foot from the first; plant in the same manner, and so on until you have four rows to a bed. Cut down the stems the last of Autumn, and, after clearing off the weeds, cover with a dressing of manure or rich compost, which is to be forked in early Spring; the plants must be properly established before cutting for use, which will require at least two seasons. As the alleys between the beds will be so much ground idle the first two years, they can be planted with Cabbage, Lettuce, Radish or other similar crops; but nothing should be planted on the beds, as it would rob the ground of a great portion of its nutriment.

THE ASPARAGUS.

The New York Market Gardeners, at Oyster Bay, who make Asparagus-growing a specialty, grow it in the following manner:

"They select a good sandy loam, which is the best adapted for an early cutting for market. The ground should be thoroughly plowed as deep as possible, and furrowed off each way from four to five feet. At each intersection dig the dirt out so as to make the hole at least twelve inches deep, then put in about a half-bushel of good strong stable manure, and press down; cover with soil, and set the plant so that the crown will be about eight or ten inches from the top of the ground when levelled off; spread the roots out flat in setting, and cover with soil; keep the ground loose by cultivating; hoe out all grass and weeds. They can be set out either in the Fall or Spring; the Fall is best, as the roots get ready to start sooner in the Spring. They will want no additional manure until the second Spring after setting, when they should have a liberal dressing of manure plowed in, and the ground kept loose and clean. The third Spring give the plants a sprinkling of guano; as soon as frost is out of the ground, cultivate and loosen the soil. This season you will cut, but not too heavy, as it is better to cut light to strengthen the roots. After cutting, give a heavy dressing of manure, and keep loose and clean. In the Fall, before the seed drops, cut the tops and burn, to prevent filling the ground with small plants. All that is necessary after this is to use guano early in Spring, and plow and work in; and after cutting, to apply a good coating of manure between the rows, keeping the ground loose and clean. One-year-old plants are best for setting. Any kind of manure is good, with occasionally a dressing of salt. The very best manure, where it can be obtained, is night-soil, plowed in; but any kind will do if you use enough of it; there need be no fear of giving it too much, as the crop will pay fourfold to the quantity of manure used. For marketing, the sprouts should be all large, as green as possible, and cut, when bunched, eight inches long. The bunches should be five inches across the butt end, and tied with basswood-tie near each end. If to be kept over night, wet the butts and stand on the ground in a cool cellar; keep the tops dry after bunching.

BEANS (Dwarf, Snap, or Bush).

HARICOT (Fr.). BOHNE (Ger.). FRIJOL ENANO (Sp.).

To afford a regular succession of crops throughout the season, plant every two weeks, from the middle of Spring to the end of Summer; but not until the soil becomes warm, as they are very sensitive to both heat and cold. Plant in rows, eighteen inches apart, two inches deep; cultivate frequently, but only when dry, as the scattering of earth on the foliage or pods, when moist, will cause them to become damaged with rust. This crop will flourish between the ridges of Celery, rows of Corn or Cabbage, when they are first planted, as the Beans would be ready for the table before the other crops attain any size.

Wax or Stringless Beans have now become a universal favorite throughout the country; so much so, that we have not yet been able to grow sufficient to supply the increasing demand; they are, without an exception, the best of the entire Bean family, and in saying this, we do not make the famous Lima an exception; they are entirely free from strings, the pods are of a beautiful waxy yellow color; boil down as rich as butter, and taste more like a tenderloin beefsteak than a vegetable. The German Wax Pole we regard as superior to the Dwarf, being more fleshy and richer. It amply repays the extra trouble and expense of furnishing rods or poles; they luxuriate in rich soil, but will produce a fair crop in poor ground. It is merely a question of time when they will almost supersede all other varieties; and they will also mature their crops as far north as the Northern Lakes, which is a very important feature. They should be used while young, or just as soon as the pods assume their waxy color. Our city markets are now daily canvassed especially for this vegetable, and market gardeners who were fortunate enough in securing and planting pure seed last Spring have met with a ready sale for their entire product at more than double the price of the ordinary varieties. We say, "securing pure seed," from the fact that two-thirds of the Beans sold under this name are *spurious*, being badly mixed with a tough green-podded variety.

DWARF GERMAN WAX BEANS.

Seed-growers are not careful enough in growing this crop; they frequently grow it side by side with other varieties, and do not even trouble themselves in weeding out the plants producing green pods. A crop grown in this manner will become entirely mixed in a single season, and there are hundreds of such crops grown every year, and sold to the seed-stores of the East and West, and supplied by them, very innocently, to their customers as pure seed (as their purity cannot be distinguished when matured); therefore be careful in purchasing, as our stock is always of our own growth, our customers will always find it strictly pure.

Early Dwarf German Wax.—The finest of all Snapshorts; pods transparent, waxy yellow, and snap like pipe stems; boil as rich as butter, and, when highly seasoned, are luscious; they are thick and very tender, entirely stringless, and fully as early as the Valentine; one of the best market varieties. The bean, when ripe, is black.

Dwarf Golden Wax.—Similar in character to the German Wax, with pods rather more fleshy, and color of them more brilliant; this has become the most popular of all the wax varieties; it is especially the most profitable for market gardening.

DWARF GOLDEN WAX BEAN.

Dwarf White Wax.—Similar in every respect to the Dwarf German Wax; the pods are, however, not quite so round, and the bean is pure white when ripe. Highly recommended.

Ivory-Pod Wax.—This desirable variety is fully a week earlier than the old favorite German Black Wax. It produces long, transparent, waxy-white pods, which are entirely stringless. It is very productive, of very rich flavor and white-seeded.

Crystal White Wax.—A very beautiful, distinct and desirable variety, producing pods of good size. Color, waxy-white, and almost transparent. Are stringless, crisp and tender, and of rich flavor. The pods develop quickly, but mature slowly, and remain in condition for table use longer than any other variety.

Early Valentine is one of the best and oldest varieties; will be ready for the table in about six weeks from the time of planting; the pods are round, smaller in size than the Mohawk, but not quite as productive; it is a first-class market variety, the best and most popular of all the green podded varieties.

Improved Early Red Valentine.—A selection made from this old and popular variety for its extreme earliness and productiveness, specially desirable for market gardeners.

Early Round-Podded White Valentine.—Similar to the Early Valentine in every respect, but having a more robust habit in its growth. The beans, when dry, are pure white.

Best of All.—This is not only a very early variety but one of the most productive and largest green-podding varieties known; as a profitable shipping sort it has few equals; cannot recommend it too highly.

Early Mohawk Six Weeks.—This is a long, flat-podded variety; withstands considerable frost, and on that account is preferred for first planting; is also an excellent variety for pickling, and for which purpose it should be planted about the last of August.

IMPROVED EARLY VALENTINE BEAN.

Early Yellow Six Weeks, in growth and maturity, is very similar to the Mohawk; pods long and flat, very productive, and ripens about the same time.

Newington Wonder, a very productive early variety, producing its pods in bunches which are small and round; is a very desirable variety for forcing, and is esteemed very highly in England especially for this purpose.

Refugee, Thousand-to-One, or Brown-Speckled Valentine, a very excellent variety, very similar to the Valentine when green, though a stronger grower; is fit for the table in about seven weeks; very productive.

Early China Red-Eye, an old favorite, is very early, of good quality, and quite popular in the South.

White Kidney, or Royal Dwarf, a good late variety, can be used as a snap-short or as a shelling-bean for winter use, for which purpose it has no equal.

White Marrow, a large, round, oval, white Bean, of good quality, either green or dry; it is generally cultivated, however, for winter use, being a fine soup Bean.

Red French is a very strong-growing variety, but is seldom used as a snapshort, being generally shelled, and used as a winter vegetable; is also an excellent variety for soup.

The Shippers' Favorite.

This is one of the earliest and most desirable market varieties, with unsurpassed shipping qualities, and is the best green-podded Snap-Short ever introduced. It begins bearing when quite small, and produces a succession of pods which are delicate, tender, and while young, entirely stringless; the size of its pods is very much larger than any other dwarf variety. In making out your seed order do not overlook it, and more especially if you are a market gardener.

BEANS (Pole or Running).

STANGEN BOHNE (Ger.).   HARICOTS A RAMES (Fr.).   FRIJOL VASTAGO (Sp.).

These are usually planted in hills and trained to poles, which should be eight or ten feet long, and firmly set in the ground from three and a half to four feet apart each way; draw around them a hill of earth, and plant four or five beans to each hill, one inch deep, always observing to plant the eye of the bean down, which will cause it to produce a stronger plant, and grow more freely.

48 BUIST'S ALMANAC AND GARDEN MANUAL.

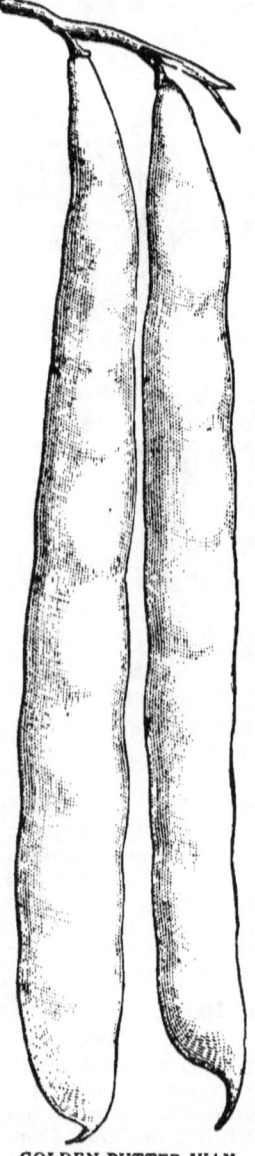

GOLDEN BUTTER WAX POLE BEANS

Large Lima.—The Large Lima is a general favorite wherever it can be cultivated; the germ of this bean is very delicate, and sometimes the first planting is destroyed by cold or wet weather; to insure against this, the beans can be sprouted in small flower-pots, or by placing them on sods of earth, placed in a frame, covered lightly with soil, and planting them out when the weather becomes warm; this will increase their earliness fully two or three weeks.

The Salem Mammoth Lima. —This is the largest and most productive variety ever introduced, and is the result of a constant selection for a number of years of the earliest and largest beans for seed stock. It produces Pods and Beans of immense size, and we regard it as the best and most profitable variety to grow.

Dreer's Improved Lima.—The distinctive improvements are its remarkable productiveness, delicious flavor, and forming the beans closely in the pod.

Carolina, or Sewee.—This variety is similar to the Lima, growing fully as strong, but producing beans but half the size; as a market variety it is not so desirable, but we consider it more productive; there is no difference in flavor.

London Horticultural, or Wren's Egg, is a very hardy and productive variety, very popular in the East, and other sections of the country where the Lima cannot be cultivated; it grows from six to eight feet high, producing purple blossoms, and pods about six inches in length; can be used either for snapping or shelling; it is also an excellent winter variety; as a baking variety it has no equal.

German Wax, or Butter (Stringless).—This variety is of unsurpassed quality, producing pods of a beautiful golden, waxen color, entirely stringless, and very productive; they should be used as a snap-short when young. Cannot recommend it too highly. Beans, when ripe, are indigo-blue.

Golden Butter Wax Pole.— A famous variety, recently introduced from Germany, where it is one of the most popular sorts; it is of the same character as the German Wax Pole, but somewhat earlier, and producing much larger pods of a bright golden waxy color; seeds when ripe are very dark purple, almost black. A very desirable variety.

Giant Wax, or Butter (Stringless).—The pods of this variety are longer than the German Wax, but not so thick; it has all its good qualities, but is rather more delicate in its growth; the beans are red when ripe.

Dutch Case-Knife is an excellent pole-bean, and very productive; is of fine flavor, and much earlier than the Lima or the Carolina; it can be used as a snap-short, or shelled, and is well adapted for Winter use. It is also an excellent variety to grow on Corn, and is sometimes called the Corn-field bean.

Southern Prolific.—An excellent bean for cooking in the pod. The pods are produced in clusters, the growth is rapid and the pods brittle and tender. It is one of the most popular beans in the Southern States, where it is better known than in the North.

Scarlet Runner.—This variety grows about twelve or fifteen feet, foliage bright green, and flowers brilliant scarlet; it is generally cultivated as an ornamental climber, and is really very attractive; it is used in many localities as a vegetable; the pods are of a bright scarlet color, and, when young, are very tender and excellent when shelled.

White Dutch Runner.—Similar to Scarlet Runner, except in color of seed and flower.

ENGLISH BEANS.

FEVE DE MARAIS (Fr.).   GARTENBOHNE (Ger.).   HABA COMUN (Sp.).

These varieties are not popular in this country, but are as highly prized in England as the Lima is here; they require a cool climate, and, if planted early on a rich, loamy soil, will produce a very good crop. They should be planted in drills, eighteen inches wide and two inches apart in the row. The Broad Windsor is the best variety, it grows about four feet, and is self-supporting.

BEET.

BETTERAVE (Fr.).   RUNKLERUEBE (Ger.).   REMOLACHA (Sp.).

Little art is necessary for the cultivation of this vegetable. One grand essential for an early crop is to dig or plow deep and manure well, and sow as early in the Spring as the soil will admit of working; draw drills half an inch deep, and eighteen inches apart; sow the seeds thinly, cover them lightly, and rake finely; before raking, sow a sprinkling broadcast of Early Radish seed, as they will be fit for pulling before the Beets are ready for thinning, which will be in about four weeks; as soon as the Beets have formed a few leaves, thin them out to six inches apart, allowing the strongest plants to remain. For a Winter crop, sow Buist's Long Blood, or Red Turnip Beet, late in Spring, or early in Summer; on the approach of frost, take up the roots and cut the leaves off to about two inches of the crown, and store them in pits secure from frost, or in a cool, dry cellar, covered with earth or sand. The seeds will always vegetate much sooner by soaking them in water six to twelve hours before sowing.

Extra Early, or Bassano.—This is the earliest variety, and is always sown for the first crop; the flesh is white, circled with bright pink, very sweet and delicate in flavor; it should not be sown at any other season of the year, as the color is generally objectionable.

50 BUIST'S ALMANAC AND GARDEN MANUAL.

Bastian's Extra Early.—A very desirable variety, following the Extra Early, and darker in color. A good market sort.

Philadelphia Red Turnip.—A very popular variety about Philadelphia; it follows the Extra Early, and is ready for pulling before the Blood Turnip; it is rather light in color.

Early Egyptian Red Turnip.—This is a very popular market variety, is very early, of beautiful smooth form, quite dark in color, and very desirable.

Eclipse.—A German variety of recent introduction, similar in character, habit and earliness to the Early Egyptian; it is, however, more of a globe shape, a very good early market variety, producing a small growth of tops, and roots of a bright red color; it can, however, be very much improved by making its color of a darker red, which can readily be done by selection.

Dewing's Early Red Turnip.—A very popular variety in the Eastern markets, of a beautiful and uniform shape, good color, and quite early.

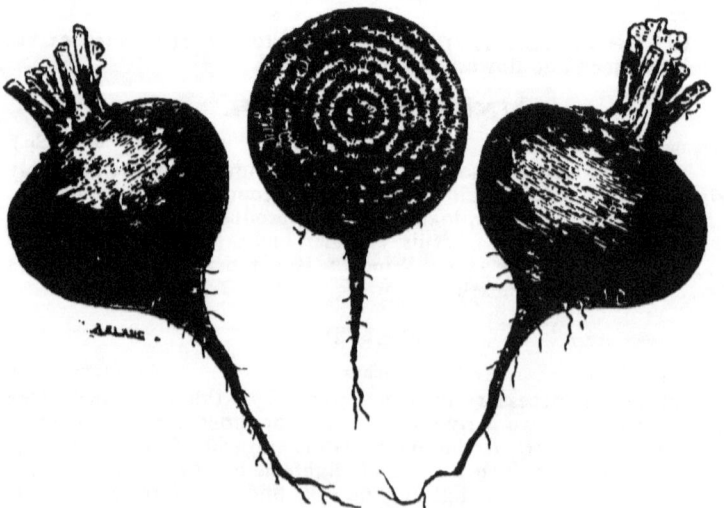

BUIST'S EXTRA EARLY RED TURNIP BEET.

Buist's Extra Early Red Turnip.—This variety surpasses all others for its extreme earliness, richness of color, perfection of form and sweetness of flavor. It is much earlier than the Othello, but not nearly so dark in color. We recommend it to all market gardeners as the most profitable Turnip variety to grow for early market. For forcing in frames or for out-door culture it is unsurpassed.

Early Blood Turnip is the most popular, but ten days later than the above variety, flesh deep blood-red, very sweet and delicate in flavor, and, as a market variety, excepting Othello, it is superior to all; it is adapted for either Summer or Winter use.

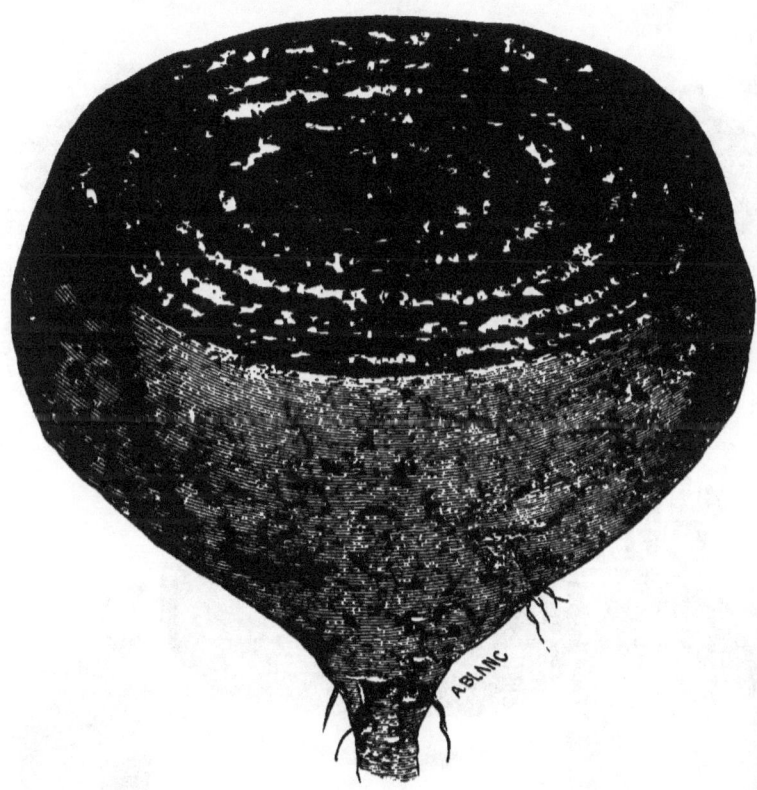

EARLY OTHELLO DARK BLOOD TURNIP BEET.

Early Othello Dark Blood Turnip.—This very desirable variety was introduced by us a few years since, and has already become very popular with the market gardeners, who require a variety of the darkest color for their main crop. It is the result of a very careful selection of the finest formed and very darkest roots, having been annually selected for the past five years for our own seed stock; and we venture to say that there is no stock in this country equal to it for its dark rich color, perfection of form or sweetness of flavor; foliage, dark crimson.

Long Blood grows from twelve to fourteen inches long, and from four to five inches thick; it is very productive, but not of such good flavor as the Red Turnip.

Improved Long Blood.—We selected this variety, a few years since, from Henderson's Pine-Apple, a celebrated English sort, and by care we have produced the finest and smoothest variety known; the foliage is of a beautiful crimson color, and the flesh dark-blood; we consider it a very valuable variety.

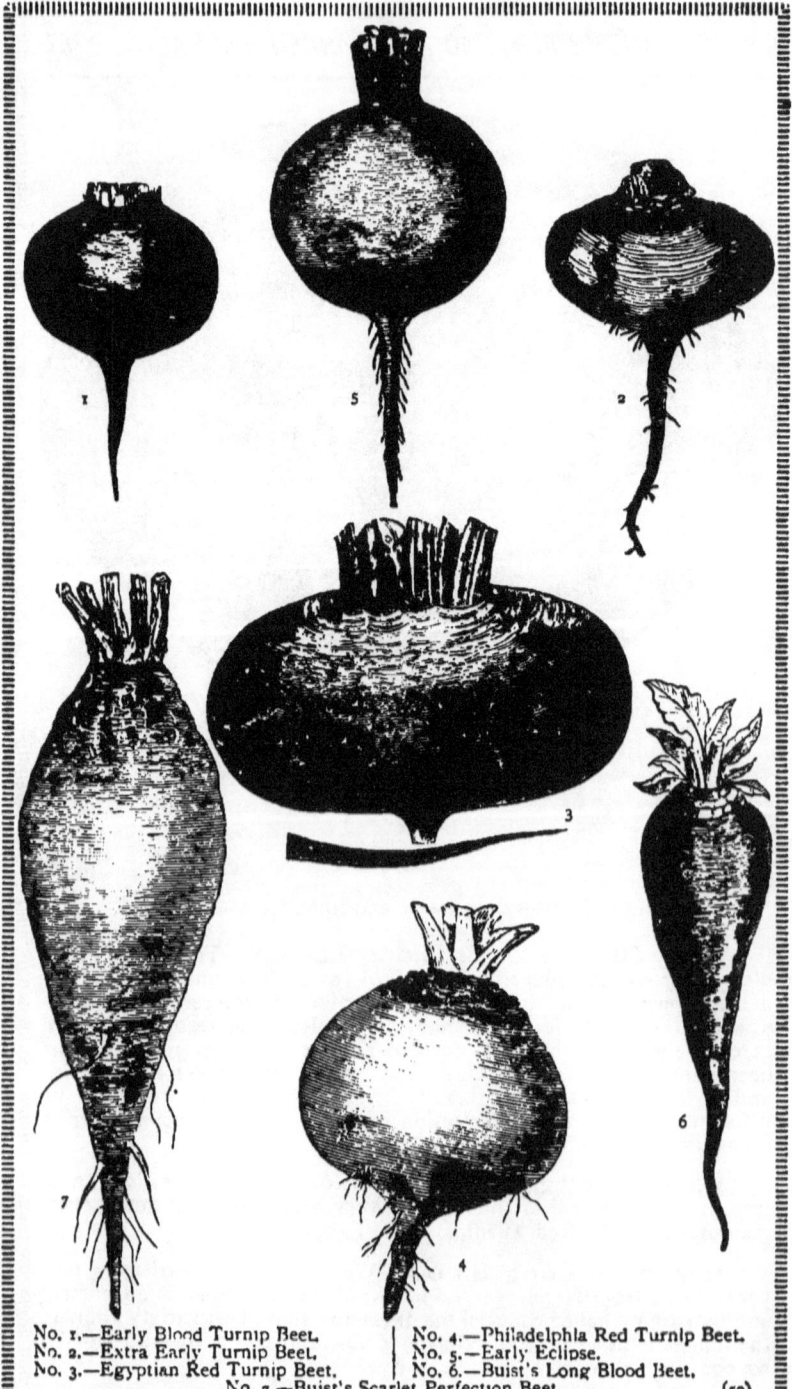

No. 1.—Early Blood Turnip Beet.
No. 2.—Extra Early Turnip Beet.
No. 3.—Egyptian Red Turnip Beet.
No. 4.—Philadelphia Red Turnip Beet.
No. 5.—Early Eclipse.
No. 6.—Buist's Long Blood Beet.
No. 7.—Buist's Scarlet Perfection Beet.

Half-Long Blood.—A very highly appreciated variety wherever grown; it follows the Early Red Turnip Beet, is of a half-long shape, and of a very dark blood-red color; it is also an excellent variety for Winter use.

Buist's Scarlet Perfection.—One of the most beautiful varieties grown, of half-long shape, dark-blood color, with a deep, rich crimson foliage; a very desirable and elegant variety, and has become very popular.

Dell's Ornamental Foliage.—A variety very extensively used in England as an ornamental border-plant; the foliage is very dark crimson (darker than any Coleus), and the root dark blood; is a very beautiful variety.

Silver or Swiss Chard.—This variety is cultivated entirely for its leaf-stalks, which are prepared similar to Asparagus, and its leaves used as Spinach. Cut often, as new and tender stalks will be produced.

BEETS (for Stock Feeding).

MANGEL WURZEL AND SUGAR.

About the Cultivation of Mangel Wurzel.

The cultivation of Mangels has long been one of the most extensive root crops grown in Great Britain, and is becoming a very popular crop with the farmers of this country who are gradually learning, by experience, that it is not only the cheapest food for stock during our long winter months, but one that is greatly enjoyed and eagerly devoured, beside this, they keep the cattle in fine and healthy condition. Their cultivation is simple and after sowing and thinning out the young plants, they will require no more care than a crop of potatoes. Cultivating and keeping clear of weeds is all that is necessary. On good rich sub-soiled ground, from 600 to 1000 bushels can be grown to the acre. In England where the climate is more favorable, the mammoth varieties have produced as much as from 60 to 100 tons per acre. In feeding them they should be sliced, and if steamed and mixed with a little bran, so much the better. Five pounds of seed is required to sow an acre.

Buist's Prize Golden Globe Mangel.—This popular and well-known variety is acknowledged to be the best and heaviest-cropping Globe Mangel in cultivation. It is remarkable for its immense size, beautiful shape, small top, fine, clear skin, and single tap-root, as well as for its most excellent feeding properties. It succeeds well on all soils, and is an eminently profitable variety, as very little labor is required in lifting and storing the crop; it will produce from fifty to sixty tons of roots to the acre, and keeps perfectly sound until late in Spring. If your soil is inclined to be shallow, this is the variety to grow to produce the largest yield.

Orange Globe Mangel Wurzel.—This variety, which is yearly coming into more general favor, is especially adapted for shallow soils, as half of it grows above ground; it is similar in shape to the Ruta Baga or Swede Turnip; the flesh is white, circled with yellow, and keeps perfectly sound until very late in Spring.

Buist's Prize Golden Globe Mangel Wurzel.
(For Stock-Feeding.)

THE LARGEST AND FINEST GLOBE MANGEL IN THE WORLD.

Buist's Mammoth Prize Long Red Mangel.—This excellent variety is the result of continuous and careful selection. It is not only distinct from, but far superior to any other Long Red Mangel in cultivation. The great characteristic of our improved stock is the broad shoulder and massive character of the bulb, by which a greater weight is obtained, without that coarseness which appears

BUIST'S ALMANAC AND GARDEN MANUAL. 55

to be inherent to many stocks of Long Mangel. It is rich in feeding properties, and is much appreciated by the leading agriculturists of the country. Is especially adapted for deep rich soil, and its production is enormous; single roots frequently weighing from 25 to 35 pounds.

Champion Yellow Globe Mangel.—This is another famous English variety of large size, globe form, solid, productive, and a good keeper.

Carter's Warden Orange Globe Mangel, a celebrated English Variety of beautiful form, flesh solid, keeps well, and very productive; average weight from 15 to 20 pounds.

Carter's Mammoth Prize Long Red Mangel.—This is the most celebrated English Variety, producing roots of prodigious size, immensely productive, and keeps as solid as a rock until late in Spring.

Long Red Mangel.—A variety requiring deep rich soil; flesh white, circled with red, very nutritious, and a good keeper.

Golden Tankard Mangel Wurzel.—This is an entirely distinct type of Mangels, of recent introduction, and highly prized wherever introduced. In England it is largely grown by

CARTER'S WARDEN ORANGE GLOBE MANGEL.

56 BUIST'S ALMANAC AND GARDEN MANUAL.

GOLDEN TANKARD MANGEL.

dairymen and sheep raisers, the former prize it not only for its great yield, but for the rich character of the milk it produces; while the latter claim, sheep fed on it thrive better and appear in much finer condition. It differs from all other Mangels, being deep yellow-color flesh to the very core; has small top, broad shoulders, smooth, rich skin, very solid fleshed and golden stemmed; admits of close culture, and is a very heavy producer.

White French Sugar Beet.—This is also a good stock beet, highly prized throughout the world; is both productive, nutritious, and has good keeping qualities. It is extensively grown in France, both for feeding purposes and for the manufacture of sugar, which is more extensively used there than that made from the cane.

Lane's Imperial Sugar Beet.—A variety produced by repeated selections made from the French Sugar; is of fine form, very productive, and a most desirable stock.

BORECOLE, OR KALE.

Chou-rest (Fr.).   Gruener Kohl (Ger.).   Breton (Sp.).

This variety of the Cabbage tribe is known as curly greens, or Kale. Sow the seeds in Spring, or in broadcast drills, thin out or transplant with the late Cabbage in early Summer; the leaves are fit for use as soon as they get a touch of frost. To preserve them during early Winter, treat them the same as Cabbage; the seed can also be sown in September; transplant like Cabbage, and they will continue growing all Winter.

DWARF GERMAN GREENS, OR CURLED BORECOLE.

BUIST'S ALMANAC AND GARDEN MANUAL. 57

Dwarf German Greens, or Curled Borecole is a dwarf, very hardy and popular variety with market gardeners; sow broadcast in early Fall, and cover with litter during Winter; the tops will be ready for use in Spring. The tall German Greens only differs from this in its growth, being twice as tall, but not nearly as desirable.

New Dwarf Erfurt.—This is without question the handsomest variety ever introduced. Is exceedingly dwarf in habit, and produces large and luxuriant leaves, which are as curly as moss-curled parsley. Very desirable for market gardeners.

Scotch or Green Curled Kale is a choice selection of Dwarf German Greens.

Curled Siberian a very beautiful and valuable market variety, is of dwarf habit, producing beautiful curled leaves, and is quite hardy.

DWARF ERFURT KALE.

BROCOLI.

CHOU BROCOLI (Fr.).   BROCOLI, SPARGEL-KOHL (Ger.).   BROCULI (Sp.).

Brocoli is a variety of Cabbage closely related to the Cauliflower, though not so delicate in flavor as that vegetable, but more hardy, and can be cultivated with greater assurance of its heading. It is supposed to have come originally from the island of Cyprus, and was cultivated nearly two hundred years ago. In mild climates it is extensively used from November to March, the various early and late sorts coming to maturity in the very middle of Winter. The most desirable for this climate are the Purple Cape and the Walcheren. Sow the seeds on a hot-bed late in Spring, transplant in early Summer into very rich ground, and water frequently to encourage their growth; they will head early in Fall; the heads should always be cut before they become open.

Walcheren.—One of the hardiest and best, with very large, firm heads.

Southampton.—A celebrated English variety, which attains great perfection in this country.

Early Purple Cabbage.—This is the most valuable kind for the North, producing large, close heads, of a brownish purple and has an excellent flavor.

BRUSSELS SPROUTS.

CHOU DE BRUXELLES (Fr.).   GRUENER SPROSSEN (Ger.).   BRETON DE BRUSELAS (Sp.).

A very desirable vegetable, requiring no special culture different from the Cabbage. The sprouts or miniature heads, which grow around

the upper part of the stem, are ready for use as soon as they have a touch of frost, and when properly prepared are exceedingly delicate in flavor; this dish is very popular in France, and called Choux de Bruxelles, but in this country its cultivation is confined to private families, and not for market. The following is the manner of preparing it for the table: place the sprouts in cold water for an hour, then boil them quickly for about twenty minutes, using plenty of water; when soft take them up and drain them well, then put them in a stew-pan with cream, or a little butter thickened with flour; stir thoroughly, and season to taste.

CABBAGE.

Chou Pomm ou Cabus (Fr.).   Kopfkohl (Ger.).   Repollo (Sp.).

For early Cabbage (where a supply of plants has not been secured in the Fall) sow on a gentle hot-bed very early in the season, and, as the plants grow, harden them to the full exposure of the air, protecting them from frost until the middle of Spring, when they should be planted in rows, fifteen inches apart and ten inches distant in the row. It may be observed that good heads can only be obtained when the ground has been well worked and highly manured. To obtain a good supply of Cabbage, the seed should be sown in September, from the fifteenth to the twentieth, in Pennsylvania. In mild climates they should be planted out late in Autumn, to remain for heading, but in cold latitudes they must be protected in beds or frames, and transplant early in Spring.

The Fall and late Winter Cabbage should be sown from the middle to the end of Spring, in beds of rich earth, and transplanted in June or July during moist weather, giving them a thorough watering in time of removal. The late Spring sowings are, in many situations, destroyed by the cabbage-fly as fast as the plants appear. So many nostrums have been recommended to preserve Cabbage plants from this pest, that we have ceased to recommend any of them. The Haltica or black-fly, which also infests the turnip crop, is checked by any application which will create a nauseous odor over the plants, such as soap-suds, tobacco-water or a sprinkling of guano, plaster or lime, early in the morning, while the dew is on them. Others adopt the method of cooping a few hens, giving their brood access among the plants, which most effectually keeps them down; but it is always the best plan to sow plenty of seed. Where there are only a few plants required, sow the seeds in boxes elevated three or four feet above the ground, and they will be entirely exempt from the attacks of the fly; in such a position the plants must have a copious watering every day until they are transplanted.

Wintering Cabbage.—In the Fall, before severe frost sets in, lift the plants from the rows, select a dry and sheltered part of the garden, and bury the roots, stock and part of the head in the earth in rows closely together, and in severe weather cover with straw or cornfodder; in Southern latitudes this is unnecessary.

To Destroy the Cabbage Worm.—Syringe the plants with strong tobacco-water. A few applications will destroy the worms entirely. A mixture of Paris green and plaster is still more effective, but should not be used after the heads are forming.

About Late Cabbage.

Among the entire list of vegetables there is no class more generally cultivated than the Late Cabbage, and none more frequently found degenerated or spurious; to cultivate a crop the entire season, anticipating a certain profit to be derived from it, and find you are only remunerated by long spindling shanks without solid heads, is certainly very provoking, to say nothing about the distress it frequently occasions to parties who are depending upon marketing their crop for support. For this reason we have made the cultivation and improvement of Cabbage a specialty for a number of years, by selecting each year the largest and most perfectly formed heads for our own seed stock. This repeated selection, extending over a period of twenty-five successive years, has produced what is considered by experienced cabbage-growers as the finest strain of late cabbage in the world. (See page 3.)

They have also proved to be the best varieties for the SOUTHERN STATES, where so much difficulty is always experienced in heading cabbage; and in the Eastern and Western country, where the weather is more favorable for the growth of Cabbage than in the South, whole fields have averaged heads weighing over thirty pounds, and many as high as fifty pounds each. In good, rich soil, and a favorable season, the heads will grow to an enormous size, frequently attaining fifteen to twenty inches in diameter. Thousands of acres of these varieties are annually cultivated in this vicinity for supplying our city markets, and for shipping. They are large, spreading varieties, generally very broad and flat at the top, and of a close and firm nature. Early Summer sowings will commence heading in October, seeds sown in April will head in July and August. Seeds of these varieties can be sown in the South in Early Fall, or as late as December; the plants will continue growing all Winter, and head up in early Spring.

To produce good heads of Cabbage, pure seed must be planted, and too much care cannot be exercised in obtaining it. Low-priced seed, or seed of doubtful quality, will never prove a profitable investment to the purchaser. For our own planting we would rather pay a hundred dollars a pound for pure seed than receive a pound of a doubtful quality as a gift. It would be painful, indeed, to find, at the close of the season, that you have been cultivating a worthless crop the entire Summer, to say nothing of the loss sustained in manure, labor, etc.; yet such are the misfortunes of the inexperienced, year after year. Thousands of pounds of English or imported seed are annually sold in this country (because cheap?), and not one plant in a thousand ever heads, in fact, this is the only kind of seed that the COMMISSION SEED HOUSES put up in their papers, and which occasion so much disappointment.

Now, if you wish a quality of Late Flat Dutch or Drumhead Cabbage that is RELIABLE and is GUARANTEED to give entire satisfaction in every respect, sow **Buist's Improved,** it is sold only by us under our seal, in papers, ½ and 1 oz. packages, and ¼, ½ and 1 lb. sealed cartoons, each of which bears the name of Robert Buist, Jr. We send out no seed of our choice stock in bulk.

BUIST'S EARLY LARGE YORK CABBAGE.   EARLY WINNIGSTADT CABBAGE.

Buist's Early York.—This is a very valuable early variety, producing heads fully two weeks earlier than any other sort. The heads are small, round, slightly heart-shaped, and very firm; its dwarf growth will permit them being planted closely together, say in rows one foot apart, and eight inches from plant to plant.

Early York (English), a cheaper grade of the above variety, but not so desirable, as the seed is imported.

Buist's Early Large York.—The most desirable second early variety, which produces heads twice the size of Early York, and very solid; it is the variety cultivated extensively for the Philadelphia market, and is a great favorite with all market gardeners.

Early Large York (English), a cheaper grade of the above variety, but not so desirable, as the seed is imported.

Buist's Earliest Cabbage.—This variety has given such great satisfaction, that we consider it peerless among the early sorts, combined with its earliness it unites compactness and excellent quality; forming conical heads, and quite large for an early strain, quite a short stem and few outside leaves, permitting close culture.

Early Paris Market.—A variety esteemed very highly in Paris, produces small solid heads and quite desirable for an early sort.

Early Etamps.—A popular early variety recently introduced from France, producing heads of fair sizes, of conical shape and quite solid.

Early Winnigstadt.—This has become one of our most popular varieties; there is no early sort which heads with greater certainty, or more solid; the heads are of good size, cone form, broad at the base, and twisted top, and succeeds the large York. To those who have never tried this variety, we say, by all means, plant it; it is invaluable for either market or family use.

Early Winnigstadt Cabbage.—(The Prussian Prize Stock.) This stock of Winnigstadt is famous for its earliness, size of head and great uniformity in heading. We have again secured this season the entire crop of a celebrated grower in Northern Prussia, which will be found far superior to any ever sold in this country.

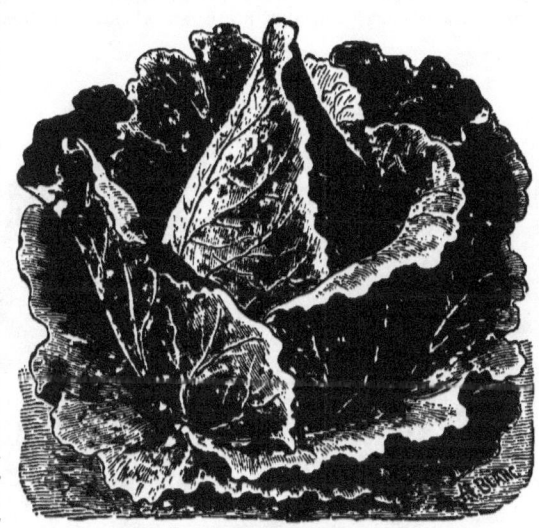

EARLY WINNIGSTADT CABBAGE.
(Prussian Prize Stock.)

Early Bonanza Cabbage.—This variety was introduced by us a few years since, which has proved itself a very large and profitable early market variety. We called it "The Bonanza," from the fact that we consider it more valuable than any other early variety, and one that will make greater returns to the market gardener than even the Jersey Wakefield, which matures about the same time; it forms heads weighing from 10 to 15 pounds each; it is of very fine grain and heads as solid as a bullet.

EARLY BONANZA CABBAGE.

Early Jersey Wakefield Cabbage.—Every year this variety is becoming more popular than ever. It has not been very long since its growth was confined almost exclusively to the market gardeners of New Jersey, but was gradually disseminated in other sections, and now is well known and highly appreciated by all the leading market gardeners of this country. We regard it as one of the best and most profitable early market varieties, always producing fine, large, solid heads. *Our stock is a selection made and grown by us from the finest stock in this country.*

EARLY JERSEY WAKEFIELD CABBAGE.

Early Summer Cabbage (BUIST'S IMPROVED STRAIN).— In introducing this improved strain of Cabbage, we will state that for

EARLY SUMMER CABBAGE.

the past five years we have been making selections from a very choice stock, selecting the earliest and largest heads, and now offer seed grown from this, which cannot fail in proving a very valuable acquisition. It is from ten days to two weeks later than the Wakefield and Bonanza, but produces much larger heads than either of them, frequently weighing from twenty to twenty-five pounds each. Its habit is dwarf, compact, and heads solid.

Early Heartwell.—A celebrated English variety of great merit, and very highly recommended by the leading market gardeners of both Europe and this country. We have grown it very extensively, and cannot recommend it too highly. It heads about the same time as the Large York.

Early Market.—A new early variety of recent introduction and highly recommended, produces large solid heads; a good market sort.

BUIST'S EARLY DRUMHEAD CABBAGE.

Early Bullock-heart.—A very desirable early market variety, forming heads of large size, and as solid as a bullet; very desirable.

Early Ox-heart.—This variety succeeds the Large York in heading, producing a medium-sized solid head, and consider it one of the best varieties.

Early Battersea is a roundish oval-headed variety; it is most excellent while young, and continues a considerable time fit for use; very desirable variety for the South.

Early Nonpareil.—This is quite an early sort, forming very fine, solid heads, with very few loose leaves; it is quite desirable.

Early Sugar Loaf is a very distinct sort; the heads are conical, and the leaves are erect and spoon-shaped; the heads are not so firm as those already described, and is only recommended as a variety, as the heat impairs its quality.

Buist's Early Drumhead.—This variety will follow the Winnigstadt in heading, and is one of the most profitable second and third early market varieties grown, producing fine large solid heads, frequently weighing over twenty pounds.

BUIST'S EARLY FLAT DUTCH CABBAGE.

Buist's Early Flat Dutch.—A very desirable third early variety, about two or three weeks earlier than the Late Flat Dutch, forming large, flat, solid heads; a very desirable market variety, standing the heat of the Southern States.

64 BUIST'S ALMANAC AND GARDEN MANUAL.

Buist's Improved Late Flat Dutch.—The popularity of this variety with market gardeners and private growers increases with each year. The large illustration in this Catalogue was taken from the growing crop at our Waterford farm, in New Jersey, which is a fair representation of an entire field; this readily shows to what perfection it has attained by proper selection and care in growing our seed. (See pages 3 and 66).

Buist's Improved Late Drumhead.—This variety is perfection, and produced by annually selecting, for over twenty-five successive years, our choicest heads for our own seed stock. It has been awarded as many as twenty-two premiums in a single season. (See pages 3 and 66).

Premium Large Late Flat Dutch.—One of the oldest varieties in existence, and more largely planted than any other sort, producing large, solid heads of bluish-green, with a broad and flat surface. When touched with frost, the outer leaves become tinted with reddish-brown; the head is white, crisp and tender. Too much care cannot be taken in the selection of your seed, as one-half sold of this and the Premium Drumhead are spurious. PLANT BUIST'S IMPROVED, which is grown from our choicest selected heads.

Premium Large Late Drumhead.—Similar in every respect to the Flat Dutch in its growth and general habit, but producing heads which have a more rounded top. Plant Buist's Improved; it is always grown from selected heads.

Large Late Bergen.—A variety very similar to the Late Drumhead, forming large and fine heads, but rather coarse; is an excellent variety for making saur-kraut.

Brunswick Drumhead.—A very desirable variety, with a very short stem, producing large, solid heads, frequently weighing twenty pounds; is earlier than the Premium Drumhead.

Red Dutch.—This sort is principally used for pickling, and is sometimes sliced in salads; it is also an excellent dish when boiled; the head is of medium size, very solid, of a heart-shape, and of a red, purplish color. The darker the color and the more thick and fleshy the leaves, the more valuable; it is in perfection from October until Christmas.

Stone Mason Drumhead.—A desirable market variety, producing medium-sized, solid heads; quite a popular variety in the Eastern States.

Marblehead Mammoth Drumhead.—This is a coarse-growing variety, and inferior to the Late Drumhead of this market; it heads very well in cool sections, but it has not proved to be a reliable heading variety for the Southern States.

Green Glazed.—A coarse, loose-headed variety, but very popular in the South, as it is supposed to withstand the attacks of the cabbage-worm better than any other variety; color, dark, shining-green.

Green Curled and Globe Savoy.—These varieties are very similar to each other; they do not, however, head firm, but the whole of the head can be used; are much improved in quality by frost. Per oz., 25 cts.; ¼ lb., 75 cts.; lb., $2.50.

Drumhead Savoy. —A variety of Cabbage producing beautiful curled leaves, which, when touched by frost, becomes very tender and delicious in flavor, closely resembling the delicacy of the Cauliflower. This variety forms quite a compact head. Per oz., 30 cts.; ¼ lb. $1.00; lb., $3.00.

GREEN CURLED SAVOY CABBAGE.

Golden Globe Savoy.—A very beautiful variety, of very attractive appearance, on account of its golden-tinted heads; is of dwarf habit, and delicate in flavor. Per oz., 25 cts.; ¼ lb., 75 cts.; lb. $2.50.

Early Dwarf Ulm Savoy.—A very early variety, producing small but compact heads; very desirable. Per oz., 25 cts.; ¼ lb., 75 cts.; lb. $2.00.

Early Paris Savoy.—A very early and popular French variety, forming fine heads. Per oz., 30 cts.; ¼ lb., $1.00; lb., $3.00.

GOLDEN GLOBE SAVOY CABBAGE.

BUIST'S ALMANAC AND GARDEN MANUAL.

Eight Specimens, Weighing 262 Pounds, of
BUIST'S IMPROVED LATE FLAT DUTCH AND DRUMHEAD CABBAGE.

SHOWING WHAT BUIST'S SEED WILL PRODUCE.

This STOCK has been awarded 22 FIRST PREMIUMS in a single season. No other Brand has ever gained such a World-wide Reputation. We sell this Seed only in our Sealed Packages and Cartoons. (See page 3.)

CARROT.

Carotte (Fr.). Moehre (Ger.). Zanahoria (Sp.).

This vegetable requires a deep, rich, light, sandy soil, well manured; if the ground is not of this quality, it should be dug deep and well broken the year previous; if for field culture, the ground .ould be subsoiled, as in all shallow or hard soils the roots fork or spread in a lateral direction, injuring both their size and quality. Sow early in Spring, in shallow drills, half an inch deep, and nine to twelve inches apart, which admits of the hoe being made use of in thinning out the crop and clearing off the weeds. As soon as the plants are up and can be distinctly observed in the rows, take a three-inch hoe and thin them out to three or four inches apart; the main crop, intended for Fall and Winter, should be thinned to six inches apart; frequent stirring of the soil is very essential to the growth of the roots; should the surface of the soil become baked before the youi g plants appear, loosen it by gentle raking. From the first of May to the first of June is the period to sow for a main crop, which will be ready to harvest about the first of November. In the Southern States they can be sown in the Fall, and will continue growing all Winter, and be fit for the table in early Spring. The seed will germinate more freely in dry weather, by soaking it twelve hours in cold water, and mixed with sand before sowing. The crop is ready for harvesting as soon as the tops commence turning yellow; they should be taken up in dry weather; cut off the tops to about an inch of the crown, and pack the roots in dry earth or sand in the cellar, for Winter use; or they may be pitted out of doors, covered with two inches of straw and a foot of earth, to keep them from frost, when they can be used until the following April. Beets, and all similar roots, can be kept in the same manner.

Extra Early French Forcing.—A favorite little Carrot, prized on account of its extreme earliness and superior flavor; best for forcing.

Early Scarlet Horn.—This has always been the general favorite for an early crop; it is of a bright orange color, of delicate flavor, and will grow in less depth of soil than any other variety, owing to the shortness of the root; the seed which we grow has a very great reputation among market gardeners for its high color and beautiful form.

Early Half-Long, or French Intermediate.—This is not only a very popular variety in France, but one that is regarded with great favor in this country; it is two weeks later than the Early Horn, but of twice its size; is of a deep-red color of perfect form, and exceedingly delicate in flavor. Knowing its great superiority, we have taken great pains to introduce our choice stock among market gardeners the past few years, and it has now become so popular among them, that we sell annually to gardeners alone, over two thousand pounds of seed; as a market variety, it has no superior.

Danvers Half-Long Scarlet.—An intermediate or half-long variety, of handsome form, of a bright orange-red color and very productive. A very desirable variety for market gardeners.

Early Half-Long Luc.—A new French variety, of a beautiful half-long shape, bright orange-red color and stump-rooted. Is quite early and a desirable market variety.

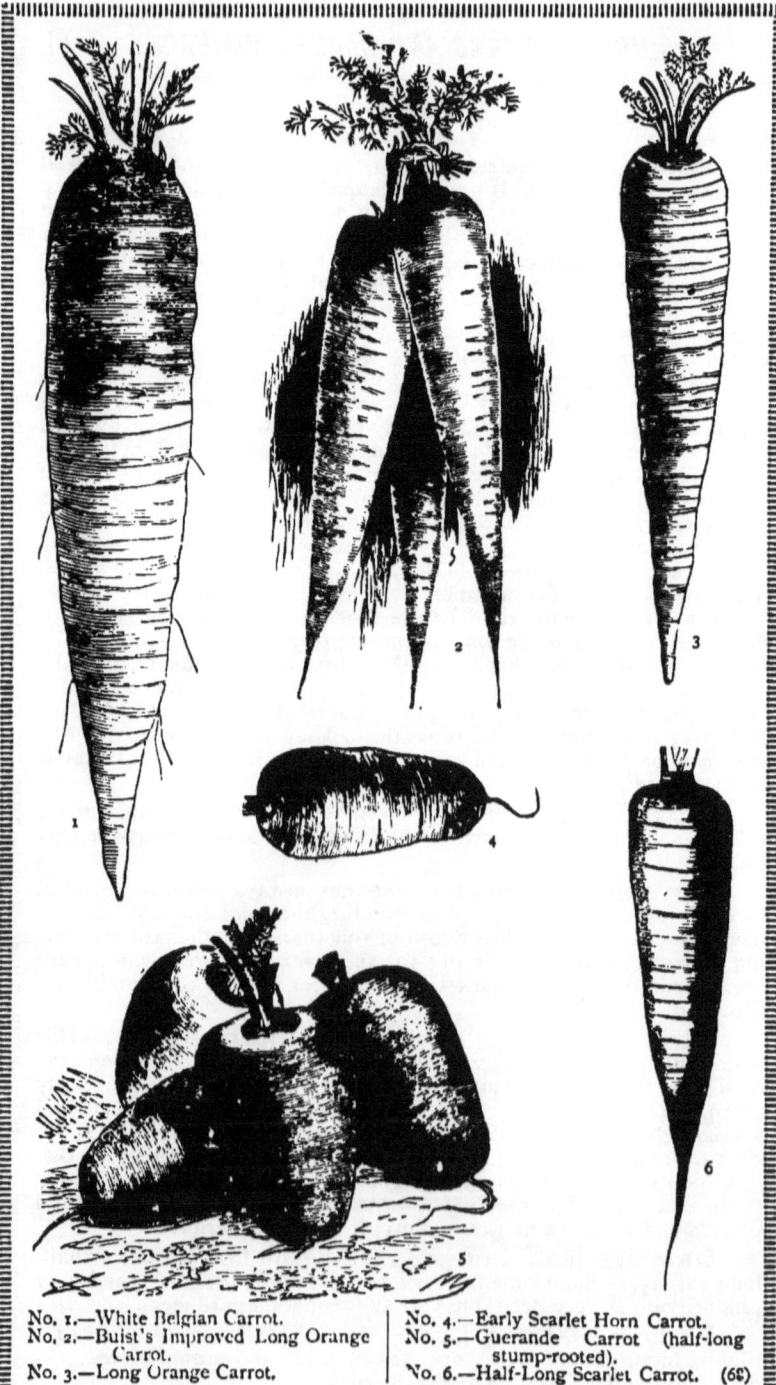

No. 1.—White Belgian Carrot.
No. 2.—Buist's Improved Long Orange Carrot.
No. 3.—Long Orange Carrot.
No. 4.—Early Scarlet Horn Carrot.
No. 5.—Guerande Carrot (half-long stump-rooted).
No. 6.—Half-Long Scarlet Carrot. (69)

Improved, or Prize Long Orange is the most popular variety in this country; it is not so bright in color as the former, and flesh much coarser; but is very productive, and, in deep rich soil, will frequently grow two feet in length, and produce six hundred bushels to the acre.

New Long Red, without Core.—A very fine new variety of a peculiar habit, growing about nine inches in length and cylindrical in shape, stump-rooted and almost entirely free from heart.

Scarlet Altringham is a bright red variety, peculiar in growing from one to two inches above the ground; is very popular in England for a general crop, but is grown to a very limited extent in this country; it is our favorite of all varieties for a field crop.

White Belgian, or Large White.—This is the most productive of all other varieties, but exceedingly coarse, and is less nutritious than any other field Carrot.

Guerande, Half-Long Stump Rooted.—A short half-long scarlet variety, in size between the Early Horn and Short Horn. A very desirable and attractive sort.

NEW LONG RED CARROT.
(without core).

HALF-LONG LUC CARROT.

The IMPORTANT ADVANTAGE purchasers of Seeds have in planting Buist's cannot be overestimated. The improvement of the various varieties of vegetables has been made a specialty by us for many years, introducing varieties that have made Buist's brand famous not only for the fine quality of vegetables they produce, but for the strong germinating qualities of their Seeds; besides, we annually grow only what we can annually sell, and, as we commission no Seeds, those sent out by us are always fresh and reliable. This is why Buist's Seeds are so satisfactory to all who plant them.

CAULIFLOWER.

CHOUFLEUR (Fr.).   BLUMEN-KOHL (Ger.).   COLIFLOR (Sp.).

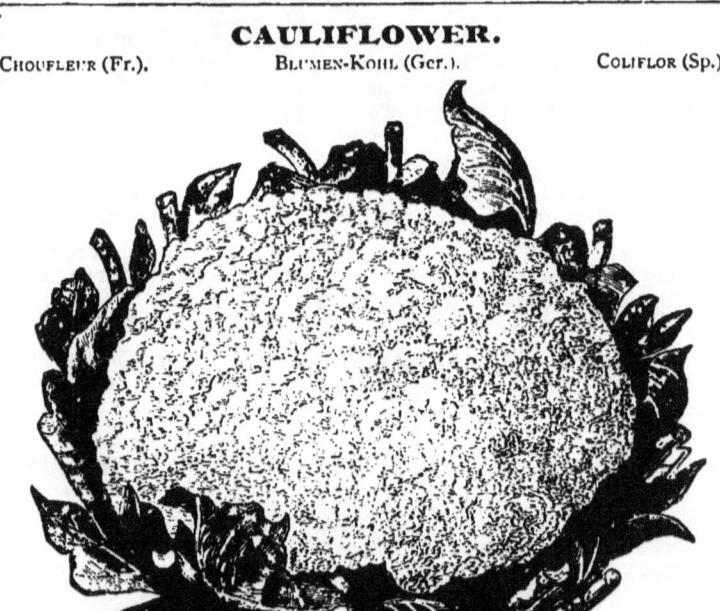

MONT BLANC CAULIFLOWER.

The Cauliflower is considered the most delicate of the entire class of vegetables, and is much sought after in every market; its cultivation is not generally understood, even by some of our most intelligent growers. Our Philadelphia markets have always been famous for the display of beautiful vegetables, grown by our gardeners, but strange to say they can rarely produce a first-class Cauliflower of their own growth, but are obliged to depend on the growers of Long Island for their supplies. For an early crop sow in September, and transplant in frames hereafter described; for Fall crop sow in a hot-bed early in Spring, and transplant into light, rich soil, when the season is favorable.

To grow the Cauliflower to perfection, prepare a bed of light, rich soil, two feet deep, and one-third of it to be composed of well-decomposed manure; select an open exposure, sheltered from the northwest; the whole to be surrounded with a close frame, and covered with glass or shutters; it should be prepared about the 1st of October, and allow the beds to settle two weeks before planting; lift the plants carefully from the seed-bed, and plant them into the frame eighteen inches apart each way; give a gentle watering to the soil around the plants, press them down firmly, and little or no more water will be required until Spring. Between each of these plants, Lettuce can be planted, which will head during the Winter, or early Spring, before the Cauliflowers form any size. The frame should be banked up on the outside with manure or dry litter, to exclude the frost, and cover the sash or shutters with dry straw or mats during severe weather, observing to give plenty of air on clear, mild days, which will prevent the plants from damping off. When they commence growing in Spring, they should receive copious waterings, to promote their growth, as when once checked by draught they rarely recover; should the flowers open more rapidly than they can be used, they can be retarded by closing the leaves over the heads, which will also cause them to blanch, and be more tender.

Mont Blanc.—This variety is one of the largest and finest Cauliflowers known. Is suitable either for forcing or for a general crop, producing large snow-white heads, which are well protected by its leaves, and of the most delicate flavor. Stem of medium growth; leaves long and smooth. It has become a very popular variety.

Early Snowball.—This is another very desirable variety for either forcing or out-door culture, producing fine large heads. Is a certain cropper and very early.

Early Dutch —This is one of the oldest varieties and frequently produces very good heads.

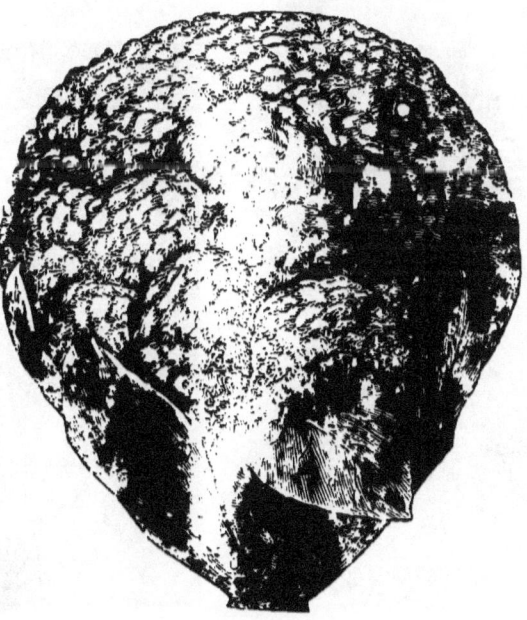

EARLY ERFURT CAULIFLOWER.

Carter's Defiance.—A very distinct and valuable extra early Cauliflower. It is earlier than any other variety. Very dwarf and compact in habit, producing fine heads, and one of the best for forcing.

Extra Early Erfurt, the earliest of all varieties, and very desirable for forcing, producing fine sized heads.

Early Erfurt.—An excellent variety, producing large, white, compact heads, of fine quality.

Early London.—An excellent early variety; heads large, very white and tender.

Early Paris.—The best known of all the early varieties; tender and delicious.

Nonpareil.—A well known variety, highly esteemed; always sure to head.

Half Early Paris.—One of the most popular varieties; heads very white and compact; good for an early or late crop.

Lenormand Short Stemmed.—A superior variety, with fine, large, and well formed heads.

Veitch's Autumn Giant.—A valuable and distinct late variety, producing large white firm heads; well protected by the foliage.

Walcheren.—A favorite late variety, very hardy, and produces large, white firm heads, of uniform closeness.

CELERY.

CELERIE (Fr.). SELLERI (Ger.). APIO (Sp.).

GOLDEN DWARF CELERY. WHITE PLUME CELERY.

A much-esteemed esculent, when produced in perfection. Sow in the garden very early in Spring, in moist, rich ground; when the plants are from four to six inches high, cut off the tops and transplant them six inches apart, into trenches four inches deep, nine wide, and three feet from trench to trench. The soil for Celery can scarcely be too rich in manure of the proper description; it should be well decayed, and not of a drying nature. In dry weather, a good supply of water or soapsuds is essential, the latter the best material that can be used; never allow the plants to become stunted, but keep them growing. Some cultivators earth up at intervals, while others permit the plants to retain their full growth, and earth up all at once; the latter is the best method. About the 1st of October, earthing up may proceed without injury; but let it be done firmly and evenly, and in a slanting direction, from the base to nearly the top of the leaves; in this state it will remain sound for a long time; should the weather become very severe, dry litter or straw should be spread over the plants; it is well, on the approach of cold weather, to lift a quantity, and bury it in sand or earth in a cellar, which will keep for several weeks. To grow large and crisp Celery, give copious waterings daily of soapsuds or liquid manure. Celery which is earthed or banked up early is liable to rust, which destroys the stalks.

Buist's Mammoth White Solid.—A variety of our own introduction, producing immense stalks, which, when blanched, are solid, crisp and tender. It is undoubtedly the best large variety.

Large White Solid.—A medium-sized, white, solid, crisp variety, which is most generally cultivated.

Golden Dwarf.—A very valuable variety, of recent introduction. In habit and growth it is similar to the Half-Dwarf kinds, except when blanched. The heart is large and of a waxy golden yellow, making its appearance exceedingly attractive. It is quite solid, of fine flavor, and keeps well.

Incomparable Dwarf White and Dwarf Crimson.—Very dwarf varieties, producing close, solid stalks, which are crisp and tender; the difference in them is only in the color.

Sandringham Dwarf White.—An English variety, which originated in the garden of the Prince of Wales; is an improvement on the Incomparable Dwarf, being rather larger in its growth, and of finer quality; we consider it one of the best dwarf varieties.

Boston Market.—A variety grown almost exclusively by the Boston market gardeners; it has the peculiarity of forming miniature stalks by its branching habit; is solid, crisp and desirable.

Wright's Grove Dwarf White.—This is the finest of all the dwarfs. Blanches almost snow-white, is very solid and of a shellbark flavor.

Wright's Grove Dwarf Crimson.—Similar to the above; only of a beautiful red color. Very desirable.

Henderson's White Plume.—A recently introduced variety of great merit, self-blanching, solid, crisp and tender, and of fine flavor.

CELERIAC.

German or Turnip-Rooted Celery.—Sow early in Spring, in light, rich soil, transplant in May into beds (not into trenches like other celery), water freely in dry weather; the roots, which form something like turnips, will be ready for use in October. This vegetable is very popular with the Germans, and is called by them the German Celery.

CELERIAC, OR TURNIP-ROOTED CELERY.

CHERVIL.

Cerfeuil. (Fr.). Gartenkerbel (Ger.). Perifolio (Sp.).

This is a warm, mild and aromatic plant, popular with the French, who use it as a salad, but it is seldom grown in this country. Sow thinly in drills eight inches apart early in Spring, and for a later crop sow early in Summer.

CORN SALAD.

Mache, Salade de Ble (Fr.). Ackersalat La' z Srsal.: (Ger). Macha (Sp).

Vettikost, or Lamb's Lettuce, as it is sometimes called, is used during the Winter and Spring as a salad; the leaves should always be picked, not cut; sow thickly in drills nine inches apart, early in Autumn, and cover thinly with straw when cold weather approaches.

CORN SALAD. SOUTHERN COLLARDS.

COLLARDS OR COLEWORT.

This variety of the Cabbage tribe is used only in the South, where it is cultivated for *Greens*. There are seasons in the South when a stand of Cabbage is hardly possible; it is then the Collard, which is a hardy, robust, vigorous plant, comes in as a substitute for head-cabbage. Sow late in Spring for early Autumn use, and again in Midsummer for Winter use; it continues growing all Winter.

CRESS, OR PEPPER GRASS.

Cresson (Fr.). Kresse (Ger.).
Mastuerzo (Sp.).

Extensively used as a small salad; for early Spring use, sow thickly on a gentle hot-bed, in shallow drills two inches apart. Sow in the garden as soon as the weather will admit; when the crop is from a half to one inch in height, it is ready for use; cut close to the roots; as it soon runs to seed, frequent sowings should be made.

BUIST'S ALMANAC AND GARDEN MANUAL. 75

CRESS (Water.)
CRESSON DE FONTAINE (Fr.).　　BRUNNENKRESSE (Ger.).　　　　　　BERRO (Sp.).

The most reliable way of cultivating the Water Cress is to sow the seed in moist soil, and when a few inches high transplant into running brooks, but protected from the current; when the plants become once established they will last for years. The leaves and stalks are used as a salad, and is considered a very wholesome dish.

SUGAR CORN (for Garden Culture).
MAIS (Fr.).　　　　　WELSCHKORN (Ger.).　　　　　　MAIZ (Sp.).

Plant about the last of Spring, in hills, about three feet apart; place a shovelful of manure or a handful of good phosphate in each; five or six grains to a hill is sufficient; when up, thin them out, allowing three of the strongest plants to remain; thorough cultivation is necessary to secure a good crop. Where a succession is required for the table, plant every two weeks until the middle of Summer.

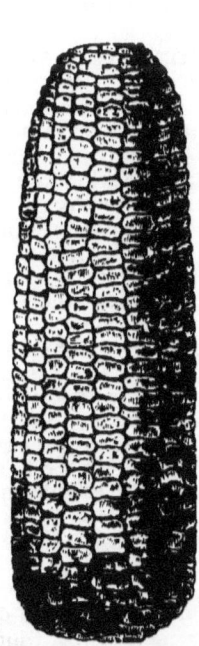

CROSBY'S EXTRA EARLY DWARF SUGAR CORN.　　STOWEL'S EVERGREEN SUGAR CORN.　　NEW ENGLAND EARLY SUGAR CORN.

Crosby's Extra Early Dwarf Sugar.—An improved variety, equally as early as the Adam's Extra Early, and having all the fine qualities of the Sugar; it is exceedingly dwarf, and requires good, rich soil; the ears are small, but luscious in flavor; never grow the Adam's Early if you can obtain this variety.

Extra Early Minnesota.—Very early, of dwarf habit, producing rather small ears, but of very choice quality.

Adams Extra Early, or Early Burlington.—This is the earliest of all varieties; it will be ready for the table in about six weeks after planting; it is not, by any means, a desirable variety, further than for its earliness; it lacks sweetness, and should only be used for first planting.

Adams Early.—A larger growing variety than the former, producing much larger ears, but not as early.

Early Narragansett.—A celebrated Eastern variety, quite early, but ears are frequently imperfect; when dry, the corn has a peculiar reddish color.

Early Marblehead.—A new and very popular Eastern variety. This new variety, tested with the Early Minnesota, Narragansett and other early sorts, proved a week earlier than any of them. The stalk is of dwarf growth, and ears set very low down; it is of fair market size and very sweet.

New England Eight-Rowed Early Sugar.—This variety we have cultivated for a number of years, and find it unequaled for an early sort; the ears are of large size, has but eight rows and of delicious quality.

Moore's Early Concord.—An early variety, forming good-sized ears, with from twelve to twenty rows.

Triumph.—An early and very desirable variety, of sweet and delicate flavor, producing a large ear and small-sized cob.

Egyptian Sugar.—This is one of the best of the large varieties, of vigorous habit; ears large, having from twelve to fifteen rows, kernels of good size, and very productive; it is very sweet and tender, and of delicious flavor; invaluable for canning.

Mammoth Sugar.—The largest of all the Sugar varieties producing perfect ears of immense size, ! ving from twelve to sixteen rows; a fine market variety, and follows the New England eight-rowed Sugar in ripening. Sweet and delicious.

Stowel's Evergreen Sugar.—Although not an early sort, it is, without any exception, the best for table use of the entire lot, although quite late. Some may observe they have tried it, and find it not equal to the ordinary Sugar; to such we say, you have not had the pure stock, as no variety degenerates so quickly as this, without the grower is exceedingly careful; we have very frequently observed samples sent out by some seed establishments, as Stowel's Evergreen, that were composed of several varieties; caused by being grown in the vicinity of other sorts. It is also the best variety for canning purposes.

Black Mexican.—A very peculiar-looking variety, from its bluish-black grains, but is quite early, and of delicious quality.

Tuscarora.—A large eight-rowed, white variety, ears of good size, cob red, grains white; was formerly a very popular variety, but is now superseded by the various varieties of sugar.

Sugar Corn for Fodder.—This is a very valuable crop for almost every cultivator; even those who have but a single cow will be much benefited by sowing a small patch for cutting when the pasture becomes short.

INDIAN CORN (for Field Culture).

Early Yellow Canada has eight rows, and ripens very early; it is generally used with us for replanting where the Gourd seed has failed. It is not very productive, but well adapted to sections where the season is short, or soils poor.

Early Yellow Dutton is also an early variety; has from ten to fourteen rows; ripens equally as early as the Canada, but more productive. We consider it one of the best field varieties.

Compton's Early Field.—A very early and prolific variety, eight to ten feet in height, ears well-filled to the end; kernel medium, bright yellow, and of the flinty order.

Pennsylvania Early Eight-Rowed Yellow.—One of the most valuable and productive varieties for late planting, producing very large ears, many measuring sixteen inches, and well filled out; it can be planted in this section as late as June 15th, and insure a crop.

Early Leaming.—A very popular yellow variety, recommended for its earliness and productiveness, grains small, but ears of good size, a desirable variety for planting late, or in localities where the seasons are short.

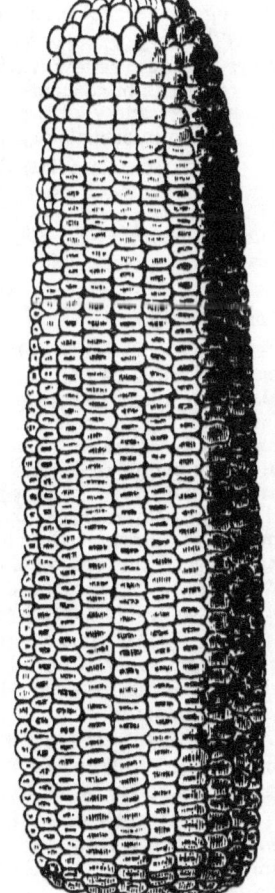

EARLY GOLDEN DENT GOURD SEED.
(The Best Field Corn for the South.)

Early Golden Dent Gourd Seed.—This is the best field corn for the South, and was introduced by us several years ago, especially for the Southern States, where it has become equally as popular as in the North. It is not quite as productive a variety as the Chester County, but we regard it as far superior. It is earlier, requires less strength of ground, and makes a fine quality of golden-colored meal. Those who desire to plant the best field corn should select it; when pure the grains are very deep, very thin cobs, and will shell more to a given weight of corn on the cob than any other variety.

Early Golden Beauty.— A beautiful golden yellow variety, with a broader grain, but not as deep as the Golden Dent, is early and productive, a fine field variety.

Buist's Improved Large White Flint.—This is distinct from the ordinary White Flint, being more productive, and ears of a much larger size; is an excellent field sort, has from ten to fourteen rows, and of a beautiful pearly appearance; it is a superior variety for hominy, and the stock which we cultivate is unsurpassed.

Maryland White.—A very popular variety in the South, and is the best of all the soft white varieties for that section; is not however, very productive, but is highly esteemed for grinding purposes, making a very choice quality of meal.

Clouds Early Mammoth Dent.—One of the best and most popular yellow varieties, has been awarded first premiums wherever exhibited; ears large, and grains very deep; it is the most productive variety known; will yield in a favorable season, on good soil, over 110 bushels per acre; cannot recommend it too highly.

Mammoth Chester County Gourd Seed.—This is the famous corn of Pennsylvania, producing ears of prodigious size, of very strong growth, and very productive, yielding upwards of one hundred bushels per acre. It is late in ripening, requiring the full season and strong soil.

CUCUMBER.

CONCOMBRE (Fr.).   GURKE (Ger.).   PEPINO (Sp.)

The Cucumber delights in rich, sandy soil. Dig out a hole about one foot wide, and one foot deep, and fill in with good soil, raise it above the surface about three inches; the hills should be about three feet apart; plant a few seeds in each during May, or earlier if the weather is favorable. Should a cold snap of weather be apprehended after the plants are up, cover each hill at night with a flower-pot, or any similar covering, as a protection, and remove the covering during the day. Make three or four plantings for a succession before the middle of Summer; the vines will always fruit better by occasionally pinching off the leading shoots. The cucumbers should be taken off when large enough for use, whether you require them or not, for if permitted to mature, it greatly reduces their productiveness.

Early White Spine.—The best early variety, producing a short light-green Cucumber covered with white spines, and when ripening turns to a very light color. As an early market variety it is unsurpassed.

Improved Early White Spine.—A marked improvement on the well-known White Spine variety, being longer, far more prolific, superior for table use.

Buist's Perfection Early White Spine.—A selection made from the Improved White Spine for its large size, perfection of form and earliness. As the earliest and most productive market variety it has no equal, and will be found far more profitable to grow than the Improved White Spine. The first and most important feature in growing cucumbers for market is to obtain the choicest seed stock for planting. Most of the crops grown are very much mixed, and of inferior quality. Buist's Perfection is regarded by growers as the finest and purest stock known. It is not only the very earliest, but it produces Cucumbers of the finest form and most salable size for shipping purposes. It was introduced by us two years since, and is already being grown by the most extensive Cucumber cultivators in this country. Our crop the past season, grown especially for seed, was over 150 acres. The seed of this variety is sold only in our sealed packages and cartoons, we sell no seed of it in bulk.

Early Frame follows the above in earliness; it is not so desirable a variety, and is cultivated to a limited extent; is of a deep-green color, and changes to a bright yellow when ripening.

Early Russian.—Very similar to the Cluster, but earlier and smaller in size, being but three inches long when fit for use; it sets its fruit in pairs, and the first blossoms usually bear.

Early Short Green is very similar to the Early Frame.

Early Green Cluster is quite early and very productive, medium size, and of a pale-green color, turning to a brownish-yellow when ripe; it is a favorite variety with some, but is not as crisp as other sorts.

Buist's Long Green.—This is very similar to Cuthill's Black Spine, but better adapted for outdoor culture, has but very few seeds, grows frequently to twenty-four inches in length, and very crisp; as a late market sort it is superior to all others.

London Long Green is the standard late sort, quite crisp, and of good size; it is not so early as either the Spine or Frame, but it is more desirable for a late crop. It is the variety also grown very extensively in New Jersey and other sections for pickling, and for that purpose should not be planted until late in July or early in August, and when of a proper size picked and put in salt and water.

Jersey Pickle.—A variety grown exclusively for pickling purposes by the market gardeners of New Jersey; it is very productive, and makes a very beautiful shaped pickle, and is the best variety for that purpose.

Long Prickly is shorter and thicker than the Long Green, equally as productive, and makes a good pickle, but is not so fine a table variety, being less crisp.

Green Prolific Pickling.—A splendid variety, selected with great care by one of the largest growers of pickling cucumbers in the country; with good culture 200,000 can be grown on one acre.

Gherkin, or Burr, or West India Gherkin, is exclusively grown for pickling; it is the smallest of all varieties, and should always be picked while young and tender, and put in salt water until required for pickling.

English Fancy Frame Cucumber.

FOR FORCING UNDER GLASS.

The following are the best varieties: Price per package of 10 seeds, 25 cts., or 5 for $1.00:

Telegraph, Star of the West,
Blue Gown, Carter's Model,
Lord Kenyon, Marquis of Lorne.

Forcing Cucumbers in Frames.—During the Winter and Spring months Cucumbers are considered by many a very great luxury; if they are a wholesome vegetable at any time, it is when they have been quickly forced and prepared for the table fresh from the vines. The last few years many of our gardeners in this vicinity have paid great attention to their forcing; finding ready sale in our fruit stores and markets for as many as they could produce, at prices ranging from twenty-five to seventy-five cents each. With very little care and attention the table can be supplied with them from February until they ripen in the open air, frequently attaining from twenty to twenty-six inches in length.

Prepare a hot-bed during January or February, as we have before described, taking care that the reduction of heat in the manure, is not carried too far before making up the bed; as, when that is the case, too little heat will afterwards be produced, and the young plants will be of a yellow color, instead of a deep rich green. In two or three days after preparing the bed, according to previous directions, the earth will be sufficiently warm for planting the seeds; place a barrowful of rich earth in the centre of each sash, form it into a neat mound, plant thereon several seeds to allow sufficient to replace any that may damp off, as is frequently the case during a spell of cloudy weather; but if all grow, thin them out to four plants. Cover the sash at night with straw mats, or any similar protection, and surround the bed with litter or boards to prevent the wind from carrying off the heat. The seed will germinate in a day or two, and before a week will form strong plants. During their growth admit fresh air every day at the back of the frame (allowing the temperature to be between seventy and one hundred degrees). When they have formed their third rough leaf, nip the point of the vine, which will cause the plant to branch. If the soil or plants appear to be dry, give them a watering with milk-warm water. As the plants grow, roots will protrude from their stems and through the hill, to which earth should be added. When the sun is very warm, a slight sprinkle of straw over the sash will prevent the the plants from drooping. By following the above directions the forcing of the Cucumber will be found both easy and profitable.

RECEIPT FOR PICKLING CUCUMBERS.—As many are not familiar with the proper mode of putting up pickles, I give the following receipt, which will be found one of the best. Cucumbers for pickling should be very small, and as free from spots as possible; wash them with a soft cloth in cold water, put them to drain, then make a brine of salt and water strong enough to bear an egg; place the pickles in and allow them to remain for about three weeks; then take them out and drain them; have your vinegar and spices boiling hot, place the pickles in jars with an onion stuck full of cloves in each; pour the vinegar boiling hot into the jar of pickles, keep them closely covered so that none of the steam may escape, as its retention promotes their greenness and prevents the flavor from evaporating. Repeat the boiling daily for four or five days; then, if a fine, green color, and the pickles are completely covered with vinegar, secure the jars with large flat corks or bladders, and put them away. Vinegar for pickles must always be of the very best kind, and should only boil for five minutes, as too much boiling reduces its strength; never, on any consideration, use brass or copper kettles for pickling; bell metal is the best; avoid stone jars also, as the lead, which is an ingredient in the glazing of common earthenware, is rendered pernicious by the action of the vinegar.

Another receipt has been sent to us by a Virginia lady, which is highly recommended.

"Make a brine of one-third of a pint of salt, and four pints of water. Drop as many cucumbers in the brine as it will cover, in which let them remain forty-eight hours; drain the brine off, place them in a porcelain kettle, covered with vinegar (good cider-vinegar, only moderately strong). Let the vinegar come to the boiling-point very slowly; then pack the pickles in glass jars, pour the *hot* vinegar over them, and seal up air-tight."

BUIST'S ALMANAC AND GARDEN MANUAL. 81

No. 1.—Early Short Green Cucumber.
No. 2.—Jersey Pickle Cucumber.
No. 3.—London Long Green Cucumber.
No. 4.—Buist's Long Green Cucumber.
No. 5.—Buist's Perfection Early White Spine Cucumber.

82 BUIST'S ALMANAC AND GARDEN MANUAL.

BUIST'S IMPROVED LARGE PURPLE EGG-PLANT. (IT HAS NO EQUAL.)

EGG-PLANT.

AUBERGINE (Fr.).   EIERPFLANZE (Ger.).   BERENGENA (Sp.).

No seed is more difficult to vegetate than the Egg-Plant; it always requires the strongest heat. For early use sow in a hot-bed early in Spring; after sowing, give them a good watering, and keep the frame closed until the plants appear, when admit fresh air in fine weather; cover the frame at night with mats, to protect against frost; after the plants attain two or three inches, they should be transplanted into another frame three inches apart, in order to make strong plants before it is time for planting out; it is a very good plan to put them singly in small flower-pots, and place them in a frame where they will become thoroughly established, and ready for setting out as soon as all cold weather is over, after which they can be planted from the pots without disturbing the roots; plant them in rows twenty inches apart, and two feet from row to row; they luxuriate in rich, loamy soil.

Buist's Improved Large Purple.—This is an improvement in earliness, productiveness, and size of fruit, over the ordinary large purple variety, or what is known as the New York Purple. When full grown it is of mammoth proportions, and is especially recommended to market gardeners.

New York Improved Purple.—This is grown very largely by the market gardeners of New York; it is of a large oval shape, with smooth stems, quite productive and of good size.

Early Long Purple.—The earliest variety, a strong grower, producing fruit of an oblong shape, very productive, and stem perfectly smooth; is always very full of seeds, and is not by any means as desirable as the Large Purple.

Black Pekin.—A variety of recent introduction from China, a very strong grower, producing bronzy-purple foliage; is used very extensively abroad as an ornamental plant for the flower garden. The fruit is round, and of a very dark-purple color, desirable only as a distinct variety.

ENDIVE.

CHICOREE ENDIVE (Fr.).   ENDIVEN (Ger.).   ENDIVIA (Sp.).

For a succession sow in very shallow drills, from the beginning to the middle of Summer; when the plants are up, thin them out to stand twelve inches apart; when the leaves have attained about eight inches long, they are fit for blanching; for this purpose a dry day must be selected. Gather the leaves up in your hand in a close and rounded form, observing there is no earth or litter in their centre, tie them up closely to prevent the rain from penetrating, which would cause the heart to decay; in ten days or two weeks they will be blanched ready for use. For a Winter crop, transplant into frames during October, and treat them in the same manner as the directions given for Lettuce.

GREEN CURLED ENDIVE.

Green Curled.—The most popular variety, producing beautifully curled dark green leaves, crisp, tender and blanches cream white.

White Curled.—This resembles the green except in color, but is not quite as hardy; the foliage is light green, blanches white.

Moss Curled.—A very beautiful and attractive variety, when full grown closely resembles a tuft of moss.

New Green Fringe.—A new variety that should have been classed with our Novelties, is one of the finest market varieties; the leaves are beautifully fringed and very attractive.

GARLIC.

AIL (Fr.).   KNOBLAUCH (Ger.).   AJO (Sp.).

Grown very extensively, for flavoring soups, stews, and other dishes, and also for medicinal purposes; they require light rich soil. Plant in drills early in Spring, one inch deep and four inches apart, and twelve inches between rows. Cultivate and treat as an onion, and when the tops wither, they are ready for harvesting, and should be stored in a dry, airy situation.

KOHL-RABI, OR TURNIP-ROOTED CABBAGE.

Chou-Rave (Fr.).   Kohl-Rabi (Ger.).   Colinabo (Sp.).

KOHL-RABI, OR TURNIP-ROOTED CABBAGE.

This vegetable has always been a very great favorite with the European gardener, and is gradually gaining great popularity in this country. When young and tender, and properly prepared for the table, it is almost equal to Cauliflower; besides, it is a certain crop, requiring no more care or attention in cultivation than a crop of Cabbage. For an early crop, sow in a hot-bed early in Spring, and treat the same as directions given for early Cabbage; for a Fall crop, sow in June. As there are many who are not familiar with the manner of preparing this vegetable for the table, I give the following receipt: Pare thinly and cut off the points, place in boiling water, and throw in a small quantity of salt; boil from two hours to two hours and a quarter, according to their size, after which cut in thin slices, season to taste, and serve up with drawn butter.

Market gardeners now find ready sale for all they can cultivate, and those who have tasted them, properly prepared, will agree with us in pronouncing it a very desirable vegetable.

The Large Growing Varieties are cultivated very extensively in Europe as a root crop for stock feeding during the Winter and Spring months, and are valued almost as highly as the Ruta Baga or Swedish turnip; producing from five to six hundred bushels to the acre; they keep perfectly sound until late in Spring, and cattle and other stock are exceedingly fond of them. They require a full season to mature their crop; should be cultivated in drills, the same as Ruta Bagas, and in harvesting them, merely strip off the leaves, and pull up the roots, storing them as any other root crop.

Early White Vienna.—This is the best and earliest variety for table use.

Early Purple Vienna.—Similar to the above except in color; on that account is not so desirable.

Large Green or White.—These are coarse growing varieties, and more generally grown for feeding cattle.

LEEK.

Poireau (Fr.).   Lauch (Ger.).   Puerro (Sp.).

This vegetable is especially desirable for soups, and is considered by many to have a better flavor than the Onion; it may be cultivated in two ways, either by sowing early in Spring in a seed-bed, to be transplanted, or into a permanent situation, where they are intended to be grown; if sown in a seed-bed, when about five to six inches high, select moist weather, and transplant them into deep, rich soil,

BUIST'S ALMANAC AND GARDEN MANUAL. 85

to stand from five to six inches apart; in planting them, use a dibble, and plant them deeply, close to their leaves, that the neck, by being covered with earth, may become blanched; after transplanting, they should have a good watering, in order to settle the soil, and thoroughly establish them; if sown in a situation where they are to be cultivated, sow the seed early in the Spring, in rows eighteen inches apart; and when four inches high, thin out to stand four inches apart. TRANSPLANTED PLANTS ALWAYS PRODUCE THE LARGEST LEEKS.

BUIST'S MAMMOTH LEEK.

Large Rouen.—A variety grown very extensively by the market gardeners of Paris, producing a short, thick stem, with dark-green foliage.

Large London Flag.—This is the ordinary variety, producing good-sized Leeks.

Buist's Mammoth.—A very large, strong-growing variety; selected from the London Flag; especially adapted for market gardeners, producing the largest Leek known.

Large Carenten.—A celebrated French variety, of strong growth, and very desirable.

Musselburgh.—An English variety of great merit, producing fan-shaped foliage; quite a strong grower, and a desirable market variety.

LETTUCE.

LAITUE (Fr.).   LATTICH (Ger.).   LECHUGA (Sp.).

From early Spring to early Summer sow thinly, in drills, every two weeks, a portion of some varieties for a succession. When up, thin them out to eight inches apart, but to form good heads they must have rich soil. For Winter forcing, or early Spring heads, sow in September, and transplant into rows, in a sheltered spot, in October; cover lightly with straw during Winter, which remove early in Spring, or transplant into glass frames, eight inches apart each way, very near to the glass; protect from frost, and they will head during Winter.

EARLY CABBAGE LETTUCE.

EARLY DUTCH LETTUCE.

Early Cabbage, or White Butter.—This is a very popular sort for either forcing or sowing in the open ground early in the season; it forms a beautiful, solid head, is very crisp and tender; but as soon as the season becomes warm it shoots to seed; it should, therefore, only be planted for first crop in the open ground, but can be sown broadcast in September, and transplanted into cold frames for heading during Winter It is really the standard variety, and will always give great satisfaction.

EARLY CURLED SIMPSON LETTUCE.

Early Dutch Butter.—A celebrated and entirely distinct variety; very popular in the Philadelphia market, producing crisp, white, solid heads, almost equal to a cabbage; the outer leaves are speckled with a brownish tinge. It is an elegant forcing variety, or for growing in cold frames, and stands the heat and cold to a remaikable degree; regard it as one of the very best and most profitable varieties to grow.

Early Curled Simpson.—An improved variety of the Curled Silesia, is quite early, but does not produce a solid head; leaves beautifully curled, and forces well.

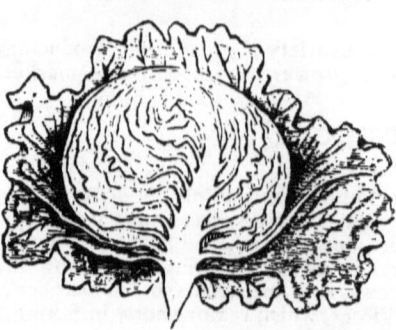
EARLY HANSON LETTUCE.

Early Hanson.—A curled variety, forming fine, large, solid heads, which are both crisp and tender. They frequently attain two or three pounds each. We regard it as a very valuable variety.

EARLY PRIZE HEAD LETTUCE.

Early Prize Head.—One of the finest varieties ever introduced, forming a very large head, but not a solid one; the leaves are slightly tinged with brown, and is remarkable for its crispness and delicacy of flavor; is well adapted for either forcing or outdoor culture; is not liable to run to seed unless far advanced, and is also quite hardy; is suitable for planting at any season of the year; cannot be too highly recommended.

Black-Seeded Simpson.—A new and desirable variety of the Curled Simpson. Does not produce a solid head, but a compact mass of leaves, which are of a much lighter color than the ordinary Simpson, and forms heads double the size. It is not only a good variety, but a desirable sort for early Summer, as it stands the heat remarkably well.

Oak Leaved.— This is an entirely distinctive variety, producing oak-shaped leaves, of a light green color, slightly curled, forming quite a compact, solid head, and very desirable for forcing. It is slow in running to seed; in fact, will remain in head for a month before its shoots appear. These shoots are in turn covered with small leaves as delicate and tender as those on young plants.

OAK-LEAVED LETTUCE

88 BUIST'S ALMANAC AND GARDEN MANUAL.

Early Curled Silesia is an early variety, and is generally sown thickly, to cut when but a few inches high; it will, however, form a very good head, if thinned out; it is quite hardy, and withstands heat and drought.

Salamander.—A desirable variety for Summer use, forming good-sized, compact heads. Color light green; stands both heat and drought remarkably well.

Early Boston Market.—A very popular and early variety, forming a fine solid head, which is both crisp and tender; very desirable for forcing, and a profitable variety for market gardeners.

Yellow-Seeded Butter.—Quite a distinct early Summer variety, forming large, dense yellow heads. Is both crisp and tender.

Improved Royal Cabbage.—A very celebrated variety, forming fine, large, solid heads, both crisp and fine flavor; stands the heat remarkably well, and is especially adapted to the Southern States, or for planting to succeed the early varieties in the North.

IMPROVED ROYAL CABBAGE LETTUCE.

Drumhead Cabbage is quite hardy, and an excellent Summer variety; forms a solid head, quite crisp and tender.

Large Passion (Black Seeded).—This variety cannot be too highly recommended to either private growers or market gardeners, it is destined to become one of our most popular varieties, and requires only to be tested once to be convinced of its superiority; it is not only fine for forcing, but desirable for a first and second crop in the open garden. It is quite early, forming a very fine sized head, the outer leaves of which have a delicate brown tinge.

Perpignan, or Early Green Summer.—A German variety that will really stand the heat without shooting to seed; produces a large and firm head; it is very highly prized by all who grow it. As a Summer variety it has no equal, and will even stand the Southern heat without flinching; fine for market.

Large India Curled.—This forms the most noble head in the whole Lettuce tribe; it is not early, but requires heat to make it crisp; the leaves are beautifully curled, and when well grown, the heads will frequently attain eighteen inches in diameter. It is, without doubt, the best Summer variety for either family use or market gardeners.

Brown Dutch Cabbage is one of the hardiest varieties; forms a very fine head, and withstands the heat and cold.

INDIA CURLED LETTUCE.

White and Green Paris Cos.

—These varieties grow strong and upright, producing long leaves, which should be tied up and blanched before cutting, which makes them very crisp and tender. They are quite hardy, and will force well. They are the most popular varieties in France, where they are frequently served without dressing and simply eaten, like celery, with salt.

Balloon White Cos.

—Quite an improvement on the old variety, producing a larger and finer head. Blanches white; is very tender and of delicate flavor.

WHITE PARIS COS LETTUCE.

Roman White Summer.

—An Italian variety, producing fine, large, solid heads. Does well either for forcing or for a general out-door crop.

Marvel or Red Besson.

—A new red tinged variety from France; highly recommended for early summer use. Is both crisp and tender.

Laciniated Beauregard.

—A very peculiar variety, of quite a distinct type. Leaves laciniated and quite ornamental; heads quite solid and of good flavor.

Improved Hanson.

—An improved strain of this superior curled, heading variety, of large size, often weighing from two to three pounds; sweet tender and crisp, even to the outer leaves, of a beautiful green without and white within. Resisting heat and drought well.

MELON (Musk or Cantaloupe.)

MELON (Fr.).   MELONE (Ger.).   MELON (Sp.).

The Melon, like the Cucumber, delights in rich, sandy soil, but grows to greater perfection in a drier atmosphere, and should never be cultivated in the vicinity of Cucumbers, Squashes, Gourds or Pumpkins, as it will invariably become impregnated with them, and produce fruit of an inferior quality. Sow about the last of Spring or first of Summer, in hills of light, rich soil, four feet apart, allowing but three plants to grow in each hill; after they have grown about a foot long, pinch off the points of shoots, which causes the vines not only to become stronger, but makes them produce lateral branches, and prove more productive and mature earlier.

NETTED GREEN CITRON MELON.

Netted Green Citron.—This variety is cultivated to a greater extent for market than any other sort, and for this purpose it has no superior. When grown from seed that has been well selected, it is of very fine flavor; fruit round flattened at both ends, roughly netted, and of a pale yellow green when ripe.

Netted Nutmeg is of an oval shape, roughly netted, but not attaining so large a size as the Netted Citron; it is equally as fine in flavor.

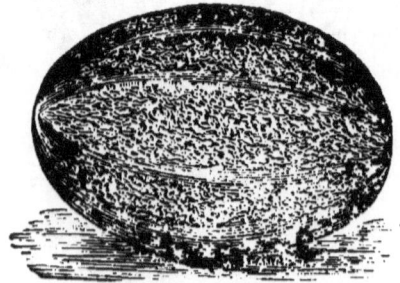

PINE-APPLE MELON.

Pine-Apple.—A medium-sized, early variety, of an oval shape; delicious flavor and highly perfumed with the fragrance of pine-apple.

Surprise.—This melon has a thin, cream-colored skin, thickly netted; flesh deep salmon-color, of exquisite flavor and very prolific.

Skillman's Netted Citron.—A medium-size, roughly-netted variety of good flavor.

Early Jenny Lind.—The earliest of all varieties, and also the smallest, but possessing a rich and delightful flavor and fragrance, and highly recommended.

New German Citron.—This new variety, which we introduced, has proved itself to be one of the best and most salable melons for market. It is quite early, of medium size, nearly round, very roughly netted, very fragrant, and of delicious flavor.

PERSIAN, OR CASABA MELON.

Large Persian, or Casaba.—This has become a very popular variety; it is large in size, oval in shape, luscious in flavor, and very fragrant; the best variety for private growers. It has a very delicate thin rind, and on this account it cannot become a profitable market variety, as it will not bear transportation.

Hackensack or Turk's Cap.—A variety of the *Green Citron;* deeply netted, very large and productive, of excellent flavor; profitable and fine for market.

Montreal Green Nutmeg.—Nearly round, flattened at the ends; deep, regular ribs; skin densely netted; flesh thick and of delicious flavor.

Bay View.—The largest, most prolific, best flavored, and finest cantaloupe in cultivation; luscious and sweet, and very hardy; picked green it will ripen up finely, and carry safely for a long distance.

HACKENSACK CITRON MELON.

Golden Gem, or Golden Jenny.—A recently introduced variety, of medium size, but one of the most popular varieties with the melon growers of New Jersey; it is early, roughly netted, and of delightful flavor.

MELON (Water).

Melon d'Eau (Fr.). Wasser-melone (Ger.). Zandia (Sp.).

KOLB GEM WATER-MELON.

Kolb Gem.—This has proved itself to be the best variety of Water-melon introduced during our experience of the past forty years; it originated with R. F. Kolb, of Alabama, one of the largest Melon growers of the South; we were so favorably impressed with its fine appearance and good qualities combined, that we considered it a very great favor to receive from him our seed stock even at $4 per lb. We were the first to introduce it and plant it in the North, and its great popularity in this section emanated from a 50 acre crop, which we grew in New Jersey; it is now the Melon that almost every grower raises for market in that State. Its strong points are many, the most important of which are its fine qualities with a remarkably thin and tough rind, which stands shipping and handling better than any variety we know of. It is a hybrid of the Scaly Bark and Rattlesnake, of a roundish, oval shape, dark skin, which is beautifully marbled, flesh bright scarlet, crisp and of a delicious flavor; it will always be a popular variety.

SOUTHERN RATTLESNAKE WATER-MELON.

Southern Rattlesnake.—A variety which has gained great popularity throughout the entire country for its large size and fine shipping qualities, and especially so in the Southern States, where melons are raised in immense quantities for the Northern market; shape oblong, of light green color, and beautifully mottled and striped with a lighter shade; flesh scarlet, rind thin, very solid, and both sweet and delicious. Stands transit well. Seeds white, with two black tips.

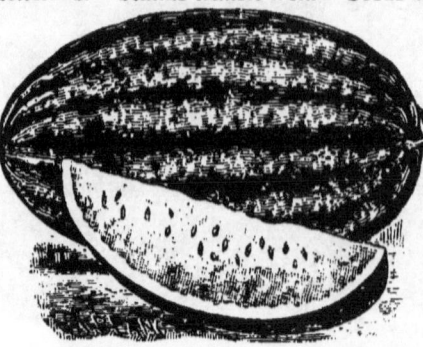

SCALY BARK WATER-MELON.

Scaly Bark.—A variety recently introduced and recommended for the great strength of its rind, and on that account will prove a valuable shipping variety. We do not regard it as some do, superior to the Georgia Rattlesnake, it will never equal it in popularity with melon growers. Flesh crimson, good flavor, thin rind, will average 30 to 35 lbs. Our seed was saved from the largest specimens only.

Jordan's Gray Monarch.

—This is one of the largest and sweetest varieties known, it originated with W. B. Jordan, of Virginia and was introduced by us. We have received many flattering testimonials of its fine qualities and it appears to be well adapted to the Southern States; in some sections, especially in Georgia and Florida, it has gained great favor; in other sections it has not come up to expectation, owing in a great measure to unfavorable weather; we regard it, however, as one of the best varieties ever introduced. Its size is immense, frequently producing melons weighing over ninety pounds each. Its quality is unequalled, and the most productive variety we have ever seen. The skin is of a very beautiful mottled-gray color, long and symmetrically formed, with an exceedingly thin rind; flesh bright crimson, and of the sweetest and most delicious flavor. Its shipping qualities are unsurpassed, and is destined to become one of our most popular varieties. Plant it by all means.

JORDAN'S GRAY MONARCH WATER-MELON.
(Weight 94 pounds.)

Florida Favorite.

—A new variety introduced by W. M. Girardeau of Florida, one of the most extensive melon growers in that state. Very desirable (see Novelties).

Mountain Sweet.

—This is the most productive and one of the best varieties for either market gardeners or private growers; thousands of acres are annually grown in the State of New Jersey for the Philadelphia and New York markets. When pure and properly grown, will attain a very large size; has a very thin rind, and flesh sweet and juicy. Seeds gray.

Mountain Sprout.

—This variety differs from the Mountain Sweet in color, being striped with different shades of green, is rather late, and will keep until quite late in the Fall; the seeds are of a brownish-yellow color; it is not, however, so desirable as the former.

Cuban Queen.—This is one of the largest and most productive varieties grown. Rind thin and solid, with dark and light green stripes; flesh bright scarlet, crisp and sweet. A good keeper and stands transit well.

The Boss is a recently introduced variety of medium size, skin dark green, thin rind, flesh deep scarlet of sweet and delightful flavor.

Dark Icing.—A very desirable variety. Dark skin, crimson flesh, thin rind, quite solid and of delicious flavor. A fine market sort.

Light Icing.—Similar to the above, only a difference in the color of the melons.

Mammoth Iron Clad.—This variety, recently introduced and highly extolled, is well worthy of cultivation. Produces melons of large size and very solid. Flesh crimson, crisp and luscious. Very desirable for market. Keeps quite late in the season.

Odella.—A variety grown very extensively in New Jersey by the market gardeners, and by many of them considered superior to the Mountain Sweet as a market variety; shape from round to oval, dark-green color, and scarlet flesh. Seeds gray.

Orange is an entirely distinct sort; its rind will peel off like that of an orange, and its flesh is separated into segments in a similar manner. A peculiar and very attractive variety.

Ice Cream (WHITE SEEDED).—This variety is annually increasing in popularity; it grows to a medium size, nearly oval, of a pale-green color, and has a thinner rind than any other variety; flesh is bright crimson, crisp, and of delicious flavor. Seeds white.

Ice Cream (GRAY SEEDED).—A variety resembling the Mountain Sweet in both form and color, very productive, scarlet flesh, and of sweet flavor.

Peerless.—A very handsome variety of medium size, mottled and striped with light green; thin rind, scarlet flesh, and of good flavor.

Black Spanish.—This is cultivated to a very limited extent, most growers preferring other varieties; it is of a round shape, color very dark green, and seeds black.

Early Phinney.—The earliest of all varieties; form oval; rind, rather thick; flesh bright red, and quite productive; but its earliness we regard as its only good quality.

GREEN CITRON (for preserving only). As this preserve is a great favorite with many, we have thought a receipt which we have followed for years would perhaps be appreciated. Select sound fruit, pare and divide them into quarters, and cut each quarter into several pieces, taking the seeds out carefully; weigh the Citron, and to every pound allow a half-pound of the best loaf sugar; place the Citron into a preserving-kettle and boil in water for half an hour, or until they become quite clear; drain them, and place them on a large dish; put the weighed sugar into the kettle and add sufficient water to dampen it, and boil until quite clear; then add the Citron, and boil slowly until they become almost transparent and sufficiently soft to allow a straw to pierce through them without breaking. A few lemons should be cut into thin slices of uniform size and shape, and boiled with the Citrons in the syrup; a few ginger-roots cut into small pieces will also greatly improve the flavor. After all is finished, put the Citron into glass jars, pour the hot syrup over them, and cork and seal tightly.

MUSTARD.

Moutarde (Fr.).   Senf (Ger.).   Mostaza (Sp.).

For early salad, sow thickly on a gentle hot-bed in February and March, and for general crop, at intervals during Spring, on very fine soil, in rows six inches apart; it should be cut when about one inch high. A mixture of Mustard and Cress makes a very delightful salad, which is very popular with the English. The White is also used for medicinal purposes, and we always have on hand a very superior article for druggist's sales; it is also a simple and efficacious cure for dyspepsia; take a tablespoonful of the whole White Mustard, stirred in a glass of cold water, and drink before each meal.

White or Yellow London.—This is the common White Mustard of commerce, used both as a salad and for flavoring purposes.

Giant Southern Creole.—The growing of mustard as a salad is very largely increasing in this country, and especially so in the Southern States. This variety is far superior to any other, producing immense leaves, which are beautifully curled, and of very rapid growth.

Black or Brown London.—Used for the same purposes as the above; the difference being in the color of the seed.

GIANT SOUTHERN CREOLE CURLED MUSTARD.

Chinese.—A variety, lately introduced, producing larger foliage, and more succulent stems than the Common White, of a deeper green color, and more desirable for salad.

MUSHROOM SPAWN.

FRENCH SPAWN IN BOXES.   ENGLISH SPAWN IN BRICKS.

Mushrooms may be cultivated much easier than is generally supposed. They can be grown in a cellar or shed, or in beds prepared in the open air in the same manner as hot beds. Take fresh horse manure, shake it well apart, and lay it into a heap to ferment; turn and mix it well every three or four days, by shaking the outside of the heap, which is cold, and the inside, which is hot, together, so that every part of it may be equally fermented, and deprived of its noxious quality. When the dung is in a fit state to be made into a bed, which will be in two or three weeks after it has been put together

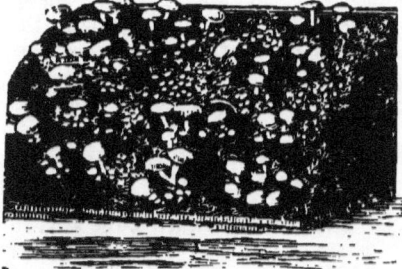

FRENCH MUSHROOM BEDS.

to ferment, select a dry spot for a foundation; mark out the bed, which should be four feet wide, and as long as you choose to make it. In forming the bed, mix the dung well together, beating it down with a fork until from eighteen to twenty-four inches thick. In this state it may remain until the temperature is sufficiently moderate for spawning, which may be ascertained by trial-sticks thrust into different parts of the bed. Divide the large cakes of spawn into small lumps, plant them two inches below the surface, and six inches apart, covering with two inches of fine light soil, and press down evenly. When finished, cover the bed a foot thick with clean straw, and protect from heavy rains. The Mushrooms will make their appearance in from four to six weeks, according to the season.

NASTURTIUM, OR INDIAN CRESS.

CAPUCINE GRANDE (Fr.).   KRESSE, INDIANISCHE (Ger.).   MARANUELIA (Sp.).

Sow early in Spring, in good, rich ground; the plants should be trained to a trellis, or rods; the leaves and flowers are used in salads; the seed-pods are picked while young and pickled, the yellow is the best for this purpose; the crimson is generally cultivated for its flowers.

Tall Yellow.—This variety is principally used for pickling.

Dwarf Crimson.—This variety produces dark rich crimson flowers; the seed-pods can also be used for pickling.

OKRA, OR GOMBO.

GOMBO (Fr.).   ESBARRE HIBISCUS (Ger.).   QUIMBOMBO (Sp.).

This is a highly esteemed vegetable throughout the entire country. The seed-pods are used in soups, while young and tender, to which it imparts an aromatic flavor; it is also stewed and served up with butter. Sow the seed late in Spring in very rich soil, in drills two feet apart, observing that the ground is warm; as if cold and moist, the seeds will invariably rot; and when the plants are up, thin out to a foot apart. The green pods may be preserved for Winter use by cutting them in halves, string and dry them. The seeds can also be ripened, which, when roasted, make a very excellent substitute for coffee.

The Buist's Dwarf.—The Dwarf Okra originated at our Rosedale Farm, and was introduced by us some years ago; it has become the most popular variety with all growers; its peculiarity is not only in its dwarf habit, but its earliness and great productiveness, producing pods from an inch of the ground to the top; of twice the size of the common variety, and from its dwarf habit it is also less exhausting to the soil.

Long Green.—A tall-growing variety, producing long thin pods.

Tall Southern.—The old-fashioned variety of the South which is still cultivated in many localities; it is a strong growing variety frequently attaining ten to twelve feet, is very exhausting to the soil, and a coarse growing crop. The Buist's Dwarf is the best to cultivate.

The Velvet.—A variety recently introduced, the pods of which are covered with a fine fibre resembling velvet.

THE TALL VARIETIES SHOULD NOT BE CULTIVATED WHEN THE DWARF CAN BE OBTAINED.

LONG GREEN OKRA.   BUIST'S DWARF OKRA.

ONION.

OGNON (Fr.).   ZWIEBEL (Ger.).   CEBOLLA (Sp.).

The Onion ranks with the cabbage in popularity with all cultivators, whether it be for the humble garden of the poor, or the more pretentious one of the wealthy; to grow it successfully, it must be borne in mind that the soil cannot be too rich, and however good it may be, it requires more or less manure for every crop; it is a plant producing numerous roots, which spread to a great extent, absorbing nourishment from every part of the soil. In regard to rotation of crops, the Onion is an anomalous case, for the same ground has been known to produce heavy crops yearly for over half a century. The system pursued is to manure the ground heavily, with rich, well-rotted manure, trenched or plowed early in the Spring, and leveled with the rake or harrow. In cool climates, seeds sown early in Spring produce full-grown Onions the same year; but in this vicinity and South it requires two seasons; the first produces the small sets, which ripen in July; these are carefully stored in dry situations until the following Spring, when they are planted out and form the full-grown Onion about midsummer. The large Red Wethersfield is the best variety for cultivating in large quantities, as they are more hardy and keep better; it is called the annual Onion, because it perfects itself in the Northern, Western, and Eastern States the first year from seed. Sow the seed in rows early in Spring, nine inches apart if to cultivate with the hoe, or two feet if the harrow or cultivator is to be used; cover the seed very lightly, and should the weather be favorable the rows will show themselves in about two weeks. Keep the rows clear of all weeds by hoeing; observe not to hoe deep, for the more the Onion rises out of the ground, the finer it is, and the better it keeps. As soon as the plants are three inches high, thin them out to two inches apart; if the weather is moist the thinnings can be safely transplanted, which will also attain a full size; but observe, in planting them, to put the roots only into the ground. For growing large Onions from seed, sow five pounds of seed to the acre. Sowings are now generally made by a seed drill, the best of which is called the Matthews. Be particular in the selection of your Onion seed, as failures are continually occurring from old or spurious stock. We are large growers of the finest stock, and can supply you with the best quality. Nothing further will be required until the crop is taken up, except in destroying all weeds as they appear.

In planting the small sets, draw out drills, about an inch deep, and nine inches apart, leaving a space fifteen inches between every three or four drills for convenience in hoeing and collecting weeds; plant the small sets in these drills about two inches apart, but do not cover them. In a few days they will commence growing; keep the ground clear of all weeds by frequent hoeing until the crop will be ready for lifting in July, In midsummer the grower can generally realize higher prices for his crop than later, as the Onions raised from seed do not come into market until Fall, and the demand for early shipping is generally great.

Onion Sets or Buttons.

Onion sets are produced by sowing seed very thickly, quite early in Spring, in shallow drills; the young plants form Onions about the size of peas in midsummer; when the foliage becomes brown and dry, the crop should then be harvested. Select good, rich soil, and be careful it is not weedy ground, as the labor in cultivating it would be much increased. Use the planet double-wheeled hoe in cultivating the crop, and keeping down weeds, which will do the work of six hands. To keep Onion Sets.—As soon as the crop is ready for harvesting, they should be lifted in dry weather and thoroughly dried in the shade; after which spread them out thinly in a cool, dry, airy loft; the Yellows should not be over three inches, and the White not over two inches thick, and frequently turned over.

Yellow Dutch, or Strasburg.—Color, brownish yellow; bulb quite flat, and of good size. This is the variety grown about Philadelphia for sets, thousands of bushels of which are annually shipped from this market to different parts of the United States. Seeds sown in this latitude in Spring form the small set by July; these are planted out the following Spring, and form full-grown Onions by midsummer. In the Southern States they can be planted out in Autumn, and will continue growing during the entire Winter, and in early Spring they will be fit to use for salads and stews.

BUIST'S ALMANAC AND GARDEN MANUAL. 99

YELLOW DUTCH, OR STRASBURG.

LARGE RED WETHERSFIELD.

WHITE OR SILVER SKIN.

LARGE YELLOW DANVERS.

White, or Silver Skin.—This is the mildest variety, and generally preferred for table use; it is of the same shape as the Yellow Strasburg, and is cultivated from sets in the same manner; color, pure white; does not keep well during Winter. This is the famous variety for pickling.

Large Red Wethersfield.—This is the favorite Onion in the East and West, where immense crops are grown for shipment. In cool sections it continues growing the whole Summer, and forms a full-grown Onion by Fall; is of a purplish-red color, of a round or oval shape, and is an excellent keeping variety.

Extra Early Red.—The earliest of all; smaller, and more flat-shaped than Large Red; close-grained; fit to gather last of July; keeps well.

Yellow Oval Danvers.—Onion-growers of the East, and in some parts of the West, look upon this variety with great favor; it is a large, round, straw-colored Onion, and a splendid keeping variety; like the Red Wethersfield, it perfects its Onion the first year from seed in all cool climates; but being of a coarse nature, it is liable to scale during Winter; it is, however, a very abundant cropper, frequently yielding upwards of six hundred bushels to the acre from seed sown in early Spring.

Southport Yellow Globe.—A very handsome, large, globe-shaped variety, very productive, of mild and pleasant flavor; a good keeping variety.

Southport Red Globe.—Similar to the Yellow Globe except in color.

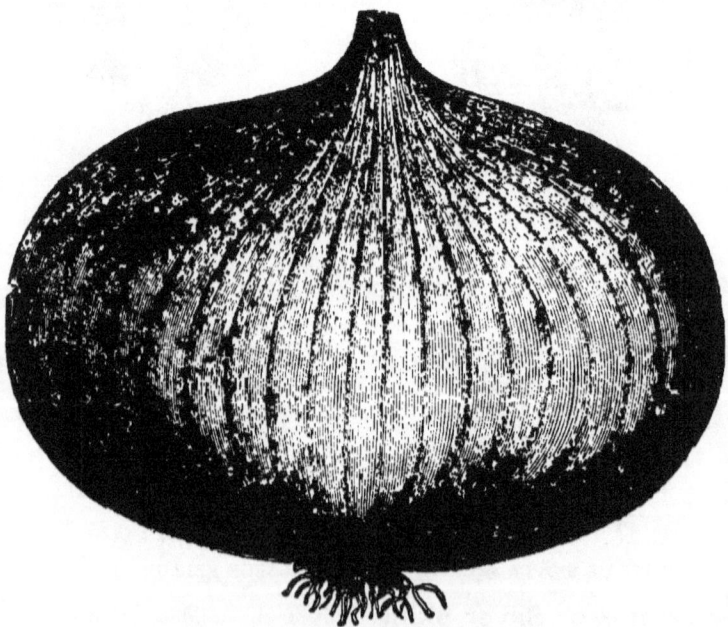

THE IMPROVED BERMUDA ONION.

The Improved Bermuda.—A very large oval, dark-red variety, selected from the Teneriff Bermuda, but possessing much finer qualities, growing full grown Onions from seed. It is quite early, very solid, does not skin in transportation, keeps better than any other variety, and is of mild, delicate flavor. In the South, seed sown in the Autumn will produce large Onions the following Spring. Highly recommended to Southern cultivators for shipping.

Large Italian Varieties.

The Italian Onions grow to a very large size in strong soil; have become quite popular, especially in the Southern States, appearing to be well adapted to warm climates; they are all of the very finest flavor and of choice quality, and produce full grown onions from seed the first year.

Giant Rocca of Naples.—A very fine, large variety, of globular shape, light-brown skin, and of very mild flavor; will frequently attain, under favorable circumstances, two pounds in weight.

Large Red Italian Tripoli.—A very large-growing variety, of blood-red color; flatter in form than the Rocca, and of mild flavor.

Large White Italian Tripoli.—A very superior variety, of flat form and large size, with a beautiful silvery white skin, and of mild flavor.

White Queen is a fine early silver-skinned variety, of beautiful form and rapid growth, and possessing fine keeping qualities; seeds sown in early Spring will produce Onions from one to two inches in diameter in early Summer, or if sown in early Summer will be fit for use by Autumn.

Extra Early Pearl.—A very early white variety, almost as transparent as a pearl, of flat form, and of very mild and pleasant flavor, and attains quite a large size.

Silver White Etna.—A new and very early silver-skin variety, of mild flavor, of flat shape and large size.

Large Brown Garganus (Mammoth).—This is the largest and finest of all the Italian varieties; it attains a prodigious size, of mild and pleasant flavor, and very desirable.

Large White Garganus (Mammoth.)—This variety is the same as the above, except in color, which is pure snow white; very desirable.

White King.—This is a very distinct and remarkably handsome white silver-skinned variety, globular in form, of large size, with a beautiful pearly skin. Mild and delicious in flavor and keeps well. We regard it as being superior to any other white variety.

PARSLEY.

Persil (Fr.)   Petersilie (Ger.).   Perejil (Sp.).

BUIST'S GARNISHING PARSLEY.

Sow in rows early in Spring, in good rich soil; it also makes a very good edging for beds or walks. Seed two years old will vegetate more freely than new seed, which will frequently require five or six weeks to germinate, so the cultivator must not be disheartened if the plants do not appear within a month. Should the weather be dry, watering will hasten their germination. The Garnishing varieties are decidedly the prettiest for ornamenting a dish; but for seasoning, they are all equally good. The seed will also germinate more freely by soaking it twenty-four hours in water, and mixed with sand before sowing.

Double Curled, or Covent Garden.—A desirable market variety; quite dwarf in habit, not as curled as the Garnishing varieties, but stands the Winter better; is very popular with the English market gardeners.

Buist's Garnishing.—This variety is a general favorite, and is especially recommended for market gardeners; is of strong growth and beautifully curled.

Champion Moss-Curled, and Myatt's Garnishing are very beautiful, fine, curled varieties.

FERN LEAVED PARSLEY.

Fern Leaved.—A variety of recent introduction; very beautiful, resembling a fern, and is used very extensively for garnishing purposes and as an ornamental plant for the garden.

Plain or Single.—This is the hardiest variety; foliage very dark green, with plain leaves, having a strong Parsley flavor, is much preferred in French cooking.

PARSNIP.

PANAIS (Fr.).   PASTINAKE (Ger.).   CHIRIVIA (Sp.).

The Parsnip luxuriates in deep, rich soil, which should be subsoiled, and the manure applied should be thoroughly decomposed; ground prepared in this manner will always produce long, smooth roots, provided the seed is pure. Sow the seed in early Spring, in drills, drawn eighteen inches apart, and cover them about half an inch with fine soil. When the young plants are about two or three inches high, thin them out to four inches apart. They require good cultivation. The roots are perfectly hardy, but improve by remaining in the ground during the Winter season. Sufficient quantities, however, should be stored in out-door pits, or in a cool cellar, to last until Spring. They are also quite desirable roots for stock feeding. The seed, like that of the Carrot, will vegetate sooner by steeping it six to twelve hours in liquid manure, diluted with water, and mixed with sand before sowing. In the Southern States it does well to sow in October.

The Student.—This variety is much in favor; it is delicate in flavor, of regular form, has a very smooth skin, and not so coarse as the Hollow Crown.

Hollow Crown, or Sugar. —This is the variety most generally grown for either table use or stock feeding; it is of uniform growth, has a very smooth, clean skin, and is easily distinguished by the leaves arising from a cavity on the top or crown of the root.

SUGAR PARSNIP.

PEAS.

Pois (Fr.).   Erbse (Ger.).   Chicaros (Sp.).

It is very essential to a well-cultivated garden to have a full supply of this indispensable vegetable throughout the season; to accomplish this, sow a succession every two weeks until the middle of Summer, commencing with Buist's Early Morning Star and Buist's Premier Extra Early, of which make two or three plantings; they are acknowledged by all growers to be the earliest and most delicate flavored varieties known; then continue with any of the early or wrinkled sorts. The last two plantings in Summer should be Buist's Early Morning Star and Buist's Premier Extra Early, as other sorts are more or less liable to mildew in the late months.

The ground should be manured the previous year; if it is heavily manured for the crop, it causes them to grow more to straw than to seed. For the first planting (which should be as early in the season as the ground can be worked), select a light, dry soil, and if possible, to be sheltered from the north-west. The drills should be from two to three feet apart, and the seed planted two inches deep; when a few inches high, draw earth to them, and repeat it again when more advanced. When the tendrils appear, provide them with suitable stakes or branches, which should be of fan form, and placed in the ground in a slanting direction; on the other side of the row, reverse the position of the stakes, which affords the vines more protection and security. If the weather be dry at the time of planting, soak the seeds twenty-four hours in water. Peas for a general crop should always be planted much deeper than for the early one; they will not only produce larger crops, but will remain in bearing condition longer; the roots penetrating to a greater depth of soil, always making a stronger growth, and are not so liable to be injured by warm, dry weather.

THE PEA BUG.—Some seasons Peas are more or less punctured with the Pea Bug, and many judge they are worthless from their appearance. These holes are caused by the sting of an insect called Bruchus Pisi, which deposits its egg while the pod is forming, and perfects the insect when the Pea is subject to heat after ripening. Strange to say, the germ is never destroyed, and those which have the largest holes

104   BUIST'S ALMANAC AND GARDEN MANUAL.

grow equal to the most perfect. We explain this from the fact that we have frequently had customers remark that Peas must be bad, as they had holes in them.

A WORD TO MARKET GARDENERS.—The Pea is one of your most important and profitable crops; you, therefore, cannot bestow too much care in selecting your seed, as the market is always over-stocked with what are called Extra Earlies, and offered at tempting low prices. These are generally grown in Canada, in a wild broadcast manner, full of runners, and sold under this name to command a better price in the market. There is no variety that deteriorates more rapidly, both in earliness and dwarfness of habit, than the Extra Early, and it requires a grower to exercise his greatest care in annually selecting his stock seed, and its proper culture, in order to keep it up to its correct standard, both for earliness and freeness from all runners. BUIST'S PREMIER EXTRA EARLY has always maintained a very high reputation with gardeners for its earliness, productiveness and fine qualities, and is to-day the best known and the most popular among all growers; it is the perfection of Peas, both for earliness and uniform dwarf habit in its growth. One of its great features is that the crop is almost ready for market at once, and the whole crop can be harvested in one or two pickings. These are very desirable features, and just what the g'dener requires. The BUIST'S EARLY MORNING STAR (our latest new variety) is the cream of all Extra Earlies, it is sold only in our sealed packages of 1, 2 and 4 quarts, also ¼, ½, 1 and 2 bushel sacks; if you are a market gardener you can't afford to be without it.

BUIST'S PREMIER EXTRA EARLY AND BUIST'S EARLY MORNING STAR PEAS
are the earliest, most productive and most profitable varieties for market.

Buist's Premier Extra Early.—A variety introduced by us a few years since, possessing all the perfections requisite to an Extra Early—being the earliest, of dwarf habit, productive, very even growth, and entirely free from all runners; it was a selection made from Buist's Extra Early, which was for many years the most popular early variety known. The Premier is one of the earliest and best for either market gardeners *or* private families. We annually grow from 150 to 200 acres of them, especially for seed, and have never yet had sufficient to meet the demand.—PLANT THEM.

Buist's Early Morning Star.—This is our latest production in the way of an Extra Early Pea. It has been raised by a three years selection from the earliest podded stock, of our famous PREMIER EXTRA EARLY, which is so celebrated with market gardeners. This has given it an established habit for extreme earliness, dwarf but robust growth, great increase in the size of its pods, and for its unusual hardiness. It is not only the earliest variety known, but the most productive and the largest podded ; but one of its greatest features is to withstand great changes and severity of weather, which of late years has proved so damaging to the early crop of Peas, especially in the South. It is sold only in our sealed packages pints and quarts, also in our leaded-sealed sacks of ¼, ½, 1 and 2 bushels. (See illustration under head of novelties.)

Buist's Extra Early is an improved Extra Early Pea, being earlier and more productive than any other variety (excepting Buist's Morning Star and Premier), and ripens almost all at once, when the ground can be cleared for a crop of Beans or Tomatoes ; they are sweet and delicate in flavor, and are a very popular market variety with all gardeners. They have a stronger growth than Buist's Premier Extra Early.

EARLY AMERICAN WONDER PEA.

Philadelphia Extra Early.—This variety originated in this city many years ago, and was known in those days as the HANCOCKS, HATCHES, or PHILADELPHIA EXTRA EARLY. They have deteriorated very much in reputation, owing to Canada Pea-growers naming almost any kind of early stock "the Philadelphia," regardless of earliness or purity. They are, therefore, frequently found not only to be late, but very full of runners. ALWAYS PLANT BUIST'S EARLY MORNING STAR AND BUIST'S PREMIER EXTRA EARLY in preference.

106 BUIST'S ALMANAC AND GARDEN MANUAL.

Improved Early Daniel O'Rourke.—A favorite English variety, which was introduced many years since as an Extra Early, to be fully as early as any variety we have in this country; but instead of which it proved a second early Pea with a smaller pod than usual. The cheap Extra Early Peas offered by many dealers throughout the country are nothing else but the Daniel O'Rourke.

Early American Wonder (Wrinkled).—The earliest wrinkled variety in cultivation. Of sweet and delicious flavor, growing from twelve to eighteen inches high and very productive. It is later than Buist's Extra Early, but is an excellent variety to plant for a succession.

Laxton's Extra Early Alpha (Wrinkled).—Each year adds still more attractive features to this desirable early wrinkled variety; it produces fine, large-sized pods, very productive, and of exquisite flavor, resembling the old Champion of England. We cannot recommend it too highly.

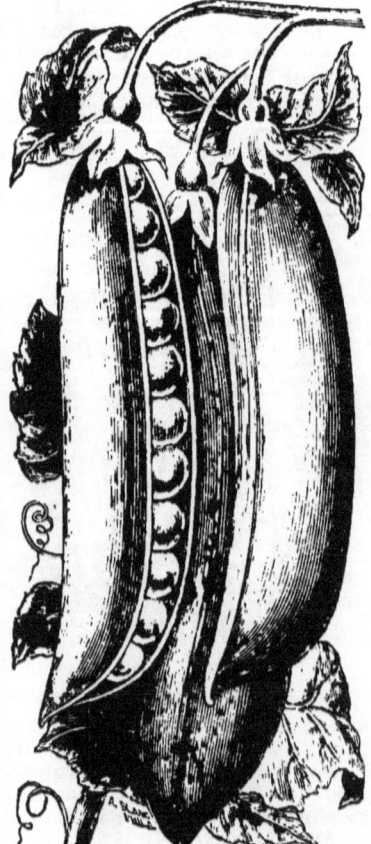

CARTER'S STRATAGEM PEA.

Carter's First Crop.—A celebrated English variety; which has gained great favor in this country; is early, a good producer, and of delicate flavor.

McLean's Little Gem (Wrinkled).—A variety having the dwarf habit of the Tom Thumb, and the delicate flavor of the Champion of England, two very important features; is very productive for its size, and especially recommended to private growers. It has become a very great favorite for its fine quality, productiveness, and dwarfness of habit.

Carter's Premium Gem (Wrinkled).—The most valuable early dwarf wrinkled Pea in cultivation; it is an improvement on the McLean's Little Gem, being more robust, and producing longer pods.

Carter's Strategem.—We cannot recommend this new English variety too highly. It is the best that has ever been introduced, and when better known will be the most popular variety for general crop. It is dwarf, growing but 2½ feet high, of strong, robust habit, requiring but slight support, enormously productive, pods large, peas sweet and of delicious flavor. Do not neglect planting it this season.

Carter's Pride of the Market.—Another English novelty. In length of pod it is equal to the Stratagem. Grows from eighteen inches to two feet high, and is of fine flavor. Its robust constitution, enormous productiveness, and superior appearance will ensure its acceptance as a favorite with the public.

Carter's Telephone.—A marvellous variety, producing pods of prodigious size, and well filled with mammoth peas of exquisite flavor. Growth, five feet; an extraordinary cropper.

Kentish Invicta is a round, blue variety, producing straight and handsome well-filled pods, and is quite early. We regard it as a market variety of unsurpassed excellence, and should be planted for a general crop, as well as an early one.

Early Tom Thumb is a favorite with all, on account of its very dwarf habit, and is really more productive than many varieties that grow twice its height; it produces a fine-sized pod; the peas are sweet and tender; and is especially adapted for small gardens.

McLean's Early Blue Peter is a remarkably dwarf variety, with dark green foliage. Splendid bearer with exquisite flavor. It is called by some the Blue Tom Thumb.

McLean's Advancer (Wrinkled).—A very fine green wrinkled variety, two weeks earlier than the Champion of England, and exceedingly luscious in flavor; it cannot be too highly recommended.

Eugenie or Alliance (Wrinkled).—A white wrinkled variety equal to the Champion of England in delicacy of flavor, two weeks earlier, and more productive. This is, without any exception, equal to the finest-flavored variety in cultivation; but many remark they do not wish for a better variety than the Champion.

Early Washington, Early Frame, Early May, are second early varieties, quite productive, tall in growth, and of good flavor.

Laxton's Prolific Long Pod.—This variety was introduced here some years since from England; it has proved a very desirable variety for second or general crop; the pods are exceedingly long, and bear abundantly.

CARTER'S PRIDE OF THE MARKET PEA.

Early Bishop's Dwarf Long Pod.—A very remarkable dwarf variety, requiring no stakes or support of any kind, except the earth drawn to its stems. It is very prolific, producing good-sized pods, and ripens about the same time as the Early Washington; a very good second or third early market variety.

Napoleon, or Climax (Wrinkled).—A green wrinkled variety, similar in flavor to the Champion of England, but more productive, and two weeks earlier.

Champion of England (Wrinkled).—A green wrinkled variety, the parent of all the celebrated English varieties, famous for its delicious flavor, but is a shy bearer. Consider it one of the finest varieties for family use, and will follow any of the second early varieties in ripening; the germ of this pea is very delicate, and should the weather be wet or damp for several days after planting, it will invariably rot in the ground, and another planting should at once be made.

Hair's Dwarf Mammoth (Wrinkled).—A light wrinkled variety of very delicate flavor, and quite productive; its good qualities are really not known, or it would be cultivated more generally.

Dwarf Blue Imperial.—A standard variety for either private use or for market gardeners; the pods are large and well filled, and when young exceedingly tender and of fine flavor; the dry peas when soaked, turn a beautiful fresh green color, and are sold in great quantities in our markets during the Winter season.

Veitche's Perfection (Wrinkled).—A large, wrinkled marrow, with large pods, fine flavor, and productive.

Dwarf and Tall Sugar.—(EDIBLE POD).—These varieties can be used either shelled or whole, the pods while young being sweet and tender; the string on the back of the pod should be drawn off before boiling.

Yorkshire Hero (Wrinkled).—An old English variety of luscious quality, and very productive. The peas when ripe are creamy-white in color, and wrinkled. Cannot recommend it too highly.

Large White Marrowfat.—Similar to the Black-eyed in all its features except in growth; it is a stronger grower, and not quite so productive.

Black-Eyed Marrowfat.—This variety is very popular in all parts of our country for its productiveness, but is very objectionable to many on account of having a strong flavor, which is peculiar to the Marrow Pea; it is a strong grower; very productive, and extensively cultivated by the market gardeners around Baltimore for their general crop, most of which are purchased by the canning establishments; the Black-Eye is far superior to the Tall White, as it makes less growth of vine; is more productive and earlier; where quantity without quality is wanted, plant Marrowfats.

Dwarf White Sugar Marrow.—This is the best of all the Marrowfats for either canning purposes or for market. The pods are not only of a larger size, but are better filled out; it ripens with the White Marrowfat, and similar to it in flavor, but dwarf in habit, requiring no sticks.

PEPPER.

Piment (Fr.).   Spanischer Pfeffer (Ger.).   Pimiento (Sp.).

Sow in a hot-bed, early in Spring, in shallow drills six inches apart; in order to make strong healthy plants they should be transplanted when a few inches high into another bed, like the Tomato, or sow in a box placed near a window, in a warm room, and transplant early in Summer. Or sow in a warm spot of the garden, about the middle of Spring, and transplant them when two inches high, in rows eighteen inches apart, and a foot from plant to plant. The Pepper delights in a rich soil, and should be well cultivated.

Spanish Monstrous, or Grossum.—A new French variety, growing six inches long by two inches thick, and of sweet flavor.

Ruby King.—A recently introduced variety of a beautiful ruby-red color, quite mild in flavor and of large size; very desirable.

Golden Bell, or Golden Dawn.—A very beautiful variety, resembling the Bell in shape and habit, but of a beautiful golden color, and of mild flavor.

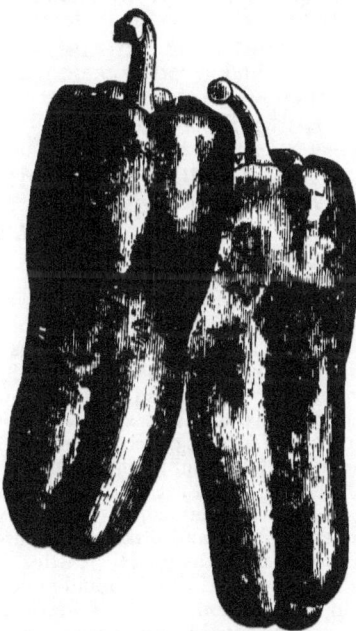

SPANISH MONSTROUS PEPPER.

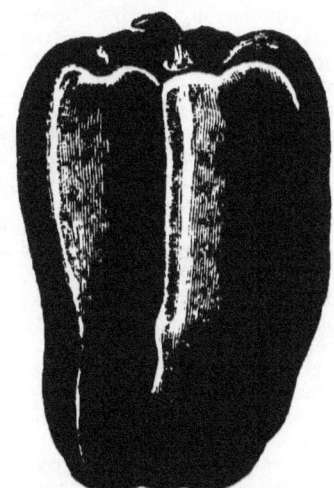

RUBY KING PEPPER.

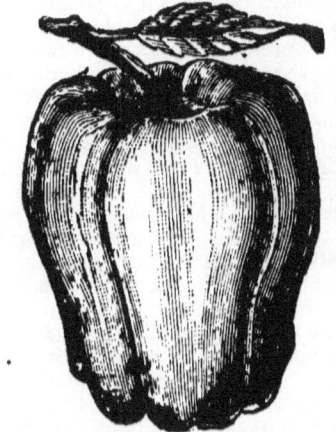

GOLDEN DAWN PEPPER.

Bell, or Bull-Nose, produces a very large-sized Pepper, which is highly esteemed for pickling, the skin being thicker than any of the other varieties,

Large Sweet, or Sweet Mountain, is similar to the Bell, but milder.

Red Cherry.—A small round variety of dwarf habit and rich scarlet color. Used for seasoning and pickling.

Tomato, or Squash.—This of a flattened shape, exceedingly hot, and generally preferred for making pepper hash, although very desirable when filled with cabbage and pickled.

Long Red Cayenne.—A long red variety, very hot, and is generally used for seasoning soups, etc.

Long Yellow Cayenne.—A long orange-yellow variety, and very desirable.

POTATOES.

POMME DE TERRE (Fr.).   KARTOFFEL (Ger.).   POTATA (Sp.).

The Potato requires a rich, sandy loam, with very liberal and clean culture; thoroughly decomposed manure is the best, and when that is not abundant, add bone-dust or guano. The crop will pay the cost, and leave the soil in splendid order. Old sod land, well turned under in the Fall, and lightly plowed and harrowed in the Spring, will produce a sound crop, and often an astonishingly large one. Clover sod for this purpose is excellent, and furnishes to the soil a large amount of vegetable substance; when turned under in August or September it will rot by the following Spring, and only a top-dressing of some well-established fertilizer will be required to carry through the crop. Wet land produces a coarse, unpalatable potato, and one of little value even as food for cattle. Barnyard manure is of little benefit to such land. Ground should never be plowed while wet or heavy; it injures the soil and does more harm than the manure can offset; the ground should be prepared as carefully and thoroughly for potatoes as for any other crop. Attention in this particular well repays the farmer. This crop requires but little manure, if the ground is rich, and that should be old and well rotted. By many, spreading the manure before plowing in the Spring is thought to be the best mode. At the time of planting, bone-dust, ashes, plaster, marl, and like fertilizers, can be used to great advantage, as they are of a dry or absorbent nature. On wet soils they are very beneficial, as they prevent disease as well as promote the growth of the tubers. On warm dry light land, muck compost may advantageously be used; decayed leaves are excellent. In seasons of disease among potatoes, in fields where ashes have been used they have suffered but little from the rot.

If you wish large well-formed roots, do not plant small ones; always select the best, cut them into four or six pieces, according to size, preserving as many eyes on each as possible; you will then have strong, healthy vines and roots. If small tubers are planted whole, the result in general is a quantity of small vines, followed with an over-proportion of small potatoes. Many cultivators in this vicinity select good-formed tubers and plant them whole. This may be an advantage should the season prove to be very dry, but we look upon it as a great waste of seed, as the product from such a crop is no better than those grown from well formed tubers cut into sets. Of late years no vegetable has been improved on as much as the Potato. Since the introduction years ago of the valuable Early Rose, new varieties flood the market every year, all claiming, either greater earliness, productiveness, or finer flavor. If they keep on in the future as they have in the past, names for them will almost be exhausted. We have now over five hundrd varieties by name, but in a few seasons these become almost unknown, and their places taken by other varieties, for which greater merit is claimed. With all the improvements in names, we have no better early varieties to-day than the Early Rose and Early Beauty of Hebron, and no better late variety for quality than the old White Peach Blow. CHANGE YOUR SEED is one of the secrets in producing good roots, and rich soil is the other. Always obtain your seed from a cooler climate and from a different character of soil. OUR ENTIRE STOCKS OF POTATOES ARE GROWN IN NEW YORK, VERMONT and NOVA SCOTIA.

HOW SHALL I KEEP MY POTATOES? It is a matter of no small importance to the farmer to be able to keep his crop of potatoes in good condition through our long Winters, and to offer them for sale, free from blemish or mildew, in the Spring. A well-kept potato generally brings three or four times its value in market in early Spring, than the same stock will if sold in the Fall, paying an extra profit over and above the cost of storing, handling, and care required. Of the three methods of storing in general use, each has its champions. They are: Storing in barrels, bins, heaps or pits. The advantage of placing in barrels is, they can be easily handled, do not suffer from abrasion, can be readily looked over, and if *disease presents itself* it can be checked or removed. When thousands of bushels are raised on one farm, this method cannot be followed on account of the time and expense involved. Bins are largely used by our large farmers, especially those near large cities, as the roots can at any time be reached and made ready for market. A dry, cool, well-ventilated cellar, with the light excluded, is the best place for storing them. It has been found very advantageous in preventing decay to sprinkle lime in the barrels or bin at the rate, say, of one pound to each barrel. It acts as an absorbent, and neutralizes the earthy odors, thus directly acting as a preventive of decay to the roots. The importance of excluding light from potatoes and keeping them as cool as possible, cannot be over-estimated as means of preserving the crop.

Early Sunrise.

EARLY SUNRISE.

—A variety possessing extreme earliness and great productiveness, producing potatoes fit for the table in fifty-two days from time of planting. The tubers are oblong, large, solid, uniform and handsome; flesh white, fine-grained and dry, cooking well even when first dug; very productive and of fine keeping qualities; vines dark green, of strong growth.

Early Rose.—Every cultivator of the Potato, both far and near, is familiar with the Early Rose. It was the pioneer of almost all the improved varieties of the present day; its highly extolled character when first introduced has not depreciated in the least; in fact, cultivators cannot speak too highly of it; it pleases the market gardener equally as well as the private grower; and in reputation to-day it equals that of any other variety. To keep it in perfection, it is always necessary to obtain your seed from potatoes grown in an Eastern climate, and those from Vermont or Nova Scotia are always the best; to keep planting from your own seed greatly deteriorates the quality, and decreases its productiveness.

Early Ohio.—A seedling of the rose, resembling it in color, but oblong in shape, and round instead of oval. It is of fine quality, about a week earlier than the Rose, and is a larger yielder, and one of the very finest varieties for the table.

EARLY OHIO.

Early Mayflower.—This very desirable early variety is a seedling of the Snowflake. We regard it as one of our very best, possessing more perfect qualities than any other variety; it is of uniform size, slightly flattened oval shape, color light lemon, skin netted, pure white, and cooks splendidly; it is also an admirable keeper.

Extra Early Vermont.—This variety is similar in color, form and general appearance to the Early Rose; it is, however, considered by many rather more hardy, a better keeper, more productive and earlier; it always proves a great favorite with all who cultivate it.

Clark's No. 1.— A very highly esteemed variety, resembling the Early Rose; regarded by some as being more productive.

Telephone.—A vigorous grower, very productive, an excellent keeper; flesh, pure white, floury, and of excellent flavor.

EARLY MAYFLOWER.

Triumph.—A very early variety of fine quality; handsome form and very productive.

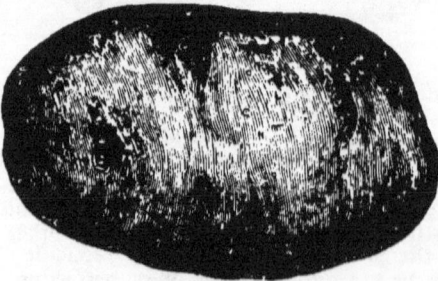

CLARK'S NO. 1

Early Snowflake. —It is one of the earliest varieties, ripening about the same time as the Early Rose. The tubers are of a good, medium and uniform size; shape elongated oval, compressed, exceedingly symmetrical and remarkably uniform; eyes few, entirely flat on the base and body of the tuber, and but slightly and sharply depressed near the seed end; skin white, with a russety tinge. Its flesh is of exceedingly fine grain, snow-white when boiled, and of a lightness and porosity almost approaching a snowflake. The tubers have attained the full developement of their quality as soon as they are fit to dig.

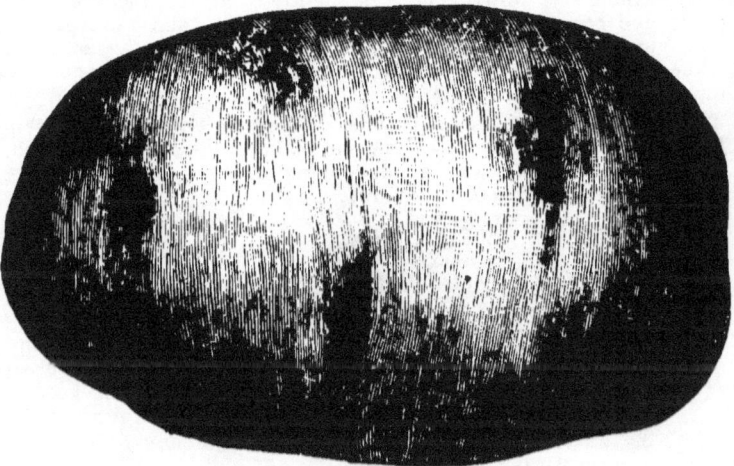

EARLY BEAUTY OF HEBRON.

Early Beauty of Hebron.—One of the best of the early varieties. In some sections it proves earlier than the Early Rose. Vine vigorous, growing very rapidly; very productive, the tubers lying compactly in the hill. Tubers similar in shape to the Early Rose, but shorter. Skin tinged with pink at first, but becomes pure white during the Winter, Flesh solid to the centre, even in large specimens, and of the finest quality.

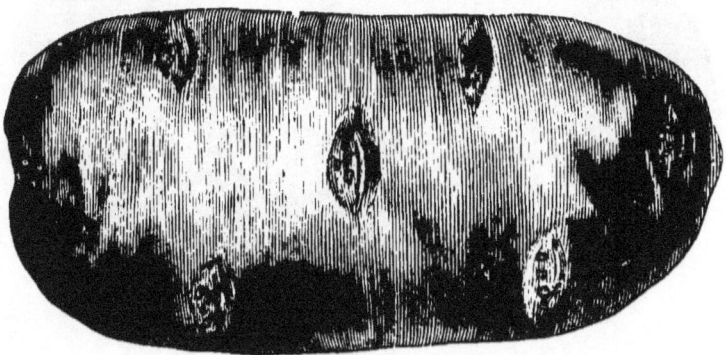

WHITE STAR.

White Star.—A very handsome and productive variety of recent introduction and of medium earliness; tubers oblong, large and uniform in size; vines strong, of a dark green color, stocky and vigorous; skin and flesh white and of fine quality; an excellent table variety, and keeps well.

State of Maine.—A cross between the early Vermont and the Peerless—combining the desirable features of both. The tuber over medium size, form cylindrical, slightly elongated, the flesh snow white and crystalline or mealy, the flavor nutty and unsurpassed. The vine erect in growth, with glossy leaf, not attractive to bugs. Tubers spread out in the hill like those of the Early Vermont—medium early. Very desirable.

Belle.—One of the handsomest formed varieties known. Skin light red, slightly netted; eyes few and shallow; tubers large, smooth, handsome and solid, with good cooking qualities. A remarkably heavy yielder and fine for main crop.

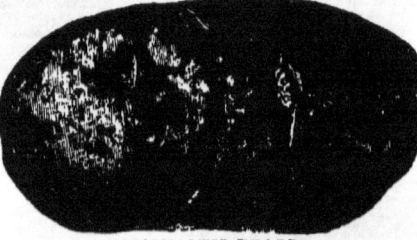

MAMMOTH PEARL.

White Elephant.—This fine late variety is a cross between the Garnet Chili and White Peach Blow. It is of excellent quality, fine flavor, wonderfully productive, of great beauty and a fine keeper. Tubers very large and solid, growing closely together in the hills.

Mammoth Pearl.—It is handsome in appearance, free from rot and never hollow; skin and flesh very white; eyes few and even with the surface, oblong to round in shape; tubers large; ripens in August; very productive, yielding twice as much as any ordinary variety.

BURBANK'S SEEDLING.

Burbank's Seedling.—A white-skinned, medium early variety, seedling of the Early Rose; of fine form and good size, it has few eyes which are but little below the surface. Either boiled or baked it is dry and floury, while the flesh is of fine grain and excellent flavor. The vines are very vigorous and healthy and in some cases have been entirely free from blight when it has destroyed crops of other varieties in the same field.

American Magnum Bonum.—It is an early variety, maturing a few days after the Early Rose, and unusually productive. Tubers large size and of excellent quality, free from disease, keeps well.

White Peach Blow.—This is the best Winter Potato for quality, but is not very productive; keeps sound until Spring, and boils dry and mealy; in our estimation it will always continue a general favorite.

Breeze's Peerless.—Is the most popular late variety in cultivation; its great beauty, superior quality and enormous productiveness have made it a great favorite; its form is oblong, skin dull white, slightly russetted, eyes shallow, flesh white and grows to a large size, frequently attaining 1½ to 2 pounds each, and producing from 300 to 400 bushels to the acre.

St. Patrick.—A second early variety. White skin, oval, oblong shape, slightly flattened, with but few eyes, almost even with the surface. Tubers of uniform size. They are excellent for table use, being dry and mealy, very white and of finest quality; grow very strong, stalks upright and branching, dark green, broad, smooth leaves; blossom very sparingly; a capital yielder; the best of keepers, and will give satisfaction.

Wall's Orange.—Excellence of quality and productiveness are the principal features claimed for this variety, and we believe experience sustains the claim.

Jumbo.—Skin and flesh white, and of fine flavor; stands continued drought well, and is an excellent keeper.

Late Beauty of Hebron.—Remarkably productive; tubers oblong and large; skin and flesh white. Keeps well and an excellent table variety.

Queen of the Valley.—Of enormous size and immensely productive; the best to raise for stock feeding.

Empire State.—A new variety, originating with Mr. E. L. Coy, the well-known originator of Beauty of Hebron and other good sorts. It grows to a fine large size, ripens late, is exceedingly productive and of fine table quality.

Chicago Market.—Large and uniform in size; productive and of good quality.

Garfield.—Of uniform, large size, and average yield; excellent table sort.

White Rose.—Shape elongated oval, of large even size, skin white and slightly russetted, eyes set well on the surface, flesh unusually white, fine grained and floury, with purest taste; cooks evenly to the centre; it is the best of keepers, and a perfect potato in every respect; ripens two weeks later than the Early Rose; cooking qualities are of the best, and is more than ordinarily productive, yielding equal to the Peerless.

Large Sweet, or New Jersey Sweet.—This is the famous Sweet Potato of Philadelphia, and is not surpassed by any other variety; sprout them in a hot-bed late in Spring, and when the weather becomes warm and pleasant, slip off the sprouts and plant them in hills two feet apart.

PUMPKIN.

Potiron (Fr.).   Kurbis (Ger.).   Calabaza (Sp.).

Pumpkins should never be grown in the kitchen garden, as they will invariably mix with Squashes, and deteriorate the quality of Melons. Plant them in the field among corn, or compost heap; they will grow in any situation, and in any kind of soil.

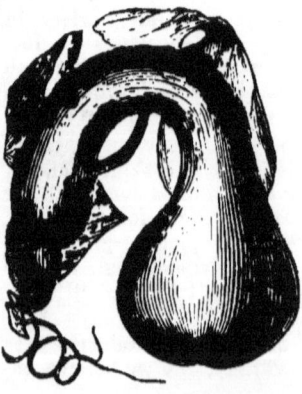

CASHAW PUMPKIN.

Cashaw Crook-Neck grows to a medium size; color, light yellow, and is the best variety for table use.

Large Cheese is of a flattened shape, color bright orange, and can be used either for stewing or stock feeding.

Connecticut Field is the common round variety cultivated by our farmers in their corn fields, for stock feeding.

Mammoth Etamps.—A variety from France, frequently attaining 150 pounds in weight, of coarse quality, only desirable for its prodigious size.

MAMMOTH KING PUMPKIN.

Mammoth King.—A variety attaining huge proportions, and frequently weighing, when attention is paid to its culture, over 225 pounds. It is very coarse, and is grown only for exhibiting.

BUIST'S ALMANAC AND GARDEN MANUAL. 117

RADISH.

Radis, Rave, Petite Rave (Fr.).   Rettig, Radies (Ger.).   Rabano (Sp.).

The Radish is one of our most popular vegetables, but contains little or no nourishment; they should never be eaten unless young and brittle, as when they become old and pithy they are very unwholesome. To have a constant supply, a sowing should be made every ten days from early in Spring until the beginning of Summer; the soil should be very rich and finely pulverized. The early varieties can be sown broadcast, very early in the season, among crops of Peas, Beets, Onions, etc.; if, however, not sown until late, they will invariably shoot to seed before forming any bulb.

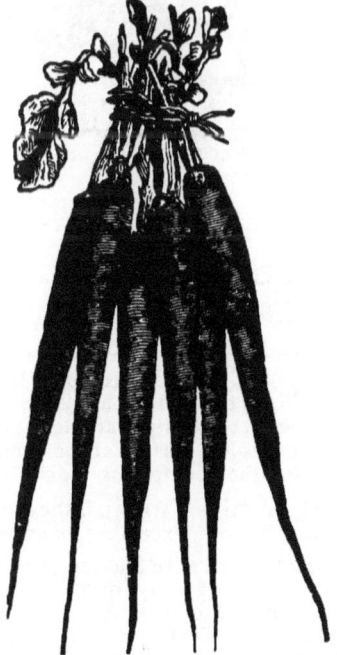

COVENT GARDEN LONG SCARLET RADISH.   BECKERT'S CHARTIER RADISH.

Early Long Scarlet Short Top (Covent Garden).—The most desirable for early forcing, or first sowing in the garden; it is of a bright scarlet color, and when grown on rich soil is very tender and brittle; do not sow in warm weather, as it will shoot to seed and form no bulb. It can also be sown early in the Fall for a late crop.

Long Salmon is of a lighter color than the former, but the same in every other respect, and should only be sown as an early crop.

Buist's Early Long White.—The same as the Early Long Scarlet, in form and earliness, but pure white. It is of fine flavor, and when grown on rich soil is very tender and brittle.

Early Scarlet Turnip.—A decided improvement both in earliness and brilliancy of color over the Scarlet Turnip, and is especially recommended to market gardeners.

Early Scarlet Turnip, White Tipped.—A beautiful scarlet variety, of handsome shape, having a white-tipped tail, or root; very desirable.

EARLY SCARLET TURNIP RADISH (WHITE TIPPED).

EARLY FRENCH BREAKFAST RADISH.

Scarlet Turnip, or Scarlet Button.—A very beautiful variety, and a general favorite; the bulb is small and is adapted for either forcing, or for early sowing in the garden, but will not stand the heat; it can also be sown early in the Fall for late crop.

EARLIEST ERFURT SCARLET TURNIP RADISH.

Earliest Erfurt Scarlet Turnip.—This is the earliest and finest of all the Scarlet Turnip varieties. Of the deepest color, perfect shape, small foliage, and the best forcing radish.

Early White Turnip is the same as the Red Turnip, excepting its color.

French Breakfast.—A very popular French variety, of very rapid growth, and one of the best varieties for early forcing; its form is oval; color, scarlet tipped with white, and small in size; it is also a beautiful variety for garnishing purposes.

Scarlet Olive-Shaped.—A very popular variety among the French and Germans; is of a half-long, or olive shape, bright scarlet color, and well adapted for either forcing, or for early sowing in the garden.

Golden Perfection.—We introduced last season this the finest strain of all the early summer turnip radishes, having been a selection made for the past three years from Buist's Yellow Summer. Its improvement consists in its earliness, its size, perfection of form, brilliancy of its golden color and fine flavor. It will be found a profitable market variety.

Buist's Yellow Summer Turnip, or Golden Globe.—This variety originated with us some years since by repeated selections made of the brightest color and most perfect formed roots from the ordinary Yellow Summer. It has become very popular, and the demand for it always exceeds the supply. The Golden Globe offered by some cultivators is Buist's Yellow Summer, with a new name.

Yellow Summer Turnip.—This variety will stand the heat, and can be sown quite late; it is a general favorite with market gardeners; is sometimes called the Mulatto Radish; flesh very crisp and tender.

White Summer Turnip is of an oval shape, white skin, and green top; is very solid, and stands the heat equal to the Yellow Summer, but is not as popular.

Chinese Rose (Winter).—This variety has become very popular with our market gardeners; it is of a half-long shape, pink color, and flesh as solid as an apple; it has not that strong flavor which is peculiar to the Black Spanish, and keeps equally as well; it should be sown during August. The White China only differs from this variety in its color.

New Early White Italian Summer.—A very remarkable early white summer radish, producing roots of twice the size of the ordinary variety, oval in shape, solid, crisp and tender; will stand longer than any other variety before shooting to seed. As a market radish it has no superior.

California Mammoth White (Winter).—A Chinese variety introduced into California; it grows to a large size; flesh quite solid, and of good flavor.

Black Spanish (Winter).—This variety is sown about the last of Summer, for Fall and Winter use; grows to a good size, of an oval shape, is quite solid, and if stored in pits, or packed away in sand, can be used the entire Winter.

RHUBARB.

Rhubarbe (Fr.).   Rhubarber (Ger.).   Ruibarbo Bastardo (Sp.).

Very familiarly known as the Pie Plant ; the footstalk is the portion that is used, and is the first article of the season from the garden ; it is now cultivated to a great extent, and indispensable wherever it is known. Sow the seed early in the Spring, in rows one foot apart, on rich ground ; the second year after planting, they can be removed, in Autumn, to the permanent spot allotted for them ; plant the roots two feet apart each way, in ground that is at least well enriched, two feet deep. No reliance can be placed on the seeds producing the identical variety. Rhubarb can be cured for Winter use by cutting the stalks into small pieces; string them, and expose to the sun until perfectly dry ; after which hang them in a dry place until wanted.

Linnæus, Victoria and Mammoth are the most desirable varieties, producing fine, large stalks.

SALSIFY, OR VEGETABLE OYSTER.

Salsifis (Fr.). Bocksbart (Ger.). Ostra Vegetal (Sp.).

Very generally known as the Oyster Plant; the roots are boiled like Carrots or Parsnips, or half boiled and grated fine, made into small flat balls, dipped in a batter, and fried like oysters, of which their flavor greatly partakes. Sow the seed in drills eight inches apart, and when up, thin them out to three inches apart in the row; those for Winter use should be taken up before severe frost, and stored the same as Carrots and Parsnips.

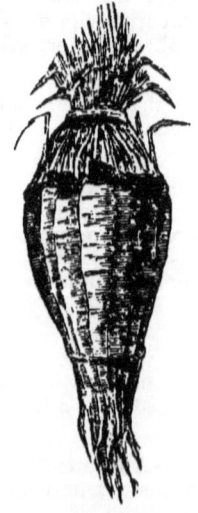
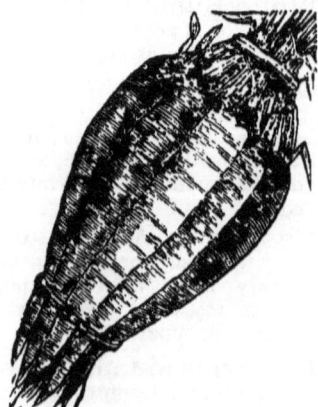

SALSIFY.   BUIST'S MAMMOTH SALSIFY.

Buist's Mammoth.—This will be found a great improvement over the ordinary variety. The roots of which are double the size and more delicate in flavor.

American Grown.—This is the common stock usually sold; its roots are only half the size of Buist's Mammoth.

Imported Seed.—There is nothing to recommend this stock but cheapness; the roots are very thin.

SCORZONERA.

Scorzonere (Fr.). Skorzonere (Ger.). Escorzonere (Sp.).

Black Salsify is a vegetable that resembles the former, and is frequently used for the same purpose, and may be treated similarly in every respect, but is by no means as desirable.

SEA KALE.

Crambe Maritime (Fr.). Selkohl Meerkohl (Ger.). Breton de Mar (Sp.).

Sow the seeds in drills one foot apart, and thin out to four inches in the row. In one year transplant them into clumps, or hills, eighteen inches apart, and three in each clump. After the second year, cover them before frost with two feet of dried leaves; they will blanch there during the Winter, and are fit for use when the stems are four inches long, and perfectly white. It is prepared like Asparagus for the table.

SPINACH.

EPINARD (Fr.). SPINAT (Ger.). ESPINSCA (Sp.).

For an early Summer crop, sow early in Spring, in drills one foot apart, and thin out to two inches in the row; the soil should be in fine order as rich ground produces large leaves. For Winter and early Spring crops, sow either broadcast or in drills, about the end of August, and again about the middle of September; as soon as severe weather sets in, cover the bed with straw or leaves, which should be raked off early in Spring.

Buist's Perfection Curled.—(NEW VARIETY FOR MARKET GARDENERS, sold only under our seal, see illustration under novelties.) This is our new curled variety of this season's introduction, brought to the present high standard, from repeated selections made from the most perfect curled plants, and is especially adapted for the market garden trade. It is a strain that produces a strong growth of leaves, which are more curled and crimped than any other variety; and also stands longer without shooting to seed, a very important requisite. It possesses all the perfections that could be desired by a market gardener in a Spinach for a popular and desirable crop. It is sold under our seal in packages, cartoons and sacks, to be had only from our house or through the merchant who handles our seeds.

American Curled.— This is an excellent curled variety introduced by us a few years since, which is now surpassed by our new strain, the BUIST'S PERFECTION CURLED.

Bloomsdale Curled.— A very popular curled variety.

Round Savoy Leaved. —This is a popular variety; the leaves are curled and quite large; it is not, however, as hardy as the Prickly, but in this vicinity it stands very well.

Broad-Leaved Flanders.—This is a much stronger growing variety than the Round; producing large, broad, thick leaves, which are more succulent, and quite as hardy.

AMERICAN CURLED SPINACH.

Prickly-Seeded.—This variety will withstand the severest weather, with only a slight protection of straw or leaves, and is generally sown in the Eastern and Western States; it is not so tender or desirable as either the Round-Leaved or American Curled.

New Thick-Leaved.—A variety producing a remarkably thick leaf, slightly crimped and quite desirable.

New Long-Standing.—A new English variety similar to the Round-Leaf, but stands longer than any other variety before seeding.

SQUASH.

Courge (Fr.).   Kürbiss (Ger.).   Calabaza Tontanera (Sp.).

About the last of Spring, or as soon as the ground becomes warm, plant in hills about three feet apart, six seeds to a hill; when up thin them out, leaving three of the strongest plants. When they are making their appearance, they are liable to be destroyed by a striped bug; to prevent this, they should be dusted two or three times with a mixture of one-third guano and two-thirds plaster; apply it early in the morning, while the dew is on them. They should be grown as far apart as possible from all other cucurbitaceous plants, so as to prevent their hybridizing.

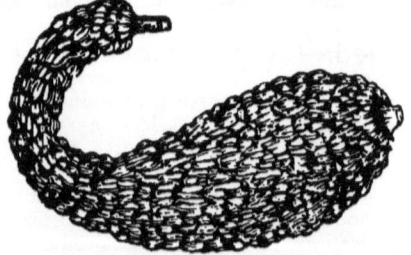

GOLDEN SUMMER CROOK-NECK SQUASH.

EARLY BUSH SQUASH.

Golden Summer Crook-Neck is a popular variety in the East, but cultivated to a limited extent elsewhere; is of a bright golden yellow color, and very much warted; it is one of the best Summer varieties and should be more largely cultivated.

Early Bush, or Patty Pan, is earlier than any other variety, of dwarf habit, very productive; grows in a bush form, and occupies less room on the ground than other sort. Summer Squashes should always be used when young and tender, which can be determined by an impression of the nail.

BOSTON MARROW SQUASH.

Boston Marrow is the favorite Winter Squash of the Eastern States; it is of fine flavor, and a good keeper; the Boston markets are completely stocked with this variety during the Fall and Winter months; a stranger is very liable to be impressed with the idea that the Bostonians live entirely on Squashes.

Buist's Improved Marrow is an improvement on the Boston Marrow, but similar to it in form; is more productive and of better flavor; for custards it cannot be surpassed, and keeps perfectly sound until late in Spring; wherever it has been introduced it becomes a general favorite.

The Hubbard as a Winter Squash cannot be too highly extolled; it boils smooth and dry, is of very rich quality, and keeps as solid as a rock. It is more popular with private growers than any other variety, but as a market sort it can never excel the Boston Marrow.

HUBBARD SQUASH.

Marblehead.—Another new variety of the Hubbard type, has a very thick and hard shell, with remarkable good keeping qualities, is of a dry, sweet and delicious flavor.

London Vegetable Marrow.—This is a very popular variety in Europe, and is gradually gaining favor in this country; it produces a succession of crops throughout the Summer; it is of a dry nature, and is superior in flavor to all other Summer Squashes; its color is of a creamy white, and is quite a strong grower.

LONDON VEGETABLE MARROW SQUASH.

White Pine Apple.—A very remarkably formed, entirely distinct and desirable variety; can be planted either as an early Summer crop, or later for Winter use; keeps remarkably well, and one of the finest for pies and custards; its flavor is very similar to that of a cocoanut.

Perfect Gem.—A very desirable variety of globular shape, but of small size, about six inches in diameter; of excellent quality.

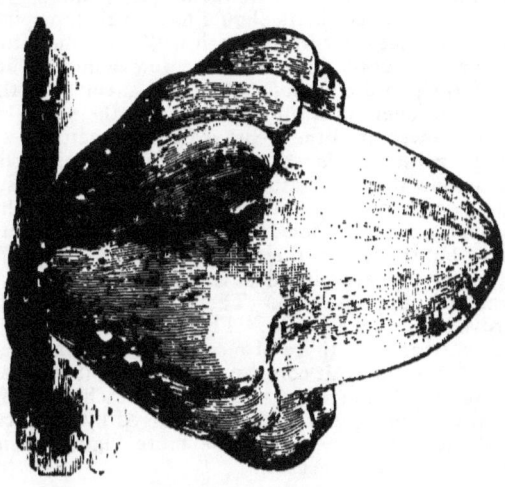

WHITE PINE APPLE SQUASH.

Butman.—A new Winter variety, possessing all the good qualities of the Hubbard, but of a very distinct color, being of a grassy-green, intermixed with white; it has a very thick shell, and is thick meated; flesh is of a light salmon color, and is dry, sweet and delicious.

BUTMAN SQUASH.

Winter Crook-Neck.—A variety resembling the Cashaw Pumpkin, but of smaller size; is of very fine quality.

Mammoth Chili.—A variety that grows to a very large size, frequently attaining over one hundred pounds, but of rather coarse flesh; only desirable for stock feeding.

TOMATO.

TOMATE (Fr.).   LIEBESAPFEL (Ger.).   TOMATE (Sp.).

Thirty-five years years ago this vegetable was considered unfit for the table; and now there is none more popular; thousands of acres are annually grown in this vicinity, and thousands of baskets are daily sold in our markets throughout the season. It is a point of good gardening to have this dish early; to accomplish which sow in a spent hot-bed early in Spring, and air freely in fine weather; for a late crop sow the seeds in a very warm spot of the garden, and cover them at night or during cold weather with boards; when the weather becomes mild and pleasant, transplant them in a sheltered part of the garden facing south or south-east; as the plants advance, support them with a few branches, or tie them up to stakes.

The earliest plants should have their tops pinched off as soon as they have set their fruit, which will cause them to ripen earlier. It is also a very good plan to plant a few plants in flower-pots or boxes, very early in the season, and place them near the glass in a greenhouse, or even on a window-sill; keep them well watered to encourage their growth until the weather becomes settled; then transplant them to the garden; this will greatly increase their earliness. Most cultivators allow their Tomato vines to grow wild and suppport themselves; they perhaps have never given it a thought, that, by training and properly pruning them, they will not only increase their productiveness, but the fruit will ripen better and be of much finer quality. This is really the case; besides, it looks more orderly and much prettier to train or support them. There has been no vegetable so highly improved as the Tomato. The old varieties are to-day valueless in comparison with those of recent introduction.

When the fruit commences ripening it is always a very good plan to place a thin layer of straw around each plant, it will not only prevent the fruit from becoming damaged by contact with the soil, but will cause the vine to become more vigorous and continue bearing much later in the season.

○ ☛**Sow the Buist's "Belle" and Buist's "Beauty," they are the two finest varieties known, for both size, solidity and productiveness.**

BUIST'S ALMANAC AND GARDEN MANUAL. 125

BUIST'S BEAUTY TOMATO

Buist's Beauty.—A new variety introduced by us a few years since, which has proved to be the best and most popular variety known. Invariably awarded first premium wherever exhibited. We annually grow fifty acres of tomatoes especially for seed, and have made the improvement of all our stocks a special study; the "Beauty" originated on our Rosedale farm from a cross made between the Paragon and the Livingstone Perfection. Its important features are solidity, large size, perfect shape, desirable color (which is brilliant scarlet), evenness of ripening without crack or wrinkle, freeness of core, and its few seeds. As a profitable market variety it has no equal.

Livingstone's Favorite.—A very desirable variety introduced by A. W. Livingstone, of Ohio, the introducer of the famous Acme and Paragon. Is large and solid, of a dark red color, not liable to crack, and a superior shipping variety.

Livingstone's Perfection.—A very desirable early variety, of dark red color, large size, perfectly smooth, ripens uniformly and bears abundantly until frost. A very valuable variety for canning purposes.

Paragon.—A very popular variety; color bright crimson; smooth, solid, of excellent flavor; bears transportation well; very productive; an excellent market variety.

BUIST'S PRIZE BELLE TOMATO.
(Weight 1½lbs.) The Largest and Best of All.

Buist's Prize Belle.—This variety is a hybrid of the famous Beauty, introduced by us, which was universally acknowledged as the largest and best variety known, having been awarded first prize wherever exhibited. The Belle is earlier than the Beauty, and still larger in size, many specimens weighing the past season 1½ lbs. each, and as solid as an apple, of a beautiful bright scarlet color, free from crack, and remaining perfect on the vine longer than any other variety. There has been no sort ever introduced that has given such perfect satisfaction, and proved such a favorite, as the Belle; in fact we cannot see how any improvement can be made on it, as it possesses not only the largest size, but the greatest solidity, finest flavor, smallest quantity of seeds, richness of color and shipping qualities unequaled.

Buist's Selected Trophy.—The popularity of the Trophy is equal that of any other variety, and will always be regarded with great favor by all growers. Our seed is saved from selected specimens, and cannot fail in producing handsome, well-formed, and desirable fruit; this variety is noted for its solidity and beauty.

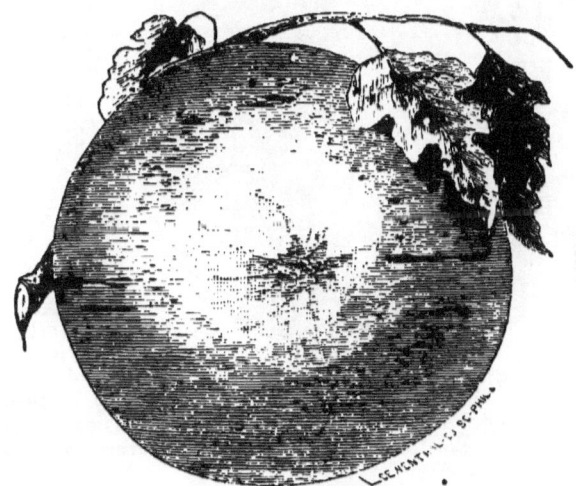

EARLY ACME TOMATO.

Acme.—With the introduction of the far-famed Trophy Tomato, many years ago, we thought that perfection in this vegetable had at last been attained, but with the introduction of the ACME the Trophy was cast in the shade. The Acme is of an entirely distinct character, and has become a very popular variety; it is perfection in its BEAUTY, SOLIDITY and EARLINESS, and has good carrying qualities, a very important requisite for a desirable market variety; it is also well adapted for Southern culture, and one of the best to grow for Northern market. The plants are of a strong and vigorous growth, very productive; fruit of medium size, large enough for any use, form perfect, round, slightly depressed at the ends, very smooth; color a glossy dark red, with a sort of purplish tinge; ripens all over and through at the same time; bears continuously until frost; delicious in flavor, has no green core, and but few seeds; unsurpassed for canning, preserving or slicing.

Mayflower.—A large early variety; of splendid shape, perfectly smooth, of a bright red color, and ripens uniformly up to the stem. The flesh is solid, free from seeds, and of a pure, rich flavor.

Cardinal.—A variety that possesses many desirable features; color brilliant cardinal red; fruit solid, of good size, and productive.

Livingstone's Beauty.—This very handsome variety grows on a vigorous vine, in clusters of five or six. Fruit large, retaining its size very late in the season. Prolific, exceptionally smooth, perfect in shape, ripens uniformly; as early as the Acme or Perfection. Being very firm and having a tough skin, it seldom rots or cracks on any class of soil. In color, a distinct glossy crimson with slight purplish tint; ripens in perfect color even when picked quite green, making it a first-class shipping sort.

LIVINGSTONE'S BEAUTY TOMATO.

Hathway's Excelsior.—This is a very desirable early variety, of perfect and regular form, medium size; grows in clusters; ripens early, and very productive; an excellent variety for early market, and also for canning purposes.

Early Smooth Red is one of the oldest varieties, quite early, of medium size, of apple-shape, and bright scarlet color.

Large, or Mammoth Red.—This is a large coarse-formed variety; very uneven and knotty, and is later in ripening than the former.

Early Conqueror.—Is an early and very popular variety, quite productive, producing fruit about three inches in diameter, and ripening very evenly and regularly.

Early Canada Victor.—A variety introduced a few years since from Canada; is very early, producing large, handsome fruit.

The Tilden.—This was the Pioneer of all the present improved varieties; it became very popular throughout the entire country both with market gardeners and private growers; color bright scarlet, of very perfect form, entirely free from all inequalities; produces abundantly; since the introduction of so many improved varieties it is now but seldom grown.

Large Yellow is similar to the Large Red in shape, but more solid in flesh; it is an excellent variety for slicing.

Golden Trophy.—A sprout from the well-known Trophy; of a beautiful light yellow, occasionally faintly streaked with red; a desirable acquisition for preserving as well as for the table.

Yellow Plum.—Shape uniformly oval, and perfectly smooth; color lemon yellow; used for preserves.

Red Pear or Plum Shaped.—Varieties producing their fruit in clusters; desirable for preserving or pickling purposes.

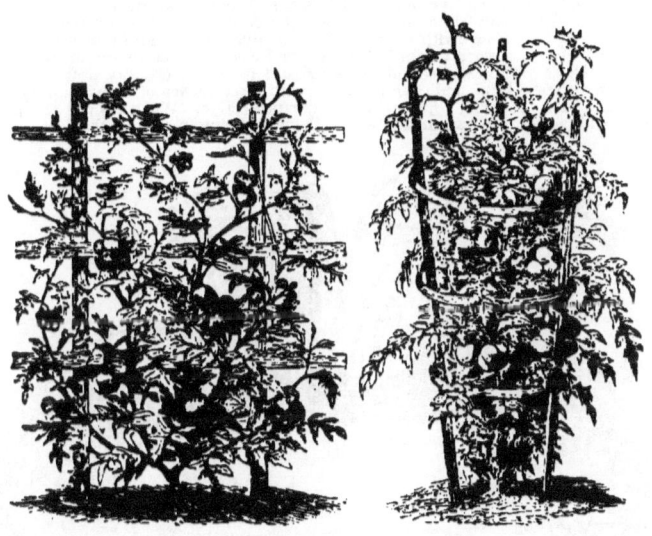

TRELLIS-TRAINING OF THE TOMATO.

TURNIP.

Navet (Fr.). Rube (Ger.). Nabo Comun (Sp.).

The cultivation of the Turnip in this country, is greatly on the increase, and is always a very desirable and profitable crop to grow; is of the easiest culture, but requires good, deep, rich soil, and should be sown before or after a rain, while the ground is moist, as on the strength of the early growth will depend in a great measure the success of the crop. The fly is very destructive to the Turnip crop, especially during warm, dry weather, and frequently they will eat off an entire field as fast as the young plants make their appearance; the best plan is to sow an abundance of seed, at the rate of two pounds to the acre, and if the plants are too thick in the drills, thin them out by hoeing, or with a light harrow if sown broadcast. As soon as the plants form their rough leaves, they are safe from the attacks of the fly; but should the crop be destroyed, loosen or harrow the ground immediately, and re-sow at once. A dusting of plaster on the plants as they appear will frequently prevent such attacks. For an early Summer crop, sow the Early White Flat Dutch or Red Top (strap-leaved) very early in Spring, in good, rich soil, either broadcast or in drills one foot apart; when the plants are up, thin them out to about four inches apart. For a general Fall crop, sow late in Summer or early Autumn, the flat, strap-leaved varieties broadcast, and the large, round varieties in drills. Ruta Baga or Swede should be sown in July, in drills twenty inches apart, and the plants thinned out to stand six inches. A seed sower should always be used for sowing Turnip seed in drills.

WINTERING TURNIPS. —Turnips may be kept perfectly sound until Spring by being taken up about the first of November or before severe frost sets in. Cut the leaves off to about half an inch of the bulb; collect the latter and put them in a dry pit or cellar; cover with straw, and earth over all. Thus protected they will be found fresh and perfect until February; the Swede will be fit for the table until April. Those for Spring use can be pitted out of doors in a dry situation, piling them in a conical form, and covering them with three inches of straw, and a foot or eighteen inches of earth, which will be ample protection. When opened in Spring, these will be found to have nearly all the flavor of being fresh from the field.

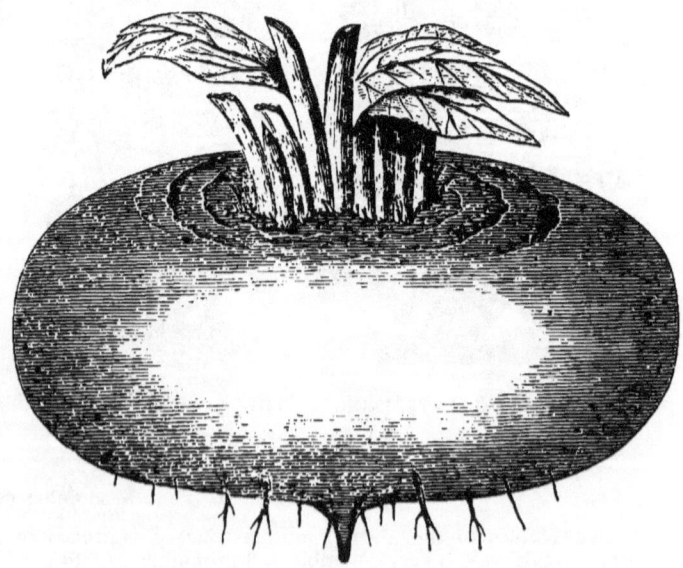

EARLY WHITE FLAT DUTCH (STRAP-LEAVED) TURNIP.

Early White Flat Dutch (Strap-leaved).—This is the earliest variety known, and can be sown either broadcast or in drills; it is, without exception, the best and most popular sort for either table use or for market; is of a beautiful, flat form, of pure white color, and of a delicate, mild flavor; it produces bulbs entirely free from small roots and with long, narrow strap-leaves growing erect, which permits close culture.

Red, or Purple-Top (Strap-leaved). A variety of the easiest culture, and a general favorite with all; will do well to sow either broadcast or in drills, and will form good-sized bulbs, in a favorable season, in about seven or eight weeks from sowing; it is of a perfectly flat form, with a small tap root, and a bright purple top; the leaves are short and narrow, growing erect from the bulb; it is a fine table variety, and excellent for feeding stock. This and the White Flat Dutch are the most popular of all the varieties. We annually grow from 150 to 200 acres of this seed to supply the demand.

BUIST'S MAMMOTH RED OR PURPLE TOP GLOBE TURNIP.
The Best of all the Globe Varieties.

Buist's Mammoth Red or Purple Top Globe.— This is a variety of recent introduction, which is becoming very popular and especially so in the South; it is of large size, globe form, of rapid growth and enormously productive; of the same character and habit as the Red Top Flat, differing only in its shape and leaves; it can be sown either broadcast or in drills, the latter method will produce the largest and finest formed roots. Flesh pure white and solid, with a reddish purple top. Regard it as one of the most valuable varieties, and cannot recommend it too highly.

Extra Early Purple Top Milan (Strap-Leaved).—This new foreign variety is the earliest strap-leaved in cultivation; flesh pure white, purple top, of flat form and excellent quality; highly recommended.

Extra Early Purple Top Munich.—A distinct and handsome variety with a bright purplish-red top; very desirable.

Early Snowball.—An early, white, round-formed variety, sweet and tender when small, but pithy when full grown.

Early White Stone.—A variety which produces enormous tops and small roots; is round in form, but inferior to the Flat Dutch in quality.

Early White French Turnip.—A very popular variety in France for early market; is pure white, sweet flavored, of handsome form, and remarkably crisp and tender.

Early White Egg, is an early variety, introduced a few years since; pure white, of egg shape, quite desirable.

Large White Globe.—A variety grown exclusively for stock feeding; should be used in the Fall or early Winter, as it becomes pithy before Spring; is one of the most productive kinds; in good, rich soil the bulbs will frequently grow to twelve pounds in weight; it is of a globe shape; flesh and skin white; the tops or leaves are inclined to make a strong growth.

Pomeranean White Globe.—This is a very handsome and popular variety, selected from the White Globe, from which it differs only in the size and beauty of its roots. It is especially adapted for the Southern States.

Early Snow-White Globe.—This is one of the most beautiful formed varieties known, of pure snow-white color, and almost as round as a ball; a very desirable and productive early market variety; is far superior to the White Globe for a general crop.

Large Green Globe.—A large, round, white-fleshed variety, with a green top, very productive.

Large White Norfolk.—There is very little distinction between this and the White Globe; they are both equally as productive, and as desirable for stock feeding.

Amber Globe.—This is a very beautiful formed variety, quite productive, solid flesh, and attractive color; it keeps well, and is desirable for either table use or for stock feeding.

Large Yellow Globe.—This is very similar to the Robertson's Golden Ball; flesh pale yellow, very solid and keeps well; grows to a medium size and is an excellent table variety.

Golden Ball.—For a Fall crop it is the best of the yellows; is very solid and of good flavor; flesh bright orange, of a globe form, and keeps well; an excellent table variety.

Purple-Top Yellow Aberdeen, or Scotch Yellow.—This is one of the most popular foreign varieties, but cultivated to a very limited extent in this country. It resembles a very handsomely formed Ruta Baga, and for feeding purposes it is fully equal to them, and keeps solid until very late in the season. It can be sown with success fully a month later than the Swede, and is also quite desirable for table use.

Long White Cow Horn.—A pure white variety, with green top, growing in shape similar to a cow's horn; is desirable for both table use and for stock feeding; keeps well.

PURPLE-TOP YELLOW ABERDEEN TURNIP.

Southern Seven Top.—This, the hardiest of all sorts, may be left standing in the open ground during Winter as far North as Philadelphia. In the Southern States it yields in the Spring abundant foliage for boiling with cured meats, and is only desirable for this purpose.

Purple Top Yellow Ruta Baga or Swede.—This is the variety from which Buist's Improved originated; it is far inferior to it, both in its size, color and productiveness; its principal recommendation is its cheapness.

Carter's Imperial Swede.—A very celebrated English variety, which has been awarded many prizes abroad; it is yellow flesh, purple top, and very productive.

134 BUIST'S ALMANAC AND GARDEN MANUAL.

Buist's Improved Purple-Top Yellow Ruta Baga or Swede.—This is the largest and most productive Swede known; there is no variety which has gained a greater reputation throughout the entire country than Buist's Improved. Testimonials are continually received by us indorsing its fine qualities and productiveness; it cannot be too highly recommended, and no sort will produce such handsomely formed roots or greater yield; it is very solid, of a beautiful orange-color, with a handsome purple top, and is the result of many years of careful selection.

BUIST'S IMPROVED PURPLE TOP YELLOW RUTA-BAGA.

Skirving's, Marshall's, Sutton's, and other special sorts, are all foreign varieties. Buist's Improved and Carter's Imperial are the best of the entire class of Ruta Bagas. The former variety, however, is better adapted to the climate of this country, as all foreign varieties produce very long, shanky necks.

White Ruta Baga, or Russian White.—A rather irregular growing variety, pure white, flesh solid, and quite sweet.

POT, SWEET AND MEDICINAL HERBS.

Angelica Garden,	*Archangelica officinalis.*
Anise,	*Pimpinella anisum.*
Arnica,	*Arnica montana.*
Balm,	*Melissa officinalis.*
Basil, Sweet,	*Ocymum basilicum.*
Bene,	*Sesamum orientale.*
Borage,	*Borago officinalis.*
Belladona,	*Atropa belladona.*
Bryonia.	*Bryonia dioica.*
Caraway,	*Carum carvi.*
Castor Oil Plant,	*Ricinus communis.*
Coriander,	*Coriandrum sativum.*
Dill,	*Anethum graveolens.*
Dock, Yellow,	*Rumex crispus.*
Fennel, Sweet,	*Anethum fœniculum.*
Fenugreek,	*Trigonella focnum græcum.*
Hellebore,	*Helleborus fœtidus.*
Hemlock,	*Conium maculatum.*
Henbane,	*Hyosciamus niger.*
Horehound,	*Marrubium vulgare.*
Hyssop,	*Hyssopus officinalis.*
Lavender,	*Lavendula vera.*
Marjoram, Sweet,	*Origanum majoram.*
Opium Poppy,	*Papaver somniferum.*
Pot Marigold,	*Calendula officinalis.*
Rosemary,	*Rosemarinus officinalis.*
Rue,	*Ruta graveolens.*
Saffron,	*Carthamus tinctorius.*
Sage,	*Salvia officinalis.*
Sage, Red,	*Salvia sclarea.*
Stramonium,	*Datura Stramonium.*
Summer Savory,	*Satureja hortensis.*
Tansy,	*Tanacetum vulgaris.*
Thyme,	*Thymus vulgaris.*
Wormwood,	*Artemisia absinthium.*

The soil for herbs should be light, rich and pulverized as finely as possible before sowing. Always plant in very shallow drills, after which rake finely, and give a gentle pressure with a board or back of the spade. They are used for seasoning and medicinal purposes, and to preserve them properly, cut the stems and leaves just as the plant is coming into bloom, dry them in the shade, and when perfectly dry wrap them up in paper and stow away in a dry room, or rub the leaves to a powder; pack in bottles and cork tightly, which will preserve them for any period.

SWEET BASIL.   SUMMER SAVORY.

BUIST'S CELEBRATED COLLECTIONS OF
KITCHEN-GARDEN SEEDS.
Complete Assortments for Family Gardens.

These assortments of seeds will be found very desirable for those who are not sufficiently experienced, or who are not familiar with the most desirable varieties, to make judicious selections from our Catalogue. They include what we regard as the very choicest varieties. We add to each collection some of our finest novelties without charge. Nos. 1, 2, 3, and 4 are sent by express or railroad at the expense of the purchaser. Nos. 5, 6, and 7 are mailed, postage paid, by us.

VARIETIES.	Col. 1 for $20 contains	Col. 2 for $15 contains	Col. 3 for $10 contains	Col. 4 for $5 contains	Col. 5 for $4.50 contains	Col. 6 for $2 contains	Col. 7 for $1 contains
Beans,	5 qts.	7½ pts	4½ pts	2 pts.	2 pkts		
Beets,	8 oz.	6 oz.	4½ oz.	2 oz.	1 oz.	3 pkts	2 pkts
Borecole, or Kale,	1 oz.	1 oz.	½ oz.	1 pkt.			
Brocoli,	1 oz.	½ oz.	2 pkts	1 pkt.	1 pkt.		
Carrot,	10 oz.	8 oz.	4 oz.	2 oz.	2 pkts	2 pkts	1 pkt.
Cauliflower,	1 oz.	¾ oz.	2 pkts	1 pkt.	1 pkt.	1 pkt.	
Cabbage,	6 oz.	4 oz.	3 oz.	2 oz.	5 pkts	4 pkts	3 pkts
Celery,	2 oz.	1½ oz.	4 pkts	3 pkts	2 pkts	1 pkt.	1 pkt.
Corn,	6 qts.	4 qts.	2 qts.	2 pts.	1 pt.	1 pkt.	
Cress,	2 oz.	1½ oz.	1 oz.	½ oz.	1 pkt.	1 pkt.	1 pkt.
Cucumber,	6 oz.	4 oz.	2 oz.	3 pkts	2 pkts	1 pkt.	1 pkt.
Egg Plant,	1 oz.	¾ oz.	½ oz.	1 pkt.	1 pkt.	1 pkt.	1 pkt.
Endive,	1 oz.	¾ oz.	½ oz.	1 pkt.	1 pkt.		
Kohl Rabi,	1 oz.	¾ oz.	½ oz.	¼ oz.			
Leek,	1 oz.	¾ oz.	½ oz.	¼ oz.	1 pkt.		
Lettuce,	4 oz.	3 oz.	1½ oz.	3 pkts	2 pkts	2 pkts	1 pkt.
Melon, Cantaloupe,	6 oz.	4 oz.	2 oz.	3 pkts	2 pkts	2 pkts	1 pkt.
Melon, Water,	1½ oz.	3 oz.	1½ oz.	3 pkts	2 pkts	1 pkt.	1 pkt.
Onion,	8 oz.	6 oz.	4 oz.	2 oz.	3 pkts	2 pkts	1 pkt.
Okra,	4 oz.	3 oz.	2 oz.	½ oz.	1 pkt.	1 pkt.	
Parsley,	2 oz.	1 oz.	½ oz.	¼ oz.	1 pkt.	1 pkt.	
Parsnip,	5 oz.	4 oz.	2 oz.	1 oz.	2 pkts	1 pkt.	1 pkt.
Peas,	11 qts.	7 qts.	5½ qts	3 pts.	1½ pts	2 pkts	
Pepper,	1 oz.	¾ oz.	½ oz.	2 pkts	1 pkt.	1 pkt.	
Radish,	14 oz.	8 oz.	6 oz.	3 oz.	2 oz.	3 pkts	1 pkt.
Spinach,	1 lb.	12 oz.	8 oz.	4 oz.	1 oz.	1 pkt.	1 pkt.
Squash,	8 oz.	6 oz.	4 oz.	2 oz.	4 pkts	2 pkts	2 pkts
Tomato,	2½ oz.	1¾ oz.	1¼ oz.	4 pkts	3 pkts	2 pkts	1 pkt.
Turnip,	1 lb.	12 oz.	8 oz.	2 oz.	1½ oz.	2 pkts	1 pkt.
Sweet and Pot Herbs	7 pkts	6 pkts	5 pkts	4 pkts	3 pkts	1 pkt.	

COLLECTIONS OF FLOWER SEEDS.
All varieties will be found in our Garden Guide.

					At Catalogue Price would cost:	
No. 1.	Contains	10	varieties	Annuals,	50 cts. for	40 cts.
No. 2.	"	10	"	Finest Annuals,	75 "	50 "
No. 3.	"	25	"	Annuals,	$1.25	$1.00
No. 4.	"	20	"	Finest Annuals,	1.50	1.25
No. 5.	"	50	"	Finest Annuals,	3.75	3.00
No. 6.	"	12	"	For Greenhouse or House Culture, 3.00		2.25

Gardeners' and Planters' Price-List.

☞ **All our Seeds** are exclusively of our own growth on our Seed Farms, ROSEDALE, WATERFORD and MORRISVILLE, OR ON THE FARMS OF OUR PRIVATE GROWERS, AND RAISED FROM THE CHOICEST SELECTED STOCKS. They will be found far superior, both in their purity and growth, to those sold by seedsmen who are obliged to purchase their supplies. IN ALL SUCH CASES THEY RARELY, IF EVER, CAN BE ASSURED OF EITHER THE AGE OR THE QUALITY OF THE SEEDS THEY SELL.

☞ **We solicit no order from localities where our seeds are sold**; in all such cases, order from the merchant who handles them, he can supply you at our prices. But should they not be kept by any of your merchants, then order direct from our house, enclosing a remittance, and it shall have our prompt attention.

☞ **Cost of Mailing Seeds.**—Orders for papers, ounce and four-ounce packages, are mailed free of postage. Orders for pounds and quarts, an advance of sixteen cents per pound, and thirty cents per quart, must be added to our quotations for postage.

☞ *Make out your orders early, before the season opens; gardeners frequently overlook ordering their seeds until they actually require them for sowing, and if they reside at a distance they are often disappointed in not receiving them in time.*

SPECIAL DISCOUNTS

THIS SEASON.

Order through the merchant who sells our seeds in your town, he will supply you at our prices and allow you our special discounts.

We offer the following special discounts this season from our prices on all Garden Seeds in bulk, that is by the OUNCE, POUND, QUART or BUSHEL, as quoted in this catalogue.

Orders Amounting to $ 5.00 and over 10 per cent. Discount.
" " " 10.00 " " 12½ " "
" " " 25.00 " " 15 " "
" " " 50.00 " " 20 " "

THIS SPECIAL OFFER GIVES YOU

Seeds to the Value of $ 5.50 for $ 5.00.
" " " " 11.25 " 10.00.
" " " " 28.75 " 25.00.
" " " " 60.00 " 50.00.

DISCOUNT ON SEEDS IN PAPERS.

We put up our Seeds in both the 5 and 10 cent size papers, SELL THEM LOWER THAN ANY HOUSE IN THE TRADE, AND MAIL THEM FREE.

FOR THE 5 CENT SIZE,

Comprising all varieties except Peas, Beans, Corn and Novelties, selections can be made by the purchaser, and may include those varieties of Flower Seeds priced at 5 cents per packet in our Flower Seed Catalogue.

25 packets for $ 1.00, costing but 4 cents per packet.
50 " " 1.88, " " 3¾ " " "
100 " " 3.50, " " 3½ " " "
200 " " 6.50, " " 3¼ " " "
500 " " 15.00, " " 3 " " "

FOR THE 10 CENT SIZE,

Comprising all varieties except the Novelties specially priced, and may also include Flower Seeds priced at 10 cents per packet.

15 packets for $ 1.00, costing but 6⅔ cents per packet.
50 " " 3.25, " " 6½ " " "
100 " " 6.38, " " 6⅜ " " "
200 " " 12.50, " " 6¼ " " "
500 " " 30.00, " " 6 " " "

VARIETIES.	Price per Ounce	Price per 4 oz.	Price per lb.
ARTICHOKE.			
Large Globe.....................................	$0 35	$1 00	$3 50
ASPARAGUS.—Colossal...................	10	20	50
Purple Top..	10	20	50
BEANS—Bush or Snapshorts.	per Quart	per Peck.	per Bush.
Early Red Speckled Valentine................	25	1 50	5 00
Improved Early Red Valentine................	30	1 75	6 00
Early White Valentine.........................	30	1 75	6 00
Early Mohawk Six Weeks......................	25	1 50	5 00
Early Yellow Six Weeks.......................	25	1 50	5 00
The Shippers Favorite.........................	60	2 50	8 00
Dwarf German Wax..............................	30	1 75	6 50
Dwarf Golden or Cream Wax.................	30	1 75	6 50
Dwarf White Wax................................	30	1 75	6 50
Crystal White Wax..............................	30	1 75	6 50
Ivory Pod Wax....................................	30	1 75	6 50
Best of All..	50	2 00	7 00
Brown Valentine or Refugee..................	25	1 50	5 00
Newington Wonder..............................	25	1 50	5 00
Early China Red Eye............................	25	1 50	5 00
White Kidney or Royal Dwarf.................	25	1 50	5 00
White Marrow....................................	20	1 50	5 00
Red French.......................................	25	1 50	5 00
BEANS—Runners or Pole.			
Large Lima..	40	2 50	9 00
Salem Mammoth Lima..........................	50	3 00	10 00
Dreer's Lima.....................................	40	2 50	9 00
Carolina or Sewee..............................	40	2 50	9 00
Giant Wax (Red Seed).........................	40	2 50	9 00
Tall German Wax (Black Seed)..............	40	2 50	9 00
Golden Butter Wax.............................	40	2 50	9 00
White Dutch Case Knife......................	40	2 00	7 00
Horticultural	35	2 00	7 00
Scarlet Runner..................................	40	2 25	8 00
Southern Crease-Back........................	60	3 50	12 00
Southern Prolific................................	40	2 50	9 00
Corn Field Bean.................................	40	2 50	9 00
BEANS—English.			
Long Pod..	40	1 90	7 00
Broad Windsor...................................	40	1 90	7 00
BEET.	per Ounce	per 4 oz.	per lb.
Extra Early Turnip or Bassano...............	10	25	70
Buist's Extra Early Red Turnip...............	15	50	1 50
Early Dark Blood Turnip.......................	10	25	75
Dewing's Early Red Turnip....................	10	25	75
Simons' Early Red Turnip.....................	10	25	75
Bastian's Early Red Turnip...................	10	25	75
Lentz's Early Red Turnip.....................	10	25	75
Early Egyptian Red Turnip...................	10	25	75

By Mail, add 30 cents per Quart for Postage.

140   BUIST'S ALMANAC AND GARDEN MANUAL.

VARIETIES.	Price per Ounce	Price per 4 oz.	Price per lb.
BEET.—Continued.			
Early Dark Othello Turnip	$ 15	$ 40	$1 25
Early Eclipse Red Turnip	15	40	1 25
Long Blood Red	10	25	75
Buist's Improved Long Blood	15	40	1 25
Bastian's Half Long Blood	10	25	75
Buist's Perfection Half Long	25	75	2 00
BEET—Stock-Feeding Varieties.			
White French Sugar	10	20	50
Lane's Imperial Sugar	10	20	50
Long Red Mangel-Wurzel	10	20	45
Orange Globe Mangel-Wurzel	10	20	45
Carter's Mammoth Long Red Mangel	10	20	50
Carter's Yellow Globe Mangel	10	20	50
Buist's Mammoth Long Red Mangel	10	20	50
Buist's Golden Globe Mangel	10	20	50
Golden Tankard	10	20	50
BORECOLE or GERMAN GREENS	10	30	1 00
BROCOLI.			
Large Early White	50	1 25	4 00
Purple Cape	50	1 25	4 00
Walcheren	60	2 00	7 00
Southampton	75	2 75	10 00
BRUSSELS SPROUTS	20	60	2 00
CABBAGE.			
Early York—English	15	40	1 50
Buist's Early Dwarf York	25	75	2 50
Early Large York—English	15	40	1 50
Buist's Early Large York	25	75	2 50
Premium Large Late Drumhead	25	75	2 50
Buist's Improved Late Drumhead (the Prize Medal Stock)	40	1 25	4 00
Premium Large Late Flat Dutch	25	75	2 50
Buist's Improved Late Flat Dutch (the Prize Medal Stock)	40	1 25	4 00
Early French Oxheart	25	75	2 50
Early Bullock Heart	25	75	2 50
Early French Winnigstadt	25	75	2 50
Early English Winnigstadt	25	75	2 50
Early Prussian Winnigstadt	40	1 00	3 00
Early Bonanza	50	1 25	4 00
Early Summer	30	1 00	3 00
Early Jersey Wakefield	30	1 00	3 00
Buist's Early Flat Dutch	40	1 25	4 00
Buist's Early Drumhead	40	1 25	4 00
Early Market	30	1 00	3 00
Early Sugar Loaf	20	75	2 00
Early Heartwell	30	1 00	3 00
Early Nonpareil	25	1 00	3 00

BUIST'S ALMANAC AND GARDEN MANUAL.

VARIETIES.	Price per Ounce	Price per 4 oz.	Price per lb.
CABBAGE. - Continued.			
Early Battersea—English	20	75	2 00
Brunswick Drumhead	25	75	2 50
Marblehead Mammoth	25	75	2 50
Stone Mason Drumhead	25	75	2 50
Buist's Large Late Bergen	25	75	2 50
Red Dutch—for Pickling	25	75	2 50
CABBAGE—Savoy.			
Green Curled Savoy	25	75	2 50
Green Globe Savoy	25	75	2 50
Early Dwarf Ulm Savoy	25	75	2 50
Large Drumhead Savoy	30	1 00	3 00
American Drumhead Savoy	40	1 25	4 00
CARROT.			
Early Scarlet Horn	15	40	1 25
Early Half-Long Scarlet—pointed root	15	35	1 00
Danvers Half-Long Scarlet	15	40	1 25
Early Half-Long Luc	15	40	1 25
Long R... ...ore	15	40	1 25
Half-Long Guerande	20	50	1 50
Long Orange	15	35	1 00
Buist's Improved Long Orange	15	35	1 00
Scarlet Altringham	10	30	1 00
Large White Belgian	10	25	75
CAULIFLOWER.			
Early London	60	2 00	7 00
Early Dutch	60	2 00	7 00
Extra Early Paris	1 00	3 50	12 00
Half Early Paris	1 00	3 00	10 00
Early Erfurt	2 00	6 00	20 00
Extra Early Erfurt	5 00	15 00	50 00
Early Snowball	3 50	12 00	40 00
Nonpareil	1 00	3 00	10 00
Lenormand's Short Stemmed	1 00	3 00	10 00
Walcheren	60	2 00	7 00
CELERY.			
Large White Solid	25	75	2 50
Buist's Mammoth White Solid	40	1 25	4 00
Dwarf White Solid	30	1 00	3 00
Sandringham Dwarf White	25	75	2 50
Incomparable White Solid	25	75	2 50
Boston Market	30	1 00	3 00
Golden Dwarf	30	1 00	3 00
White Plume	75	1 50	5 00
Wright's Grove Dwarf White	30	1 00	3 00
Wright's Grove Dwarf Crimson	30	1 00	3 00
Incomparable Dwarf Crimson	25	75	2 50
Celeriac, Turnip Rooted	20	60	2 00
Soup, or Flavoring	10	30	50

VARIETIES.	Price per Ounce	Price per 4 oz.	Price per lb.
CHERVIL—Curled...........	25	75	2 50
COLLARDS.			
Blue Stem...........	25	75	2 00
Georgia or Southern...........	25	75	2 00
CORN—For Garden Culture.......	per Quart.	per peck.	per Bush.
Adams' Early...........	20	1 25	4 00
Adams' Extra Early	20	1 25	4 00
Crosby's Extra Early Sugar...........	25	1 25	4 50
Extra Early Minnesota Sugar...........	25	1 25	4 50
Early Triumph Sugar...........	25	1 25	4 00
Early Concord...........	25	1 25	4 50
Early Egyptian Sugar...........	25	1 25	4 50
Early New England Sugar...........	25	1 25	4 50
Large Mammoth Sugar...........	25	1 25	4 50
Stowell's Evergreen Sugar...........	25	1 25	4 50
Black Mexican...........	30	1 50	5 00
Tuscarora	25	1 25	4 00
Corn—for Field Culture.			
Early Yellow Canada...........	15	75	2 50
Early Yellow Flint...........	20	75	2 50
Early Leaming...........	15	75	2 50
Early Golden Dent...........	15	75	2 50
Early Compton...........	20	1 00	2 75
Pennsylvania Eight-rowed Yellow...........	15	75	2 50
Early Golden Beauty...........	15	75	2 75
Clouds Early Mammoth Dent...........	15	75	2 50
Mammoth Chester Co. Gourd Seed...........	15	75	2 50
Buist's Large White Flint...........	15	75	2 50
Sugar for Ensilage or Fodder...........	20	75	3 00
	per Ounce	per 4 oz.	per lb.,
CORN SALAD........	10	25	90
CRESS OR PEPPER GRASS.			
Curled...........	10	20	50
Water	50	1 50	5 00
CUCUMBER.			
Early White Spine...........	15	30	1 00
Improved Early White Spine...........	15	30	1 00
Buist's Perfection White Spine	20	40	1 50
Early Frame...........	15	30	1 00
Early Cluster...........	15	30	1 00
Early Russian...........	15	40	1 25
Early Short Green...........	15	30	1 00
London Long Green...........	15	40	1 25
Long Green Turkey...........	15	50	1 75
Buist's Long Green...........	20	50	2 00
Jersey Pickle...........	15	30	1 00
Long Prickly...........	15	40	1 25
Green Prolific...........	15	40	1 25

Add 30 cents per quart for Postage.

BUIST'S ALMANAC AND GARDEN MANUAL. 143

VARIETIES.	Price per Ounce	Price per 4 oz.	Price per lb.
EGG PLANT.			
Large New York Purple	$ 60	$2 00	$7 00
Buist's Improved Large Purple	75	2 50	8 00
ENDIVE.			
Green Curled	20	60	2 00
White Curled	25	75	2 50
Broad Leaved	25	75	2 50
Moss Curled	30	1 00	3 00
New Green Fringe	30	1 00	3 00
KALE, or Borecole.			
Green Curled Scotch	10	30	1 00
Dwarf Green Curled	10	30	1 00
New Dwarf Erfurt	20	60	2 00
Curled Siberian	10	30	1 00
KOHL RABI.			
Early White Vienna	25	75	2 50
Large Green or White	25	75	2 00
Early Purple Vienna	25	75	2 50
LEEK.			
London Flag	20	60	2 00
Buist's Mammoth	30	1 00	3 00
Large Musselburgh	30	1 00	3 00
Large Rouen	30	1 00	3 00
LETTUCE.			
Early White Butter, or Cabbage	20	60	2 00
Early Prize Head	20	60	2 00
Early Dutch Butter Cabbage	20	60	2 00
Improved Royal Cabbage	20	60	2 00
French Blondé d'été	25	75	2 50
Large Passion	25	75	2 50
Early Curled Silesia	20	50	1 50
Early Curled Simpson	20	50	1 50
Curled Simpson (Black Seeded)	20	60	2 00
Early Curled Hanson	20	60	2 00
Early Tennisball	25	60	2 00
Early Boston Curled	25	60	2 00
Early Boston Market	25	60	2 00
Drumhead Cabbage	15	40	1 50
Brown Dutch—Black Seed	25	75	2 00
Perpignan, or Early Summer	25	60	2 00
Large India Curled	25	60	2 00
Marvel or Red Besson	25	60	2 00
Yellow Seeded Butter	25	60	2 00
Salamander	25	60	2 00
New Oak Leaved	50	1 25	4 00
Roman White Summer	25	60	2 00
Laciniated Beauregard	25	60	2 00
Baloon White Cos	25	60	2 00
White Paris Cos	20	60	1 75

VARIETIES.	Price per Ounce	Price per 4 oz.	Price per lb.
MELON—Water.			
Mountain Sweet	$ 10	$ 25	$ 75
Mountain Sprout	10	30	1 00
Gipsy	10	35	1 00
Improved Gipsy	15	50	1 50
Jordan's Gray Monarch	25	75	2 00
Kolb Gem (Selected)	20	50	1 50
Mammoth Iron Clad	20	50	1 50
Improved Peerless	15	35	1 00
Southern Rattlesnake	15	50	1 50
Ice Cream (White Seed)	15	35	1 00
Ice Cream (Gray Seed)	10	30	1 00
Black Spanish	10	25	75
Dark Icing	15	50	1 50
Light Icing	15	30	1 00
Cuban Queen	15	50	1 50
Early Phinney	15	30	1 00
Odella	10	25	80
Orange	15	40	1 25
Citron (for Preserving)	10	30	1 00
MELON—Cantaloupe.			
Netted Nutmeg	10	25	80
Netted Green Citron	10	25	80
Skillman's Netted Citron	15	30	1 00
Persian, or Casaba	15	40	1 25
Pine Apple	10	30	1 00
Early Jenny Lind	10	25	80
Hackensack (Selected)	10	25	1 00
Montreal Nutmeg	15	40	1 25
Golden Gem or Jenny	15	40	1 25
New Orleans Citron	20	50	2 00
MUSHROOM SPAWN.			
English in Double Bricks, each 40 cts.			
French in Boxes, $1.00 and $1.50.			
MUSTARD.			
White or Yellow London	5	15	30
English Black or Brown London	5	15	30
Southern Creole	20	50	1 50
Giant Southern Curled	20	50	1 50
NASTURTIUM.			
Tall Yellow	15	50	1 50
Dwarf Crimson	25	75	2 50
OKRA.			
Buist's Dwarf	10	35	1 00
Long Green	10	25	75
Tall Southern	10	25	75
Velvet	20	60	2 00
ONION (Our Growth).			
White, or Silver Skin	40	1 25	3 50

VARIETIES.	Price per Ounce	Price per 4 oz.	Price per lb.
ONION (Our Growth).—Continued.			
Yellow Strasburg	$ 25	$ 75	$2 00
Yellow Dutch	25	75	2 00
Large Red Wethersfield	25	75	2 00
Extra Early Red	25	75	2 00
Large Oval Yellow Danvers	25	75	2 00
ONION (Eastern Growth).			
White or Silver Skin	30	1 00	3 00
Large Red Wethersfield	20	50	1 75
Extra Early Red	25	75	2 00
Large Yellow Danvers	20	50	1 75
Yellow Dutch, or Strasburg	20	50	1 75
Southport Yellow Globe	25	75	2 00
Southport Red Globe	25	75	2 00
ONIONS (Italian).			
Brown Giant Rocca	25	75	2 50
Improved Yellow Giant Rocca	25	75	2 50
Improved Bermuda	25	1 00	3 00
Red Italian Tripoli	25	75	2 50
White Italian Tripoli	25	75	2 50
White Queen	30	1 00	3 00
Extra Early Pearl	40	1 50	5 00
Silver White Etna	35	40	3 50
PARSLEY.			
Doubled Curled	10	25	80
Buist's Garnishing	15	40	1 25
Champion Moss Curled	15	30	1 00
Myatt's Garnishing	15	30	1 00
Fern Leaved	25	75	2 00
Plain, or Single	10	25	60
PARSNIPS.			
Fine Sugar	10	25	75
Student	10	25	75
PEAS.	per Quart.	per Peck	per Bush.
Buist's Premier Extra Early	30	1 75	6 00
Buist's Extra Early	30	1 75	6 00
Buist's Early Morning Star (New)	40	2 00	6 50
Philadelphia Extra Early	25	1 50	5 00
Improved Early Daniel O'Rourke	25	1 50	5 00
Canada Extra Early	25	1 50	5 00
Early American Wonder	40	2 25	8 00
Early Tom Thumb	40	2 25	8 00
Carter's First Crop	25	1 50	5 00
Laxton's Extra Early Alpha	35	2 00	7 00
Pride of the Garden	30	1 75	6 00
Early Kent	25	1 50	4 50
Early Frame	25	1 50	4 50
Early May	25	1 50	4 50
Early Washington	25	1 50	4 50

Add 30 cts. per Qt. for Postage.

146   BUIST'S ALMANAC AND GARDEN MANUAL.

VARIETIES.		Price per Quart	Price per Peck	Price per Bush
PEAS.—(Continued.)				
Carter's Premium Gem		$ 30	$1 75	$6 50
McLean's Little Gem		30	1 75	6 50
Kentish Invicta		30	1 75	6 00
Early Blue Peter		35	2 00	7 00
McLean's Advancer		35	2 00	7 00
Eugenie	Add 30 cents per Quart for Postage.	35	2 00	7 00
Carter's Stratagem		60	3 00	10 00
Carter's Pride of the Market		40	2 50	8 00
Carter's Telephone		50	2 50	9 00
Bishop's Dwarf Long Pod		30	1 75	6 00
Veitche's Perfection		35	2 00	7 00
Champion of England		30	1 75	6 00
Yorkshire Hero		30	1 75	6 00
Fillbasket		30	1 75	6 00
Dwarf Blue Imperial		25	1 50	5 00
Dwarf White Sugar Marrow		25	1 50	5 00
Large White Marrowfat		20	1 00	3 00
Black-Eyed Marrowfat		20	1 00	3 00
Dwarf Sugar—Purple Blossom		40	3 00	10 00
Tall Sugar—Purple Blossom		40	3 00	10 00
PEPPER.		per Ounce	per 4 oz.	per lb.
Large Sweet		30	1 00	3 00
Large Bell		30	1 00	3 00
Large Ruby		40	1 25	4 00
Golden Dawn		30	1 00	3 00
Spanish Monstrous		40	1 25	4 00
Long Red Cayenne		30	1 00	3 00
POTATOES. (Market Price subject to change.)			Per Bush	Per Bbl
Vermont Early Rose			1 50	4 00
Nova Scotia Early Rose			1 50	4 00
New York Early Rose			1 50	4 00
Extra Early Vermont			1 50	4 00
Early Snowflake			1 50	4 00
Early Beauty of Hebron			1 50	4 00
King of the Earlies			1 50	4 00
Early Sunrise			1 75	4 50
Early Ohio			1 75	4 50
Early Mayflower			2 00	5 00
Telephone			1 75	4 00
Clark's No. 1			1 75	4 50
Triumph			2 25	5 00
Belle			1 50	4 00
White Elephant			1 50	4 00
St. Patrick			1 50	4 00
Wall's Orange			2 00	5 00
Jumbo			2 00	4 50
Chicago Market			2 00	4 50
Garfield			2 25	5 00
White Rose			1 75	4 00
Burbank's Seedling			1 50	4 00

VARIETIES.	Price per Bush.	Price per Bbl.
POTATOES.—(Continued.)		
State of Maine...	$1 75	$4 00
Magnum Bonum..	1 50	4 00
Breeses' Peerless.......................................	1 50	4 00
Mammoth Pearl...	1 50	4 00
White Star..	1 50	4 00
Queen of the Valley..................................	1 75	4 00
New Jersey Yellow Sweet.........................	1 75	4 00

	per Ounce	per 4 oz.	per lb.
PUMPKIN.			
Cashaw (Crook-Neck)...............................	15	40	1 25
Large Cheese...	10	30	75
Mammoth Etamps.....................................	30	1 00	3 00
Mammoth King, 25 cts. per pkt.; 5 pkts. for $1.00.			
Connecticut Field, per quart 20 cts., per peck $1.25, per bush. $4.00.			
RADISH.			
Early Long Scarlet (Short Top)..................	10	25	70
Early Long Scarlet (Strap-Leaved).............	10	25	80
Early Long Scarlet (Imported)...................	10	20	60
Early Long Salmon...................................	10	25	70
Buist's Early Long White..........................	15	50	1 50
Early Red Turnip......................................	10	25	70
Early Deep Scarlet Turnip.........................	10	25	80
Extra Early Scarlet Turnip.........................	10	30	1 00
Earliest Erfurt Scarlet Turnip.....................	15	35	1 25
Scarlet Turnip (White Tipped)..................	10	25	80
French Breakfast (White Tipped)..............	10	25	80
Deep Scarlet Olive-Shaped........................	10	25	80
French Half-Long Scarlet...........................	10	25	80
Wood's Early Frame..................................	10	25	80
Extra Early White Turnip..........................	10	30	1 00
Early White Turnip...................................	10	25	80
Buist's Yellow Summer Turnip.................	10	30	1 00
Buist's White Summer Turnip..................	10	25	80
Golden Globe..	10	25	80
Golden Perfection.....................................	15	50	1 50
Black Spanish (Winter).............................	10	25	80
Scarlet China Winter................................	15	35	1 25
White Italian Summer...............................	15	50	1 50
Long White Naples...................................	15	40	1 00
SALSIFY, or Oyster Plant.			
American Grown Seed..............................	20	50	1 75
Buist's Mammoth.....................................	25	1 00	3 00
Imported..	20	40	1 50
SPINACH.			
Buist's Perfection Curled...........................	10	20	50
American Curled Savoy............................	10	20	50
Bloomsdale Curled...................................	10	20	50
Round Savoy..	10	20	40
Broad-Leaved Flanders.............................	10	20	40
Prickly Seeded..	10	20	40

148 BUIST'S ALMANAC AND GARDEN MANUAL.

VARIETIES.	Price per Ounce	Price per 4 oz.	Price per lb.
SPINACH.—(Continued.)			
New Thick Leaved	$ 10	$ 20	$ 50
Long Standing	10	20	50
SQUASH.			
Early Bush, or Patty-Pan	10	25	1 00
Golden Summer Crook-Neck	10	25	1 00
London Vegetable Marrow	25	75	2 50
Boston Marrow	15	30	1 00
Buist's Improved Marrow	20	60	2 00
Hubbard	15	30	1 00
Perfect Gem	20	50	1 50
White Pineapple	25	75	2 50
Butman	15	30	1 25
Marblehead	15	30	1 25
Winter Crook-Neck	15	40	1 25
Mammoth Chili	30	1 00	3 00
TOBACCO.			
Havana	50	1 50	5 00
Kentucky	40	1 25	4 00
Virginia	40	1 25	4 00
Connecticut Seed-Leaf	30	1 00	3 00
TOMATO.			
Buist's Beauty	50	1 25	4 00
Buist's Belle	75	2 00	5 00
Livingston's Perfection	30	1 00	3 00
Livingston's Favorite	30	1 00	3 00
Livingston's Beauty	40	1 25	4 00
Early Acme (Selected)	30	1 00	3 00
Early Hathaway's Excelsior	30	1 00	3 00
Early Paragon	30	1 00	3 00
Buist's Selected Trophy	30	1 00	3 00
Mayflower	30	1 00	3 00
Cardinal	30	1 00	3 00
Mammoth Red	20	75	2 00
Early Conqueror	30	1 00	3 00
Early Canada Victor	30	1 00	3 00
Tilden	25	75	2 00
The Mikado	75	2 00	5 00
Large Smooth Red	20	75	2 00
Large Yellow	30	1 00	3 00
Golden Trophy	30	1 00	3 00
Yellow Plum	30	1 00	3 00
Red Pear-Shaped	25	75	2 50
TURNIP. (White Varieties).			
Red or Purple Top Flat	10	20	50
Red or Purple Top Flat (Strap-Leaved)	10	20	50
Early White Flat Dutch	10	20	50
Early White Flat Dutch (Strap-Leaved)	10	20	50
Large Red Top Globe	10	25	75
Buist's Mammoth Red Top Globe	15	30	1 00

BUIST'S ALMANAC AND GARDEN MANUAL.

VARIETIES.	Price per Ounce	Price per 4 oz.	Price per ℔
TURNIP.—(Continued.)			
Pomeranian White Globe	10	20	50
Large White Globe	10	20	50
Large White Norfolk	10	20	50
Large Green Globe	10	20	50
Large Cow Horn	10	20	60
Southern Seven Top	10	20	50
Purple Top Milan	15	30	1 00
Early Snowball	10	20	50
Early White Stone	10	20	50
Early White French	10	20	60
Early Snow White Globe	15	30	1 00
Early White Egg	10	20	60
Large White Hanover	10	20	60
Sweet German	10	20	60
TURNIP. (Yellow Varieties).			
Purple Top Yellow Aberdeen	10	20	50
Amber Globe	10	20	60
Yellow Globe	10	20	60
Yellow Stone	10	20	60
Golden Ball	10	20	60
TURNIP, RUTA-BAGA, or Swede.			
Buist's Improved Purple Top, Yellow	15	25	75
American Purple Top, Yellow	10	20	50
Imported Purple Top, Yellow	10	20	50
Carter's Imperial Purple Top, Yellow	10	20	50
Skirving's Improved Swede	10	20	50
Sutton's Champion Swede	10	20	60
Large White Swede	10	20	60
HERBS—Sweet and Medicinal.			
Anise	15	35	1 00
Balm	40	1 25	4 00
Basil, Sweet	15	50	2 00
Bene	20	60	2 00
Borage	15	60	3 00
Caraway	10	35	1 00
Coriander	10	35	1 00
Dill	15	50	1 50
Fennel	15	50	1 50
Horehound	40	1 00	3 00
Hyssop	40	1 00	3 00
Lavender	15	50	1 75
Marjoram, Sweet	25	75	2 50
Pot Marigold	40	1 00	3 00
Rosemary	30	1 25	4 00
Rue	25	75	2 00
Sage	20	75	2 50
Saffron	15	50	1 50
Savory, Summer	20	75	2 50
Savory, Winter	30	1 00	3 00
Thyme	50	1 75	6 00

150 BUIST'S ALMANAC AND GARDEN MANUAL.

FRUIT SEEDS.

Pear Pips,	Per lb., $2.00;	oz., 25 cts.
Quince Pips,	" 3.50;	" 35 "
Apricot,	" 75;	" 10 "
Cherry, Mazzard,	" 75;	" 10 "
Cherry, Common,	" 75,	" 10 "
Apple,	Per bush., $8.00;	qt., 50 "
Peach Pits,	" 1.50;	" 10 "
Plum	" 8.00;	" 30 "
Currant,	Per packet,	50 "
Strawberry Seeds,	" 25 and	50 "
Raspberry Seeds,	" 25 and	50 "

BIRD SEEDS.

Our Bird Seeds are always recleaned, and entirely free from all dust and dirt, which are so injurious to birds. They are beautifully put up in pint and pound cartoons at 10 cents each. It is the finest quality of seed and is regarded by bird dealers as the best brand in the market. If your merchant does not keep it, order direct from us; we can mail you a pound package as sample for 25 cts., or you can order a 25-pound case for $2.50, which can be sent by express or freight at a trifling cost.

	Per. Bush.	Per qt.
Canary Seed, Sicily,	$4 00	$0 20
Canary Seed, German	4 00	20
Canary Seed, Spanish,	4 00	20
Bird Seed, Mixed,	4 00	20
Hemp Seed, American,	3 00	15
Hemp Seed, Russian,	3 00	15
Millet Seed,	1 50	15
Rape Seed, London,	6 00	25
Rape Seed, German,	6 00	25
Rice, Unhulled,	4 00	25
Maw Seed,	per lb.,	30
Lettuce Seed,	oz., 10	50
Mocking-Bird Food (Prepared),	per bottle,	40
Cuttle Fish Bone,	each 5c., per lb.,	60

MISCELLANEOUS SEEDS.

Broom Corn, Improved Evergreen,	per qt., 25 cts.,	per bush.,	$4.00
Broom Corn, Dwarf,	" 25 cts.,	"	4.00
Broom Corn, California,	" 25 cts.,	"	4.00
Broom Corn, Common Tall,	" 20 cts.,	"	3.00
Buckwheat, Common Variety,	" 15 cts.,	"	1.50
Buckwheat (Silver Hull),	" 20 cts.,	"	2.50
Cotton Seed, Upland,		per lb.,	25
Cotton Seed, Sea Island,		"	25
Flax Seed,	" 25 cts.,	per bush.,	4.00
Jute Seed,	per oz., 25 cts.,	per lb.,	3.00
Locust, Honey,	" 15 cts.,	"	1.00
Locust, Yellow,	" 15 cts.,	"	1.00
Osage Orange,	per lb., 75 cts.,	per bush.,	10.00
Poppy, Opium,	per oz., 20 cts.,	per lb.,	1.50
Ramie, or China Grass,		per oz.,	2.00

MISCELLANEOUS SEEDS.—(Continued.)

Sorghum, or Sugar Cane, Early Amber,	" 25 cts., per bush.,	3.00
Spurry,	per lb.,	25
Sunflower, Russian,	"	75
Sunflower, Oscar Wild,	"	75
Tares or Vetches, Spring,	" 25 cts., per bush.,	4.00
Tares or Vetches, Winter,	" 25 cts., "	4.00

KITCHEN GARDEN ROOTS AND PLANTS.

The following Plants and Roots can be furnished from our gardens in their season, and packed for transportation:—

Asparagus Roots,	Cauliflower Plants,	Tomato Plants,
Rhubarb "	Cabbage "	Pepper "
Horse-Radish"	Brocoli "	Sweet Potato "
Garlic "	Celery "	Lettuce "
Shallot, "	Egg "	

Vegetable Plants should always be sent by Express or Mail, but Asparagus, Rhubarb, Onion Sets and all other roots can be sent by freight with perfect safety.

VARIETIES OF CLOVER.

Amerriean Red,	*Trifolium pratense,*	per lb.	$0 15
White Dutch (American),	*Trifolium repens,*	"	40
" (Imported),	" "	"	50
Lucerne, or Alfalfa (California),	*Medicago sativa,*	"	40
" (Imported),	" "	"	50
Alsike, or Hybrid,	*Trifolium hybridum,*	"	35
Scarlet,	*Trifolium incarnatum,*	"	40
Bokara,	*Melilotus alba,*	"	60
Yellow Trefoil,	*Medicago Lupulina,*	"	40

BUIST'S RECLEANED CLOVER SEED.

We call special attention to the SUPERIOR QUALITY of **Buist's Recleaned Red Clover Seeds,** which will be found superior to the samples generally handled by the trade. Special prices on application.

A Useful Hint in Purchasing. There is not sufficient care exercised by the planter or farmer in the selection of this the most valuable of all grass seed; many sow it without even examining whether or not it does not contain more seeds of weeds than of clover, and such may frequently wonder where all the daisies, docks, thistles, and other weeds that infest their farms spring from. Weeds will always make their appearance fast enough without sowing them, and to guard against this, sow no grass seed unless you examine it either with a sharp eye or a magnifying glass; no farmer should ever allow a weed to run to seed on his farm; cut them down or pull them out; weeds can't stand such harsh treatment long, and a season or two of this kind of warfare will give you a clean farm and more money in your pocket. Owners of farms who lease them out should always select the required grass seed themselves, as many tenants are really exceedingly careless in this important requisite; we know of instances where tenants on short leases annually purchase and sow the screenings of clover, which is composed of weeds and imperfect grains of Seed, simply to economize; but such economy would very soon impoverish any farm, and a tenant who exercises it is certainly a very unprofitable one.

LUCERNE, OR ALFALFA CLOVER.

(*Medicago sativa.*)

The increasing demand for this valuable forage plant from all sections of our country, and especially from the South, has induced us to give a few brief hints for its culture. Lucerne, or Alfalfa Clover, is a perennial plant, and when once properly seeded in suitable soil, will produce fine crops for several years. It has a remarkably strong growth, occasioned by its roots penetrating the ground to a great depth, until they are altogether out of reach of drought; and in the very driest and most sultry weather, when every blade of grass droops for want of moisture, Lucerne appears in luxuriant growth; and for this reason it is very desirable for all tropical countries. Its cultivation is simple, requiring no more care and attention than a crop of the ordinary red clover, excepting the first year, in preparing the soil and seeding; the ground should be thoroughly mellowed and prepared by clean and careful tillage, the seed sown with any grain crop in either Spring or Autumn, or as a separate crop, at the rate of ten or twelve pounds per acre, and the second year it will become thoroughly established; it delights in deep, loamy soil, with a sand or gravel subsoil, but will not succeed well on stiff, clayey ground, or on soil that is not properly drained; the proper time to cut it for either hay or feeding grain is just before coming into bloom, as it is then in its perfection, and makes a very delicate and desirable feed, being relished by all kinds of stock. Per lb., 40 cents.; 10 lbs., $3.50; 25 lbs., $7.50.

LUCERNE.

GERMAN, GOLDEN, OR SOUTHERN MILLET.

This variety of Millet is well disseminated throughout the entire country, and wherever introduced it has become a general favorite; it is decidedly the best variety to grow, producing large crops of fine grass, ranging in growth from 4½ to 6 feet high (according to strength of soil), which can be cut green or made into hay, which is readily eaten by all kinds of stock; its yield is from one and a half to two and a half tons to the acre; it requires three-fourths of a bushel to sow one acre.

German Millet (prices variable), about, per bushel, - $1.50
Hungarian "   "   "   "   "   -   1.25

'S ALMANAC AND GARDEN MANUAL. 153

S LAWN GRASS SEED.
s, Parks, Tennis and Croquet Grounds.

of Grass Seeds which we prepare for lawns, parks, etc.,
ighout the entire country for producing a beautiful ver-
he year. Some of the finest lawns about Philadelphia
·ere seeded down with our mixture, and are the admira-
furnished our Fairmount Park with about one thousand
round on which it was seeded has produced the finest
Park. In ordering, it is necessary for us to know on what
ed is intended to be sown.

iced the finest turf in the Fairmount Park.
d the Government Building, Fairmount Park, was universally
the handsomest within the Exhibition Grounds. The seed was a
>m the seed establishment of Robert Buist, Jr., of Philadelphia.
(Signed), JOHN WALKER.
r to the Government Agricultural Department.

	Per Qt.	Per Peck.	Per Bush.
Finest Mixture,	$0 25	$1 50	$5 00
Second Mixture,	20	1 25	4 00
Third Mixture,	20	1 00	3 50
1 Park Mixture,	20	1 50	5 00

res Four Bushels of Seed to sow an acre. One Quart
15x15 feet. Price, by mail, 35 cents per quart, includ-

HOW TO PREPARE THE GROUND FOR SEEDING LAWN GRASS.

When a lawn or park is properly planted, the next most important feature is the grass which covers it; for no matter how beautifully a lawn is situated and planted, if it lacks this one requisite, it ceases to be attractive, and is like unto a beautiful mansion furnished with rag-carpet. To accomplish this, pay great attention to the preparation of the soil; in a large extent of grounds it should be plowed, sub-soiled, and cross-plowed; in contracted spaces dug and trenched, the surface properly graded and finely prepared, taking care to collect every weed or root of a weed that can be found. Sow the seed in the months of February, March, or April, in the Spring, with a slight broadcasting of oats; and August, September, or October, in the Fall, with a small proportion of rye. What kind of seed to sow, and where to get it, is the next question, as all that is called lawn grass seed is by no means the same. Some who prepare it are really entirely ignorant of the growth and nature of the various varieties of grasses, and are frequently led into errors that prove ruinous to the lawn. An error of this kind involves a great loss and disappointment to the owner, and is almost irreparable; therefore, procure your seed from an experienced and reliable house. After preparing the ground as above, sow the seed at the rate of three to four bushels to the acre; cover in with a light seed-harrow, or thin branches tied together, to serve the purpose of harrowing, and give the whole a light roll with a field or lawn-roller. Our finest mixed lawn grass which we prepare, is well known for its superior quality in producing a succession of verdure throughout the whole season. Some of the finest lawns on the Hudson River and about Philadelphia were sown with our best preparation; but in ordering, it is essential to state the nature of the soil. Mow early, and mow frequently, is the secret of your after success, which gives strength and stability to the sward. During the warm Summer months permit the mown grass to remain on the lawn; it will greatly strengthen the roots, and prevents the young grass from being burnt out. And as a top dressing or manuring, never use stable manure, as it always contains seeds of weeds, but apply fine bone-dust at the rate of three or four hundred weight per acre, or two hundred weight of Peruvian guano.

Use lawn-mowers in preference to the scythe; it is not only a source of economy, but a lawn kept shorn with a machine is always more beautiful than one mown with a scythe, as the sod becomes more compact, the surface more even, and the grass more luxuriant. Lawn-mowers have now reached great perfection; we have them of all sizes, some even sufficiently light for ladies' use. The most improved machines are the Philadelphia and Pennsylvania. ☞ Send for Illustrated Catalogue with prices

GRASS SEEDS.

Red Top Grass (*Agrostis vulgaris*).—Valuable as a mixture in either pasture or lawn grasses; succeeds well in almost any soil. Per qt., 15 cts.; bush. of 10 lbs., $1.50; sack of 50 lbs., $5.00.

Kentucky Blue Grass (*Poa pratensis*).—Also known as June grass. A valuable variety for lawns when mixed with other grasses; thrives best in dry soils, and retains its verdure during the hottest weather. Cleaned, 15 cts. per qt., or $2.25 bush. Extra cleaned, 20 cts. per qt., or $2.50 bush.

Creeping Bent Grass (*Agrostis stolonifera*).—An excellent variety for lawns, succeeding well in moist situations. Per qt., 25 cts.; bush., $4.50.

Rhode Island Bent Grass (*Agrostis var.*). One of the finest of grasses for lawns when sown alone. Per qt., 25 cts.; bush., $3.50.

Orchard Grass (*Dactylis glomerata*).—One of the most desirable of all pasture grasses, especially valuable for grazing stock. Does well even in shaded situations; when sown with clover it makes a heavy crop of desirable hay. Per qt., 20 cts.; bush. $3.

Timothy, or Herd Seed (*Phleum pratense*).—This well-known variety is extensively grown throughout the country and makes the finest quality of hay. It will produce a larger crop, and contains more nutriment than any other kind. (Sold at market price.)

Sweet Vernal Grass (*Anthoxanthum odoratum*).- Useful as a mixture with other grasses, on account of its early growth. It emits an agreeable odor when cut for hay. Per lb., 50 cts.

Meadow Foxtail (*Alopecurus pratensis*).—One of the most desirable of all grasses for permanent pasture, being early and rapid in growth. It thrives best on rich, moist soils. Per lb., 50 cts.

Tall Meadow Oat Grass (*Avena elatior*).—Is highly recommended for soiling, being rapid and luxuriant in its growth. Per qt., 25 cts.; bush., $4.

Yellow Oat Grass (*Avena flavescens*). -Good for dry pasture and meadows. Per qt., 30 cts.; bush., $5.

Wood Meadow Grass (*Poa nemoralis*). Well adapted for either pastures or pleasure grounds, having a pure, succulent, and nutritive herbage, of early growth, and thriving well under trees. Per lb., 50 cts.

Rough-Stalked Meadow Grass (*Poa trivialis*). — Valuable for pastures and meadows, particularly on damp soils and sheltered situations, producing a constant supply of nutritive herbage, greatly liked by cattle. Per lb., 50 cts.

Hard Fescue (*Festuca duriuscula*).—One of the finest dwarf-growing grasses, thriving well in dry situations. Per lb., 30 cts.

Meadow Fescue (*Festuca pratensis*).—A valuable variety for permanent pastures. Per lb., 50 cts.

Sheep's Fescue (*Festuca ovina*). — Excellent for sheep pastures; is short and dense in growth, making it valuable for grass plots. Per lb., 30 cts.

English Perennial Rye Grass (*Lolium perenne*).—A very nutritious and valuable grass for meadows and permanent pastures. Per bush., $2.50.

Italian Rye Grass (*Lolium Italicum*).—A valuable European variety, thriving in any soil, and yielding early and abundant crops. Per bush., $2.75.

Bromus Schraderi, or Rescue Grass.—Is valuable for pastures, being hardy, productive, and of rapid growth. Per lb., 50 cts.

* **Johnson Grass** (*Sorghum Halapense*).—The Johnson Grass is especially adapted to all tropical climates, as the roots penetrate the soil to a great depth; it is perennial, a rapid grower, very nutritious, being eagerly devoured by all kinds of stock; comes early in the Spring; grows

Varieties of Grass Seeds.

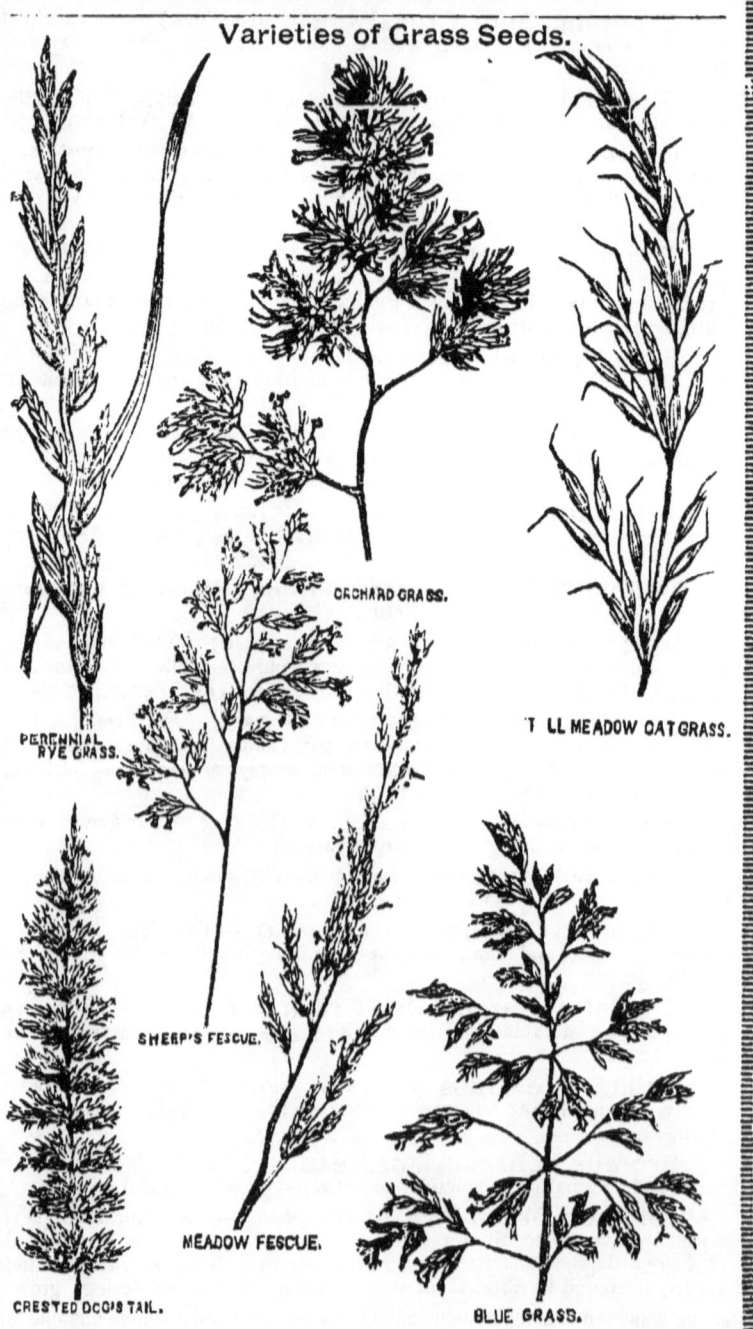

BUIST'S ALMANAC AND GARDEN MANUAL. 157

until the frost cuts it down in the Fall; stands the drought better than any grass, having long, cane-like roots which penetrate the soil for moisture; superior both as a grazing and hay grass; has abundance of roots which decay, thereby enriching the ground rather than exhausting it as Timothy does; belonging to the Sorghum family, it contains much saccharine matter, which is an important factor in the food of stock. It will grow on any land where corn will grow. On lands that will produce a bale of cotton to the acre, four to six tons of hay can be cut per annum, cutting three and four times. Heavy fertilizing would produce greater results. The best results follow sowing the seed in August and September, enabling the seed to get a good root by Fall, and forming a better turf the following season. Sow broadcast, with clean seed, at the rate of one bushel to the acre, or seed in the chaff at the rate of two bushels to the acre, and cover with a light brush, or sow just before a heavy rain. Three good crops the following season will be the result if the season is favorable. Sowing in the Spring does well, but the crop would not be as heavy the first year. Price per lb., 50 cts.; bush. of 25 lbs., $5.00.

BRUDDER SAM'S MEMORY IS WEAK SOMETIMES.

"Cur'us 'bout me, Mac—I can 'membah de mos' insignif'cant ting dat eber happened since I wah two yeah ole. F'rinstance—"

"I say, Brudder Sam, does yo' 'membah anyt'ing 'bout dat ha'f dollah yo' borr'd ob me las' yeah?"

HEAVY SEED OATS.

	Per Peck.	Per Bush.	Per 10 Bush.
American Triumph Oats	50 cts.	$1.40	$12.50
White Belgian Oats	40 "	1.00	9.00
Welcome Oats	40 "	1.25	10.00
Wide-Awake Oats	50 "	1.50	12.50
White Probstier Oats	40 "	1.00	9.00
White Russian Oats	40 "	1.00	9.00

WEBER'S EVERGREEN BROOM CORN.

The Evergreen Broom Corn has long been known as the very best variety, but of recent years it has very much deteriorated by becoming mixed by hybridization. This stock, which we introduced last season as the Weber's, is a very great improvement over the purest Evergreen in length, strength and size of heads and straightness of the brush. It is of a very bright green color without the slightest reddish tinge. Mr. Weber is one of our largest growers, and has made his stock famous by selection and improvement. Price per qt., 30 cts.; per peck, $1.50; per bush., $5.00. If by mail, add 20 cts. per qt.

THE KAFFIR CORN.
A valuable crop for both Grain and Forage.

This crop was cultivated very largely in some sections of the South the past year with great success. It should be sown or planted early in spring; when required for forage sow either broadcast or thickly in rows about three feet apart; or if desired for the grain, plant a few seed every foot in the row and thin out to three or four stalks, according to the quality of the soil. When the grain turns white clip the heads, and other heads will come; this ensures the largest yield of grain. It gives the best results by cutting the first growth for forage when in early bloom, and letting the second growth yield both grain and forage late in fall. If forage only is desired, the seed may be drilled lightly in the furrow. It withstands drought and is particularly adapted to the thin land of the Cotton Belt section. The grain when ground makes excellent food for stock, and equal to flour for bread. Price per lb., 40 cts.; 5 lbs., $1.50, or 10 lbs. for $2.50.

HYACINTHS, TULIPS, CROCUS

And all other **GERMAN BULBS,**

FOR AUTUMN PLANTING.

Orders filled from Aug. 15 to Dec. 15

FINE MIXED HYACINTHS.
Per 100 bulbs, assorted, ... $7.00

	Per doz.		Per doz.
Double Blue, *all shades*, .	$1.00	Single Blue, *all shades*, . .	$1.00
Double Red, *all shades*, .	1.00	Single Red, *all shades*, . .	1.00
Double White, *various*, .	1.00	Single White, *various*, . .	1.00
Double Yellow, *all shades*,	2.50	Single Yellow, *all shades*, .	1.00
Double Fine Named, . .	2.50	Single Fine Named, . . .	2.50
Per 100, $15.00.		Per 100, $15.00.	

Finest Selected, Per 100 bulbs, assorted, $9.00.

	Per doz.		Per doz.
Double Blue, *all shades*, .	$1.50	Single Blue, *all shades*, .	$1.50
Double Red, *all shades*, .	1.50	Single Red, *all shades*, . .	1.50
Double White, *various*, .	1.50	Single White, *various*, . .	1.50
Double Yellow, *all shades*,	2.00	Single Yellow, *all shades*, .	1.50

MIXED TULIPS, for Bedding.

	Per doz.	Per 100		Per doz.	Per 100
Mixed Single Early,	$0.40	$2.50	Mixed Double, . .	$0.40	$2.50
Finest Mix'd Single Early	50	3.50	Finest Mixed Double,	50	3.50
Mixed Duc Van Troll,	50	3.50	Mixed Parrot, . .	50	3.50

CROCUS.

	Per doz.	Per 100		Per doz.	Per 100
Large White, . . .	$0.20	$1.00	Large Yellow, . .	$0.20	$1.00
Large Blue, . . .	20	1.00	Cloth of Gold, . .	20	1.00
Large Striped, . .	20	1.00	Large Purple, . .	20	1.00

	Per doz.		Per doz.
Polyanthus Narcissus, .	$1.00	Crown Imperials, . . .	$6.00
Narcissus, Single, . . .	1.00	Anemones, Mixed, . . .	50
Narcissus, Double, . . .	75	Ranunculus, Mixed, . . .	50
Jonquils, Single, ...	50	Snowdrops, Single, . . .	25
Jonquils, Double, . . .	60	Snowdrops, Double, . . .	50
Japan Lilies, ...	4.00	Golden Japan Lilies, . . .	5.00

NOVELTIES and VEGETABLE SEEDS
OF
SPECIAL MERIT.

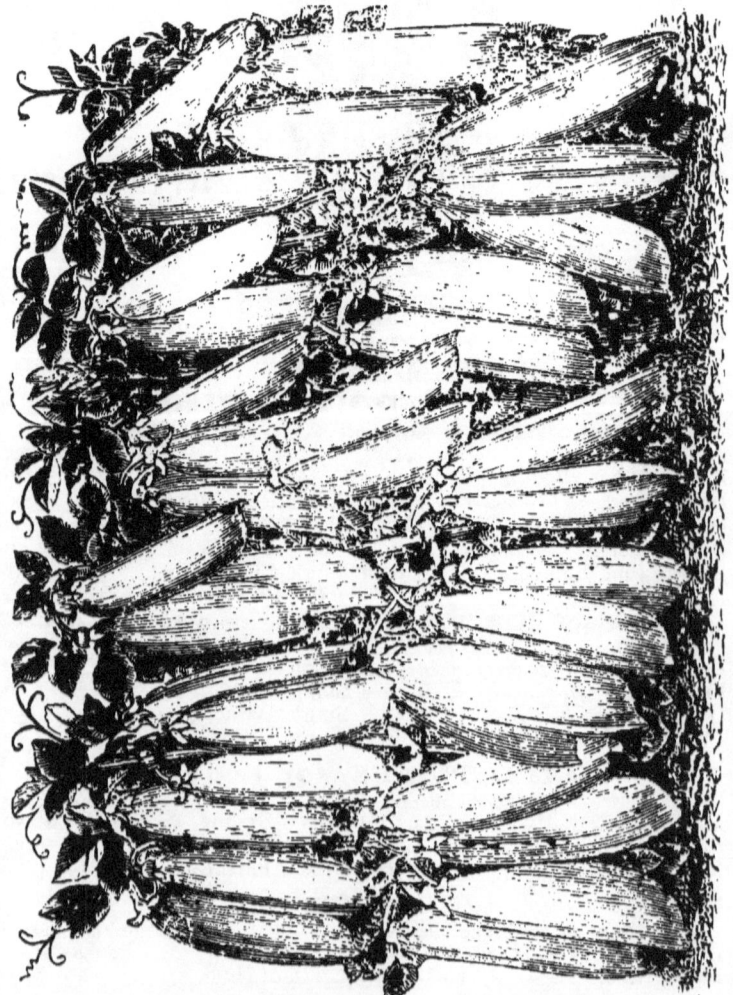

BUIST'S EARLY MORNING-STAR PEA.
THE EARLIEST PEA IN THE WORLD.
It is much hardier, more productive, and withstands greater changes of weather than any other variety.

(DESCRIPTION AND PRICES ON NEXT PAGE.)

Peas—Buist's Early Morning Star (Sealed.) We introduced this extraordinary variety of EXTRA EARLY PEA the past year, two thousand bushels of which were sold and sent to almost every section of the United States, and especially to the districts devoted to market-gardening. There has been but one verdict, and that is, "**They proved the Earliest and Best ever Grown.**"

It was raised from a three years' selection from the earliest podded stock of our famous PREMIER EXTRA EARLY, which is so celebrated with market-gardeners, this has given it an established habit for extreme earliness, dwarf but robust growth, great increase in the size of its pods, and unusual hardiness; growth of vine 2½ feet. It is not only the earliest variety known, but the most productive and the largest podded. One of its greatest features is to withstand great changes and severity of weather, which, of late years, has proved so damaging to the early crop of Peas, especially in the South. It is the most profitable variety for the market-gardener, because the earliest and most productive.

They are sold only in our Sealed Packages, as follows : Papers, 10 cts.; ½ Pint, 15 cts.; Pint, 25 cts.; Quart, 40 cts.; 4 Quarts, $1.25. Leaded Sealed Sacks, etc.: ¼ Bushel, $2.00; ½ Bushel, $3.50; Bushel, $6.50.   Lots of 10 Bushels at $6.00 per Bushel.

The opinion of one of our largest and most successful market-gardeners, who, together with his neighbors, planted over 100 bushels last spring of our Early Morning Star.

> I planted 4 Bushels of Buist's Morning Star Peas in spring of 1886 and made more money off them than on 7 Bushels of another leading brand ; they not only came earlier, but yielded better than any variety I ever planted. Last Spring I planted 13 Bushels of these with the same success. I recommend them highly to the market-gardener.
>
> HOWARD RUSS, Market-Gardener, of New Jersey.

> Your Early Morning Star Pea is all you claim for it. We have had Peas of the choicest quality and in the greatest perfection the past week.
> May 19th, 1887.   MRS. WILLIAM BINGHAM, of North Carolina.

> I planted your Early Morning Star Peas, March 12th, and every Pea has come up. They are a handsome sight and far ahead of other varieties.
> May 6th, 1887.   W. T. LILLY, of West Virginia.

Peas—Carter's Lightning (Sealed). This is one of the very best and earliest of all the foreign varieties ever introduced. It is especially adapted to this country and is destined to become a general favorite for its extreme earliness, productiveness and fine flavor ; pods are large and well filled ; growth of vine, 2½ feet.   Peas sown last spring, March 25th, were in full bloom May 15th, and ready for market June 2d.

Price : Sealed Pints, 30 cts. ; Quarts, 50 cts. ; 4 quarts, $1.50 ; ¼ Bushel, $2.25 ; ½ Bushel, $4.00 ; 1 Bushel, $7.50.

Beans.—New Golden Wax Flageolet Pole.—We regard this as the finest of all the Wax Pole varieties ; it is a new German sort of great merit, and should be planted by every cultivator of a garden. Its pods are about eight inches in length, and of a rich golden-yellow color, of round form, full and fleshy, entirely free from strings, and of superb quality; they are produced in immense clusters, and continue in bearing throughout the season. Per pkt., 15 cts. ; per qt., 75 cts. ; per 4 qts., $2.50; peck, $4.00; bush., $15.00.

Beans — Algiers Dwarf Wax.—

This is a very celebrated variety in the French markets, and is becoming very popular here. We regard it far superior to the Dwarf German Black Wax, as its pods are not only of a much larger size, but are more fleshy and of a richer flavor, of a bright golden yellow color, and entirely stringless. Per packet, 10 cts; qt., 50 cts; 4 qts., $1.50; peck, $2.25; bush., $8.00

Dwarf Bean — Early Speckled Kidney Wax Butter.—

A new variety of last season's introduction, which is equal in quality to the Golden Wax, but more productive. Any novelty in this line is always acceptable, as the Wax varieties are general favorites. The vines are of medium size, erect, hardy and productive. Pods long, broad, flat and of a delicate waxy yellow color, brittle and entirely stringless. Beans white with two shades of reddish purple more or less visible, a distinct kidney shape. Prepared for the table it has a fine buttery flavor, and is destined to become the leading snap bean, as well as a strongly endorsed winter shelled sort. Packet, 10 cts.; qt., 50 cts; 4 qts., $1.50; peck, $2.50; bush., $8.00.

Dwarf Beans — The Shippers' Favorite.—

This is one of the earliest and most desirable market varieties, with unsurpassed shipping qualities, and is the best green-podded Snap-Short ever introduced. It begins bearing when quite small, and produces a succession of pods which are delicate, tender, and, while young, entirely stringless; its pods are very much larger than any other dwarf variety. In making out your seed order do not overlook it, and, more especially, if you are a market gardener. (See illustration page 47.) Per qt., 50 cts.; 4 qts., $1.50; peck, $2.50; bush., $9.00.

Dwarf Bean — Early Golden Wax Butter.—

A German variety of great value, and the earliest of all; very productive; pods of a beautiful golden waxy color, and much larger than the other varieties; entirely stringless, and of rich flavor. The bean, when dry, is jet black, and of a kidney shape; is entirely distinct from the Golden Wax; strongly recommended. Per packet, 10 cts.; qt., 50 cts.; 4 qts., $1.50; peck, $2.25; bush., $8.00.

ALGIER'S DWARF WAX BEAN.

Pole Bean—Improved Southern Crease-Back or Fat Horse.

This variety has been the the most popular Pole Bean in some sections of the South, especially in Louisiana, for many years, and strange to say it has not been more largely disseminated; the stock which we now offer is an improvement both in the size of its pods and its productiveness; it is a strong grower and an abundant bearer, producing its handsome green pods in clusters, which are from 6 to 7 inches long; it is entirely stringless and very fleshy. As a market variety it is unequaled, always commanding the highest price; it is also celebrated for its fine shipping qualities, as it retains its polished and brilliant green appearance, longer than any other variety. The beans, when dry, are of small size and pure white. The pods round, with a deep crease in the back, from which it is

SOUTHERN CREASE-BACK POLE BEAN.

164   BUIST'S ALMANAC AND GARDEN MANUAL.

named the Crease-Back. In some sections it is also called the Fat Horse Bean. Per packet, 15 cts.; qt., 60 cts.; 4 qts., $1.50; peck, $3.50; bushel, $12.00.

Beans.—Golden Butter Wax Pole.—A famous variety, recently introduced from Germany, where it is one of the most popular sorts ; it is of the same character as the German Wax Pole, but somewhat earlier, and producing much larger pods, of a bright golden waxy color; seeds, when ripe, are very dark purple, almost black. A very desirable variety. Per packet, 10 cts.; per qt., 40 cts.; per peck, $2.50; per bush., $9.00.

THE WASHINGTON MARKET CITRON MELON.

MELON (Cantaloupe). The Washington Market. —This new variety of cantaloupe melon is not only entirely distinct from any other, but is one of the finest and most delicate flavored melons ever introduced. It originally came from Madrid, Spain, and is remarkable for its unusual size, extreme productiveness, beautiful shape, rich fragrance, and fine shipping qualities. It is more deeply netted than any other sort, and is destined to become one of our most popular market varieties. Per packet, 10 cts.; per oz., 40 cts.; 4 oz., $1.00; lb., $3.00.

Melon (Cantaloupe). The Versailles Prize.—A new variety from France, which made its appearance in the markets of that country the past year, where it was regarded as the finest of all their varieties. The French melons have always been noted by American travellers as being far superior to those grown in the United States; with a marked peculiarity, that one of inferior flavor is but seldom found. The Versailles is of very large size, roughly marked, and of a light green shade. The flesh, which is of a beautiful golden color, extends almost to the core, and is of a rich sugary flavor. Per packet, 20 cts., or 6 packets for $1.00

MELON (Cantaloupe). Prescott or Rock.—This is a very large roughly marked French cantaloupe; flesh, deep orange, a rich and delightful flavor ; it is the variety so much admired and enjoyed by the American tourist. Per packet, 10 cts. ; per oz., 30 cts. ; 4 oz., $1.00 ; per lb., $3.00.

Beet—Early Othello Dark Blood Turnip.—This very desirable variety was introduced by us a few years since, and has already become very popular with the market gardeners, who require a variety of the darkest color for their main crop. It is the result of a very careful selection of the finest formed and very darkest roots, having been annually selected for the past five years for our own seed stock ; and we venture to say that there is no stock in this country equal to it for its rich dark color, perfection of form, or sweetness of flavor ; foliage, dark crimson. (See illustration, page 51.) Per oz., 15 cts. ; 4 oz., 40 cts. ; lb., $1.25.

Beet—Buist's Extra Early Red Turnip.—This variety surpasses all others for its extreme earliness, richness of color, perfection of form and sweetness of flavor. It is much earlier than the Othello, but not nearly so dark in color. We recommend it to all market gardeners, as the most profitable Turnip variety to grow for early market. For forcing in frames or for out-door culture it is unsurpassed. (See illustration, page 50.) Per oz., 15 cts. ; 4 oz., 50 cts. ; per lb., $1.50.

Beet—Eclipse.—A German variety of recent introduction, similar in character, habit and earliness to the Early Egyptian ; it is, however, more of a globe shape; a very good early market variety, producing a small growth of tops, and roots of a bright red color ; it can, however, be very much improved by making its color of a darker red, which can readily be done by selection. Per oz., 15 cts. ; 4 oz , 40 cts. ; lb., $1.25.

Melon (Cantaloupe)—New Orleans or Creole.—We regard this as one of our very finest varieties of citron melons. It originated in Louisiana, and was grown by us in '84 from seed obtained from that section. We were so favorably impressed with its fine quality, as to be induced to grow it very largely the past season. It grows to a larger size than any other variety (which in itself is no recommendation), but its fine quality surpasses any known sort. It is very roughly netted, of beautiful shape, thickly fleshed, sweet and juicy. Per oz., 20 cts. ; per ¼ lb., 60 cts. ; per lb., $2.00.

MELON (Cantaloupe). Swedesboro Favorite.—
A very popular market variety, grown very extensively in the vicinity of Swedesboro, the great melon centre of New Jersey. It is of large size, beautifully netted and of fine flavor; very desirable. Per oz., 20 cts. ; per 4 oz., 60 cts. ; per lb., $2.00.

Mangel Wurzel Beet. Chirk Castle.—This is a new variety of the Mammoth Long Red, which originated in Scotland. Its size is prodigious, and its productiveness unequalled. Specimen roots were grown, the past year, weighing 56 pounds, and the whole crop averaged 38 pounds per root. This country is just beginning to appreciate the Mangel as a stock feeding root; and a variety that produces the greatest weight per acre, is what the agriculturist wants. Per oz., 15 cts., per 4 oz., 40 cts. ; per lb.. $1.00 ; per 5 lbs., $4.00 ; per 10 lbs., $7.50,

BUIST'S IMPROVED LATE DRUMHEAD CABBAGE.

About Cabbage.—One of the most remunerative crops of the present day for the Gardener, is the Cabbage; that is, a crop that will produce fine, solid heads, with short stocks, heading evenly and uniformly. Size is not of such importance as solidity ; but to combine them both with earliness is certainly a very profitable acquisition.

Such varieties are **Buist's Improved Drumhead and Flat Dutch.** They are the most popular varieties in this country, and are grown under an entirely different method from the stocks sold by the trade as Drumhead and Flat Dutch. We have been for over twenty-five years the largest growers of Cabbage Seed in the United States; and the annual demand of our customers for these two varieties require from eighteen to twenty thousand pounds of seed. We have been frequently asked how we have been so successful in bringing them to such a state of perfection. It is simply explained—Because WE SELECT OUR CABBAGE TO PRODUCE OUR SEED. Every year when our crop is in full head, we personally go through the crop and select from it the most perfect heads, with low stocks, and especially those that show greater earliness in heading; these are carefully lifted and planted entirely separate from the others, and the seed they produce is sown for our crop the following year. EACH YEAR WE REPEAT THIS PROCESS. Cabbage Seed of the finest quality must be grown in this manner.

Cabbage—Buist's Improved Large Drumhead.— Put up and sold only under our seal. Per oz., 40 cts; 4 oz., $1.25; per lb., $4.00.

Cabbage—Buist's Improved Large Flat Dutch.— Per oz., 40 cts; 4 oz., $1.25; per lb., $4.00.

Cabbage—Extra Early Express.—This variety was introduced the past season from France, and has proved to be the earliest in cultivation. We regard it as a very valuable acquisition, it is simply recommended to the market gardener for his earliest crop. The heads are of good size and very solid. Packet, 15 cts.; 5 pkts., 50 cts.; oz., 75 cts.; 4 oz., $2.00; per lb., $7.00.

Cabbage—Early Paris Market.—This variety is very early and grown largely by the market gardeners of Paris for their first crop. It produces a small but compact head, similar in shape to the Large Ox-heart. Per oz., 30 cts.; per 4 oz., 75 cts.; per lb., $2.50.

Cabbage—Buist's Earliest.—This variety has given such great satisfaction that we consider it peerless among the early sorts. Combined with earliness it unites compactness and excellent quality; forming conical heads, and quite large for an early strain; having a short stem and a few outside leaves, permitting close culture. Per oz., 30 cts.; 4 oz., $1.00; per lb., $3 00.

Cabbage—Blood Red Berlin.—This is the finest of all the red varieties, is of medium size and of a very dark blood-red color; it is the best for both pickling and boiling. Per oz., 40 cts., per 4 oz., $1.25; per lb., $3.50.

Cabbage—Large German Drumhead.—This is a famous variety among the German gardeners of this country, who regard it as one of the very best varieties. Its popularity is annually increasing; it produces heads of large size, great weight and solidity, and appears to be especially adapted to this country. It must be borne in mind, however, that all the German Drumhead which is imported, is by no means of the same stock and quality; some of which never will head. The choicest strain, which we import especially for our German gardeners, is obtained from but one locality in Germany, this seed we sell only under our seal. Price: Per oz., 40 cts.; 4 oz., $1.25; per lb., $4.00.

168   BUIST'S ALMANAC AND GARDEN MANUAL.

LARGE LATE RUSSIAN DRUMHEAD CABBAGE.

Cabbage—Large Late Russian Drumhead.—This variety we imported for trial two years ago from Copenhagen, Denmark, and have found it a very superior strain of cabbage for this country and especially so for the Southern States; it is similar in character to the variety cultivated so largely in Germany, but of a much finer strain ; it is a sure heading variety, producing heads weighing from 15 to 30 pounds, of the finest texture. We cannot recommend it too highly as a profitable market variety. Per oz., 40 cts.; 4 oz., $1.25 ; per lb., $4.00.

Radish—Buist's Early Short White Forc'ng.—This is a remarkable variety for early forcing or cold frame culture ; is of oval shape and snow white, producing very large roots, and very early; and is one of the best varieties for market gardeners. Per oz., 20 cts.; per 4 oz., 50 cts.; per lb., $2.00.

Radish—White Summer Strasburg.—This is a very desirable early summer variety, of an oblong tapering shape, and a pure white color, is exceedingly crisp and tender; it forms its roots very quickly, and can be sown throughout the summer, as it stands the heat remarkably well ; it is a very popular variety in the Paris market and is rapidly becoming one of our most salable varieties here. Per oz., 10 cts.; ¼ oz., 30 cts.; per lb., $1 00.

EARLY SCARLET GLOBE RADISH.

Radish—Early Scarlet Globe.—A new and very beautiful German variety, of globe shape, brilliant scarlet color, short-leaved, and very early; a desirable forcing variety. We regard it as one of the very best market varieties. Its very beautiful and distinct appearance will always insure its sale. Per oz., 15 cts.; per ¼ lb., 40 cts.; per lb., $1.25.

Radish—Early Deep Blood-Red Turnip.—This is quite distinct in color from all other varieties, is deep blood-red, very early and attractive in appearance. Per oz., 15 cts.; per ¼ lb., 40 cts.; per lb., $1.25.

Radish—New Early White Italian Summer.—A very remarkable early white summer radish, producing roots of twice the size of the ordinary variety, oval in shape, solid, crisp and tender. Will stand longer than any other sort before shooting to seed. As a market radish it has no superior. Per oz., 15 cts.; per 4 oz., 50 cts.; per lb., $1.50.

Buist's Early Long White.—This is identical with the Early Long Scarlet, in form and earliness, but pure white. It is of fine flavor, and when grown on rich soil is very tender and brittle. Per oz., 15 cts.; per 4 oz., 50 cts.; per lb., $1.50.

NEW INTERMEDIATE KALE.

Kale—New Intermediate.—This variety produces an intermediate growth between the Dwarf and Tall; we regard it as the most profitable market sort; its leaves are luxuriant and beautifully curled; cannot recommend it too highly. Per oz., 15 cts.; 4 oz., 50 cts.; per lb., $1.50.

Egg Plant—Buist's Improved Large Purple.—Until the improvement of this one of the most important market vegetables was undertaken by us, the stock generally grown was what was called the New York Purple, which, was not only of inferior size, but very much mixed, both in form and color. The seed, which we offer under the name of BUIST'S IMPROVED, is now acknowledged, by the market gardeners of New Jersey, to be the finest and purest stock in this country. Wherever exhibited it has taken first premium. When full grown the fruit attains mammoth proportions, frequently weighing from 15 to 18 pounds. Its attractive features are purity of color, perfection of form, productiveness, and fine size, which is attained very early in its growth. These are important requisites for the profitable growing of this crop. (See illustration, page 82.) Per packet, 10 and 25 cts.; per oz, 75 cts.; per ¼ lb., $2.50; per lb., $8.00.

Okra—New White Velvet.—A variety recently introduced from the South, the pods of which are covered with a fine fibre resembling velvet. It is one of the finest varieties. Per oz., 20 cts.; per 4 oz., 60 cts.; per lb., $2.00.

Salsify—Buist's Mammoth.—This is a remarkable and attractive variety, the roots attaining twice the size of the ordinary sort; it is less stringy and more delicate in flavor; it is useless to grow the old variety when this improved stock can be obtained. Per oz, 25 cts.; 4 oz., $1.00; lb., $3.00.

Lettuce—Buist's Perfection White Forcing.—This is one of the most beautiful as well as the most profitable varieties for forcing, in frames, for winter and spring heading; the heads are large, solid; and under the outside leaves is pure white, crisp and tender, making it a very attractive and salable variety; it has no equal. Price: pkt., 15 cts.; oz., 50 cts.; 4 oz., $1.25; per lb., $4.00.

BUIST'S ALMANAC AND GARDEN MANUAL. 171

PHILADELPHIA MARKET LETTUCE.

Lettuce—Philadelphia Market.—This variety made its first appearance in our markets two years ago, and has become very popular; its great feature is not only its large size, but the solidity of its heads; it is desirable for either forcing or out-door culture, and follows the Boston market in heading; but to grow it to its greatest perfection it should be sown early, in the open ground. Per pkt., 15 cts.; per oz., 50 cts.; ¼ lb. $1.25; lb., $4.00.

Lettuce—Oak Leaved.—This is an entirely distinct variety, producing oak-shaped leaves of a light green color, slightly curled; forming quite a compact, solid head, and very desirable for forcing. It is slow in running to seed; in fact, will remain in head for a month before its shoots appear. These shoots are in turn covered with small leaves as delicate and tender as those on young plants. See illustration, page 87. Per oz., 50 cts.; 4 oz., $1.25; lb., $4.00.

Lettuce—Roman White Summer.—An Italian variety, producing fine large, solid heads. Does well either for forcing or for a general out-door crop. Per oz., 25 cts.; per ¼ lb., 60 cts.; per lb., $2.00.

Radish—Early Short-Top Deep Scarlet Olive.—This is one of the best forcing varieties, and differs from the ordinary Scarlet Olive in its earliness, dwarf foliage and brilliancy of color. Per oz., 15 cts.; 4 oz , 35 cts.; per lb., $1.25.

Radish—Earliest Erfurt Scarlet Turnip.—This is the earliest and finest of all the scarlet turnip varieties. Of the deepest scarlet color, perfect shape, small foliage, and the best forcing radish. Per oz., 15 cts.; per 4 oz., 35 cts.; per lb., $1.25.

Carrot—St. Valery Long Red.—This is the finest of all the long carrots, being a perfect model in shape, and of a beautiful red color; a desirable market variety. Per oz., 15 cts.; 4 oz., 40 cts.; per lb., $1.25.

Carrot—Chantenay Half-Long Scarlet. (Stump-rooted.)—This is the best of all the stump-rooted varieties, cylindrical in its entire length, and almost entirely coreless, of a bright red color. Per oz., 20 cts.; 4 oz., 50 cts.; per lb., $1.50.

Carrot—Early Half-Long Luc. - A new French variety, of a beautiful half-long shape, bright orange-red color and stump-rooted. Is quite early and a desirable market variety. (See illustration, page 69.) Per oz., 15 cts.; ¼ lb., 40 cts.; per lb., $1.25.

Cucumber — Buist's Perfection Early White Spine.—This is the finest strain of this celebrated variety; it is not only earlier but more productive than the stock generally grown. It is the best and most profitable market variety. Sold only under our seal (see page 19). Per oz., 20 cts.; 4 oz., 40 cts.; lb., $1.50.

Celery—Golden Self-Blanching.—Similar in habit and growth to the White Plume and Self-blanching; the heart is of a rich golden yellow color, dwarf and compact in its growth, keeps well and of fine rich flavor; very desirable. Packet, 15 cts., oz., 60 cts ; 4 oz., $1.75; lb., $5.00.

Celery—New Rose or Pink.—One of the finest flavored d most beautiful varieties grown, of a delicate pink color and both crisp and tender; in richness of flavor it surpasses them all. Packet, 10 cts.; oz., 60 cts.; 4 oz., $1.75; lb., $5.00.

Celery—Buist's Mammoth White Solid.—A variety of our own introduction, producing immense stalks, which, when blanched, are solid, crisp and tender. It is undoubtedly the best large variety. Per oz., 40 cts.; 4 oz., $1.25; per lb., $4.00.

Celery—Wright's Grove Dwarf White.—This is the finest of all the dwarfs. Blanches almost snow-white, is very solid and of a shell-bark flavor. Per oz., 30 cts.; per 4 oz., $1.00; per lb., $3.00.

Celery—Wright's Grove Crimson.—Similar to the above, only of a beautiful red color. Very desirable. Per oz., 30 cts.; 4 oz., $1.00; per lb., $3.00.

Turnip—Buist's Mammoth Red or Purple Top Globe.—(See illustration, page 131.) This is a variety of recent introduction, which is becoming very popular and especially so in the South; it is of large size, globe form, of rapid growth and enormously productive; of the same character and habit as the Red Top Flat, differing only in its shape and leaves; it can be sown either broadcast or in drills, the latter method will produce the largest and finest formed roots. Flesh, pure white and solid, with a reddish purple top. We regard it as one of the most valuable varieties, and cannot recommend it too highly. Per oz., 15 cts.; 4 oz , 30 cts.; lb., $1.00.

Tomato—Buist's Prize Belle (See page 126.).—This is the largest and best of all varieties (weighing 1½ lbs.) of the most perfect form. It is a hybrid of the famous Beauty, introduced by us, which was universally acknowledged as the largest and best variety known, having been awarded first prize wherever exhibited. The Belle is earlier than the Beauty, and still larger in size, many specimens weighing, the past season, 1½ lbs. each, and as solid as an apple; of a beautiful bright scarlet color, free from crack, and remaining perfect on the vine longer than any other variety. There has been no sort ever introduced that has given such perfect satisfaction, and proved such a favorite, as the Belle; in fact we cannot see how any improvement can be made on it, as it possesses not only the largest size, but the greatest solidity and finest flavor; with the smallest quantity of seeds; and its richness of color and shipping qualities are unequalled. Per oz., 75 cts.; 4 oz., $2.00; lb., $5.00; or seed saved from selected fruit, per packet, 25 cts., or 5 packets for $1.00.

The seed bought of you gave perfect satisfaction, and the Belle Tomato was the best I ever saw.
October 10, 1886.   J. T. WADE, Jr., of Ark.

The seed bought last year proved satisfactory. The Belle Tomato eclipsed all others.
February 10, 1887.   H. L. FOSTER, of N. C.

Tomato—Buist's Beauty.—(See illustration page 125.) A new variety introduced by us a few years since, which has proved to be the best and most popular variety known. Invariably awarded first premium wherever exhibited. We anually grow fifty acres of tomatoes especially for seed, and have made the improvement of all our stocks a special study; the "Beauty" originated on our Rosedale farm from a cross made between the Paragon and the Livingstone Perfection. Its important features are solidity, large size, perfect shape, desirable color (which is brilliant scarlet), evenness of ripening, without crack or wrinkle, freeness of core, and its few seeds. As a profitable market variety it has no superior. Per oz., 50 cts.; 4 oz., $1.25; lb., $4.00; or seed saved from selected fruit, per packet, 25 cts.; or 5 packets for $1.00.

Your celebrated Beauty Tomato has given me better satisfaction than any variety I have ever tried.
March 11, 1887.   H F. TUTTLE of Mass.

Tomato—Turner's Hydrid, or The Mikado.—This is an entirely distinct sort; being a hydrid, its foliage is quite different from any other variety; it is a strong grower, very productive and producing fruit of a very large size and of a beautiful brilliant red color, highly recommended. Per packet, 10 cts.; oz., 50 cts.; 4 oz., $1.50; lb., $4.00.

Beet.—New Crimson Ball. This variety is a very great acquisition to the varieties of Turnip Beet, for its fine flavor, extreme earliness, and beautiful crimson color; it is a very desirable and salable market variety. Per oz., 20 cts.; 4 oz., 50 cts.; lb., $1.50.

Celery.—Carter's Solid Ivory. This is a Dwarf, Compact, solid, crisp variety; twice the number of plants can be cultivated in the same space of ground that a strong growing variety would require; it can also be planted on the surface, instead of trenches, as what earthing up it requires can readily be done with a hoe. Per packet, 20 cts; oz., 60 cts.; 4 oz., $2.00; lb., $6.00.

Corn—Buist's Prize Medal Southern Snow-Flake.

The South has long required a white variety of corn, which, in earliness, productiveness and quality, should be equal to the Early Golden Dent (which we introduced some years ago, especially for the Southern States, which has become the most popular variety of that country.) This new variety we have named the **Southern Snow-Flake.** It was awarded the **First Prize** for WHITE CORN AT THE PENNSYLVANIA STATE FAIR, last SEPTEMBER; it is the most perfect white variety known, for its earliness, productiveness, and fine quality of its meal—its growth is from 7 to 8 feet, producing two ears to the stalk; it is earlier than the Golden Dent, more productive and with a deeper grain; will shell more corn from a given weight on the cob, than any other variety.

Price per pkt., 10 cts.; quart, 30 cts.; peck, $1 00; bushel, $3.00 10 bushels, at $2.50 per bushel.

Spinach.—Buist's Perfection Curled.

(NEW VARIETY FOR MARKET GARDENERS, which is sold only under our seal.) This is our new curled variety, brought to the present high standard from repeated selections made from the most perfect curled plants, and is especially adapted for the market garden trade. It is a strain that produces a strong growth of leaves, which are more curled and crimped than any other variety; and also stands longer without shooting to seed, a very important requisite. It possesses all the perfections that could be desired by a market gardener in a Spinach for a popular and desirable crop. It is sold, under our seal, in packages, cartons, and in leaded-sealed sacks, to be had only from our house, or through the merchant who handles our seeds. Per oz., 10 cts.; per 4 oz., 20 cts.; per lb., 50 cts.; per 5 lbs., $2.00; per 10 lbs., $3.50; per 25 lbs., $7.50.

Lettuce.—Silver Ball or Winter Passion.

A foreign variety of fine forcing qualities, producing a solid head, of a silvery white color; very desirable. Per oz., 25 cts.; per 4 oz., 60 cts.; per lb., $2.00.

Buist's Prize Medal Southern Snow-Flake Corn

What our Customers say about the Quality of Buist's Garden Seeds.

For the past few years we have taken the liberty of publishing extracts from a few of the many complimentary letters we are continually receiving, in order to satisfy those who are strangers to our house, that BUIST'S GARDEN SEEDS will always afford them the utmost satisfaction. The disinterested opinion of our customers will certainly be more convincing than any remarks we could possibly make. All letters of this character will always be separately filed, and kept open for the inspection of any customer:—

Your Mammoth Red or Purple Top Globe Turnip has given better satisfaction than any Turnip I have ever had; cannot speak too highly in its favor.
January 13, 1887. L. G. SANDIFER, of Texas.

In a few more years all of my neighbors will be convinced that your seeds are the best, and will do as I have done for the past nine years, send to your house for all their seed. Your Tomato seeds are very fine.
March 1, 1887. MRS. F. BLALOCK, of Tennessee.

Buist's Garden Seeds take the lead in Florida.
June 23, 1887. J. A. WORLEY, of Florida.

I planted your Jordan Monarch Melon this season and can recommend them as the very best variety for this section. Took off fine crop latter part of June, and this, August 6th, same vines are green and flourishing with a full second crop on them that will be ripe in a week or ten days.
August 6, 1887. J. W. BEATON, of Georgia.

I consider you the best seed grower in the country.
March 17, 1887. L. C. JONES, of Miss.

I always use your seeds and invariably find them perfectly reliable.
January 3, 1887. J. C. MEADERS, of Alabama.

Your seeds last year, were the best we ever used.
April 8, 1887. G. A. SMITH, of Tennessee.

Since I succeeded so well with Cabbage seed, purchased of you last season, will order again.
April 23, 1887. D. L. LAPEYMIZE, of Louisiana.

Your seeds and plants have always given me satisfaction
April 30, 1887. A. BERARD, of Michigan.

Every seed that we bought of you last year grew.
March 30, 1887. M. F. BOWERS, of Delaware.

I have used your seeds for many years and find them superior to all others.
March 29, 1887. M. S. B. F. CAMP, of South Carolina.

We never failed making nice Turnip with your seed.
July 4, 1887. A. R. KANAGA, of Arkansas.

I have used your seed for two years and find them very good.
March 17, 1887. R. BRIDGE, of New Jersey.

We used your Cabbage seed last season with great success.
February 17, 1887. C. & B. HOTCHKISS, of New York.

Seeds ordered in t Spring gave entire satisfaction.
August 2, 1887. W. R. MERRILL, of New Mexico.

Am very much pleased with your seed.
March 15, 1887. B. K. BRUCE, of Kansas.

I have been buying your seeds for many years and they are the best; shall never use any others while I can get yours.
March 12, 1887. Mr. WALSER, of North Carolina.

I like your seeds very much—it pays to send for them.
April 16, 1887. JNO. GARDNER, of Illinois.

I am delighted with all your seeds that I have planted, they are giving perfect satisfaction.
March 24, 1887. MRS. C. W. WRIGHT, of Georgia.

Your seeds have given me a good profit, but I could not begin to supply the demand; my customers who complained of other seed not germinating, say they will use none but Buist's in future; they are true to their reputation.
April 29, 1887. DR. E. W. PUGH, of North Carolina.

We have used your seeds, and they proved a success.
June 4, 1887. MRS. H. MILLER, of Louisiana.

Have always found your Garden seeds the best, and prefer them to others.
July 14, 1887. MRS. M. J. Smith, of Ohio.

There is nothing better than your Turnip seed for our Southern climate.
June 18, 1887. M. L. MEHAFFEY, of Georgia.

I have tried your seeds for years and find them the best in the market. Your Lettuce seed takes the lead.
March 11, 1887. A. R. HOFFMAN, of Pennsylvania.

I use Buist's seed and grow fine vegetables.
July 22, 1887. N. J. DRAKE, of Georgia.

The seeds bought of you in the Spring were fine, especially the Turnips.
May 27, 1887. L. M. ROUNTREE, South Carolina,

I was well pleased with your seed last year.
February 26, 1887. A. SPROUSE, of Nebraska.

I used your Cabbage seed last year and was well pleased with the result.
February 24, 1887. T. HEVI, of Kansas.

All who use your seeds have good gardens.
July 4, 1887. J. M. MEADERS, of Georgia.

I have been very much pleased with your seeds—there are none like them.
March 11, 1887. J. C. MORITZ, of Ohio.

Have used your Garden seeds for two years and feel I cannot have a good garden without them—they never fail.
March 15, 1887. MRS. O. G. HAMBLETON, of Wisconsin,

Buist's Garden Seeds are not Offered as the Cheapest, but as the Best and most Reliable Brand in this Country.

Price should never be taken into consideration in the purchase of Garden Seeds, if cheapness was our motto we should never grow a pound, as we can always purchase at much less cost than we can grow them.

But what are they? Well, this is the important feature; to the eye they may appear all right and if you test them they will sometimes even grow. **But the disappointment comes at Harvest time.** You have been cultivating your crop the entire season, depending on it for a supply, but, at harvest time, to have any thing to harvest will be the exception and not the rule. It is strange, but, nevertheless a fact, that there are annually more worthless and spurious seeds sold, in value, than any other merchandise.

We care nothing for the trade of a customer for a single year, what we want and what we aim for, is, to supply him with seeds of such quality as will induce him always to purchase his supplies from us.

ROBERT BUIST, Jr.

Illustration representing the First Floor of our Market Street Warehouse, from which all Orders are Shipped.

This warehouse, located at Nos. 922 and 924 Market St., covers eight floors. It is not only the largest in Philadelphia, but it is the most centrally located, being next to the post-office. Besides this, we have two large warehouses expressly for the storage of our Seeds. Our facilities for conducting our large and increasing business are unequalled, and **the system under which we grow our Seeds insures to the patrons of Buist's Seeds the most perfect satisfaction.**

→ BUIST'S GREAT CABBAGE
FOR THE SOUTH.
Improved Drumhead and Flat Dutch.

(THREE HEADS WEIGHING, 122 POUNDS.)

THEY HEAD WHEN ALL OTHERS FAIL.
Over Five Million Packets Sold in the South the Past Year.

This stock of Seed is sent out only under our seal, with our name on each package, and mailed at the following prices:

25 Small Packets for $1.00.
15 Large Packets for $1.00.
½ Pound, $2.00; 1 Pound, $4.00.
¼-Ounce Packet, $ .20
1-Ounce Packet, .40
4-Ounce Packet, 1.25

☞ If your merchant keeps Buist's Seeds, you must order from him; if not, then order from us.

www.ingramcontent.com/pod-product-compliance
Lightning Source LLC
Chambersburg PA
CBHW032154160426
43197CB00008B/907